A MATTER OF ALLEGIANCES

THE JOHNS HOPKINS UNIVERSITY STUDIES IN HISTORICAL AND POLITICAL SCIENCE

NINETY-SECOND SERIES (1974)

1. A Matter of Allegiances: Maryland from 1850 to 1861
   BY WILLIAM J. EVITTS

2. This Sheba, Self: Attitudes toward Work in Early America
   BY J. E. CROWLEY

WILLIAM J. EVITTS

A MATTER OF ALLEGIANCES

MARYLAND FROM 1850 TO 1861

THE JOHNS HOPKINS UNIVERSITY PRESS
BALTIMORE AND LONDON

This book has been brought to publication
with the generous assistance of the
Andrew W. Mellon Foundation.

The Johns Hopkins University Press, Baltimore, Maryland 21218
The Johns Hopkins University Press, Ltd., London

Library of Congress Catalog Card Number 73-19336

ISBN 0-8018-1520-7

Manufactured in the United States of America

Library of Congress Cataloging in Publication Data
will be found on the last printed page of this book.

Because no one ever does it alone, this book is dedicated to those who prepared the way:

To my father, Charles Evitts, and the memory of my mother,

and

to Irene and Walter Allen

CONTENTS

TABLES AND MAPS

TABLES

MAPS

ACKNOWLEDGMENTS

THIS BOOK, like virtually all books, leaves its author in a state of deep indebtedness to a host of people. Librarians by the score have given me assistance, but I feel special gratitude to Ellen Bayly Marks and Nancy Boles of the Maryland Historical Society, and to the entire staff at the amazingly pleasant Eleutherian Mills Historical Library in Greenville, Delaware. And, like all historians, I am deeply obliged to those who worked the field before me; at the risk of slighting others I must mention the work of Jean H. Baker, whose meticulous and imaginative study of the Know Nothings saved me endless labor and made this book that much more complete. She also put up with my interminable questions and read a chapter of the original draft, much to its benefit. Aida DiPace Donald has been a patient but firm editor, and having her knowledge and experience behind me has helped enormously. Praise is also due to Penny James, of the Hopkins Press, for so gracefully guiding a novice author through the publishing thicket.

Special thanks are due to Dr. David Donald, now at Harvard. As the director of the dissertation from which this volume evolved he is, in a way, the intellectual godfather of the work. Like any proper godfather, he may point with pride to the offspring's merits while justly disclaiming responsibility for his faults. Throughout the course of my research and writing he pushed, cajoled, corrected, encouraged, admonished, and inspired me. He was at once understanding and uncompromising. This book is unquestionably better than it could possibly have been without his presence, and I can think of no higher aspiration than that he approve of this study and be pleased by his association with it. My debt to him goes much deeper than this book, deeper than even he (and possibly even I) can know.

I used to sneer at the seemingly automatic acknowledgment most authors gave to their wives. It seemed just a sop to keep the little women happy. Now I know better. Carole has suffered through every prepositional phrase of this effort. She has been without me when she needed me and has had to put up with my distracted state even when I was around. She deserves my unending gratitude and two weeks in Bermuda, but on our budget I am afraid she will have to settle for the gratitude.

INTRODUCTION

THIS IS A STUDY of Maryland from 1850 to 1861, or, more precisely, to that point in the summer of 1861 when it became clear that Maryland would remain in the Union. If execution is equal to the design, the book by implication will also say something about subjects which range beyond the Free State—subjects such as nativism and the Know Nothing movement, urban conditions, border-state conservatism, the condition of politics in the 1850s, and the coming of the Civil War. Yet Maryland itself is the subject.

Maryland needs study. It is a remarkably diverse state, as close to an American microcosm as any single state is likely to be. Maryland had close emotional, geographic, and economic ties to the North and the South in the 1850s. Geographically, Maryland runs from the sandy beaches and flat peninsular fields of the Eastern Shore to mountainous, wooded Allegany County in the west. The state has at least three informal geopolitical divisions—the Eastern Shore, Southern Maryland, and Western Maryland—and maybe four, if you count Baltimore separately. In 1850 Maryland had all varieties of farming, manufacturing, commerce, and trade; Marylanders themselves included old Episcopalian plantation families and brand new, unassimilated Catholic immigrants. And yet, for all this, and despite the existence of a competent, well-stocked historical society with its own magazine, Maryland remains relatively unexamined. Many of the studies which do exist are outdated in technique, sources, and outlook. Compared with such well-researched states as Massachusetts, New York, and Virginia, Maryland and its history are woefully unattended.

This study examines Marylanders primarily through their politics. Voting records are the largest single body of information we have about the lives of Marylanders in the mid-nineteenth century. Through their votes Marylanders left traces of their choices, fears, hopes, prejudices, interests, and allegiances. Of course, politics is not a pure reflection of public sentiment. Politics assumes a certain life of its own and, consequently, distorts some of the choices the voters make. The voting returns from Baltimore in the 1850s, for example, are highly suspect because of fraud and violence at the polls. Another case in point is the presidential election of 1860, when the outcome was decisively affected by purely local antagonisms, and the majority sentiment of Marylanders on national issues was, I believe, misrepresented. In addition, electoral choices usually reduce to no more than two options, two candidates representing two generalized points of view; in this way politics oversimplifies the assorted shades of individual opinion. These and other distortions caused by the political process are not only obstacles for the political historian, but also proper objects of study themselves. It can legitimately be asked how well the party system represented its constituents. This book is therefore a political history in a certain specialized sense—political history seen as a rather precise kind of social history. It looks much more at the populace than at the politicians, because politics is valued here not as an end in itself, but for what it can tell about a diverse group of Americans called Marylanders in a troubled time.

Historians dissect the 1850s primarily because these are the years of prologue to a great war; perhaps that is a mistake. Granted, we need to understand the decade and we need to do so partly for what we can learn about the way war happened. But, if we approach our study totally conditioned by foreknowledge of the war, a serious misinterpretation may occur. Marylanders feared a sectional split and civil war, and this did affect their thinking, yet their lives were not molded entirely by a concern for the coming conflict. Perhaps the secret to understanding what went wrong at the end of the 1850s lies in trying to see the decade as the participants saw it, blissfully unaware of what was ahead. From this point of view the decade offers a great deal for study that might otherwise be overlooked.

Marylanders, for one thing, turned to political nativism in the 1850s. The Know Nothing movement is a well-remarked phenomenon, but most often it is brushed aside as an aberration, a dead end, or, at best, a way station for hesitant Whigs en route to becoming Republicans. Value judgments of nativist prejudice aside, the Know Nothing phenomenon was much more crucial to Marylanders' search for values than has been commonly assumed. The American party ruled Maryland for half the decade, providing a voice for Marylanders threatened by changing times—by immigrants, by political confusion and disaffection, by sectional stress, and by a vague sense of values lost and goals misplaced. Furthermore, the nativist movement in Maryland was not a static pose which was assumed briefly and forgotten. The movement became a political party which totally restructured Marylanders' political allegiances. The party itself went through several metamorphoses before passing away from numerous causes.

Marylanders also went through a political change in the 1850s which was largely unassociated with parties and platforms. Early in the decade a pervading sense of disillusionment appeared in Marylanders' approach to politics in general. This disillusionment was the result of the changes in political behavior and morality that followed the era of Jacksonian democracy. Even beyond the repugnance felt by conservatives to the raucous tone of contemporary politics, Marylanders of all persuasions were becoming dismayed by the political process and the men who engaged in it. This subtle disenchantment with politics in general had specific consequences for party structure, hastening the end of the Whig organization and making the public mind more receptive to nativism. Besides revulsion, other political undercurrents surfaced in Maryland between 1850 and 1861. For one, a strong nostalgic theme appealed to many people. This theme was inspired by distaste for the present and was gratified by glorification of a past time whose outlines were softened by a charitable memory. Reform zeal also seized many Marylanders in this decade, as revealed in the "Maine Law" temperance drive and the crusading stage of nativism. Restoration and reform often went hand in hand, both appealing to persons who were out of sympathy with current conditions.

Maryland in the 1850s offers valuable insights into the role of the city in the mid-nineteenth century. Baltimore dominated Maryland politics, and any inquiry into political behavior necessarily leads to a consideration of the Maryland metropolis and its problems, as well as to a brief inspection of Marylanders' concepts of cities and urban life. Baltimore, it seems, was bedeviled by inadequate institutions and the invincibly negative attitudes which Americans have about cities.

The unifying theme for this study is allegiance, by which I variously mean loyalty, affiliation, endorsement, identification. Marylanders in the 1850s were a diverse group of Americans searching for something to support and believe in. The overriding question of allegiances, of course, was that of choosing between the North and the South. Marylanders desperately did not want to have to make that choice, and they worked hard to preserve the Union. Until well after the firing on Fort Sumter in April 1861, Marylanders as a group were still grappling with that decision and trying, if possible, to evade it through the fiction of "armed neutrality." But there were other choices to be made, too: choices among parties, candidates, and principles; choices between city and country; choices between volatile democracy and conservative order. Furthermore, these questions of allegiance overlapped one another. Local issues became tangled with national ones, as when the Whigs ran into an unfortunate combination of setbacks at both the state and federal level in the early fifties, or when Baltimore reform affected the presidential election of 1860.

The pursuit of this kind of history dictates certain kinds of sources and methods. Newspapers were vital to this study for several reasons—as recorders of opinion, as shapers of opinion, and as a not too distorted mirror of life. Advertisements and editorials had value for this study. Newspapers are also necessary sources of detailed facts, including statistics. The press is the collective diary of society. I also used other traditional sources, such as individual diaries and correspondence, official documents, and legislative journals. Personal papers for leading Marylanders in this period are, unfortunately, scarce. Emphasis fell on evidence pointing to trends, opinions, and—that elusive concept—allegiances.

Statistics figure prominently in this work and a word on their use is necessary. Behind statistics lurk individuals, people who are born, work, vote, move, fight, commit crime, get married, and die. The only way to handle these people in meaningful quantities is through statistics. Unfortunately, by divesting the people they represent of their humanity, statistics often obscure as much as they reveal. The only cure for this conceptual myopia is constant vigilance against allowing statistics to blind us to their real human meaning.

I

MARYLAND AT MID-CENTURY

IN 1850 MARYLAND was changing. The state began in 1634 as a Tidewater tobacco-growing enterprise which was indistinguishable, in all important aspects, from early Virginia. By the middle of the nineteenth century Maryland was nearly an American microcosm—diverse, exciting, confused, and changing. Marylanders themselves clearly sensed their drift. In business, for example, years of planning and building were about to be rewarded. The Chesapeake and Ohio Canal, started in 1828, began full-time operation in 1850; this opened the Western Maryland coal fields to international trade. The Baltimore and Ohio Railroad neared completion in 1850. When finished, the B. & O. promised to be the finest East-West trunk line on the continent. It would link Baltimore to the interior and climax half a century of effort by Baltimore merchants to build a major trading center.[1] In Cumberland, in the western part of the state, the construction of the railroad created change; rents rose sharply; old dilapidated frame houses were torn down daily, and new brick structures took their place.[2] Two new churches and a school went up in May 1850.[3] Every warehouse and vacant loft in the western canal town of Williamsport was stacked with grain that spring of 1850, and trade was heavy.[4] In politics, everyone was debating the need to rewrite Maryland's 1776

[1] See Edward Hungerford, *The Story of the Baltimore and Ohio Railroad* (New York: C. P. Putnam's Sons, 1928); Walter S. Sanderlin, *The Great National Project: A History of the Chesapeake and Ohio Canal*, The Johns Hopkins University Studies in Historical and Political Science, ser. 64, no. 1 (Baltimore: The Johns Hopkins Press, 1946); and *idem*, "The Maryland Canal Project," *Maryland Historical Magazine*, 41 (1946): 51–65.

[2] Reprinted from *Cumberland Civilian* (Cumberland, Md.) in *Baltimore Sun*, March 2, 1850; see also *ibid.*, September 13, 1850.

[3] *Baltimore Sun*, May 7, 1850.

[4] *Ibid.*, March 1, 1850.

constitution—another wrenching change. Baltimore, Maryland's proud metropolis, witnessed the most ferment of all. The city had more than doubled in size in thirty years.[5] Its prosperity was increasing, too. A few years earlier, an income of three or four thousand dollars a year had made a Baltimorean very wealthy indeed, and there had not been a dozen private carriages in the town.[6] By 1850, however, fortunes reached the millions.[7] Eventually these fortunes would give the city an excellent free library, a world-famous conservatory of music, and the first true university in America.[8] Great mansions went up in Exchange Place, along Charles Street, and at Mount Vernon Place. The city had developed a rich leisure class.[9] Yet not all Marylanders saw change as uplifting and beneficial. The *Baltimore Sun*, for example, grumbled editorially about an alarming rise in street crime and pauperism.[10] Another frightened Marylander complained of "the awe-inspiring omnipotence" of the B. & O.[11] Nonetheless, progress would not hold back for a few critics. Benjamin C. Howard, speaking before the state Democratic convention in 1850, likened Maryland to a ship in dry dock and set for a great voyage.[12] Overblown as his metaphor was, Howard was fundamentally correct; in his politician's way he tried to catch the feeling of the changing times.

The changes in Maryland affected different parts of the state in different ways—ways which were shaped by geography and history. Maryland began on the lower Chesapeake Bay in the Tidewater. At first the state looked exactly like Virginia. Isolated plantations along the coastal rivers dominated settlement. Private wharfs blunted the need for towns, which in any case were merely collection points like Port

[5] The 1820 Census listed Baltimore at 62,700 people. By 1850 the population of the city had grown to 169,054.

[6] Raphael Semmes, "Baltimore during the Time of the Old Peale Museum," *Maryland Historical Magazine*, 27 (1932): 117–18.

[7] *Herald and Torch Light* (Hagerstown, Md.), March 15, 1854, listed three citizens worth from one and one half to three million dollars, at least; they were George W. Brown, Jacob Albert, and Johns Hopkins, all from the Baltimore area.

[8] In the 1850s most people were still busy making their money; the philanthropy would come later. But eventually the George Peabody fortune established the conservatory; the public library was named after commission merchant Enoch Pratt; and Johns Hopkins, Quaker merchant, endowed the university which bears his name.

[9] An interesting glimpse of the frivolous side of the new Baltimore rich is provided by the diary of Mrs. Benjamin S. Harris, which is on file in the manuscript collection at the Maryland Historical Society, Baltimore.

[10] January 28, 1850.

[11] Letter of "Admonition," *ibid.*, March 14, 1850.

[12] *Ibid.*, May 25, 1850.

Tobacco and Port Deposit. Tobacco ruled the colonial economy, bringing with it Negro slavery. Tobacco was even used as currency in the colonial period, and Marylanders frequently faced grain shortages because they put their best land in the smoking weed. In the beginning, Maryland was Southern. A century after the original settlement on the Bay, however, a second Maryland began to develop in the West, around Frederick. German immigrants came from the North in search of good lands and better protection against Indians than Quaker-dominated Pennsylvania would provide. With the Germans came a new pattern of life, based on small-unit, diversified, nonslave agriculture.[13] The older settlements welcomed this as a useful counterweight to the tobacco mania of the Tidewater and as a source of grain, taxes, and frontier stability. But with the Germans came a split in Maryland society, a split which persisted down to 1850 and affected the politics, economy, attitudes, and allegiances of the entire state.

In the mid-nineteenth century two rural life styles existed side by side in Maryland. They were divided roughly by the Fall Line, that small but definite escarpment where Tidewater rises to become Piedmont, producing falls and rapids on the streams that cross it (see Map 1). The old society of the Tidewater, heavily involved with slavery, stable almost to the point of stagnation, fought a constant losing struggle against the more dynamic new society of the North and West, which included Baltimore. "New" and "old," of course, are relative terms, for both parts of Maryland had been established for more than a century by 1850; yet the designations are useful. The division in Maryland pitted a Northern-style economy against a Southern one for control of the state's destiny. Furthermore, the clash of societies within the state occurred during the national sectional debate. The local contest reflected many of the same concerns that agitated the nation: concerns about majority representation versus minority rights, the role of the government, protection of the society against change, the confrontation of city and country, and the overwhelming dilemma of where loyalties rightly belonged. Maryland's history down to 1850, from the old societies of the Bay settlement to the more vigorous West, was the story of two different states developing inside one political unit. Between 1850 and 1861 these debates within and without the state built to a climax.

[13] See Dieter Cunz, *The Maryland Germans* (Princeton: Princeton University Press, 1948); and Avery O. Craven, *Soil Exhaustion as a Factor in the Agricultural History of Virginia and Maryland, 1606–1860*, University of Illinois Studies in the Social Sciences, no. 13 (Urbana: University of Illinois, 1926).

Map 1. Maryland in the 1850s

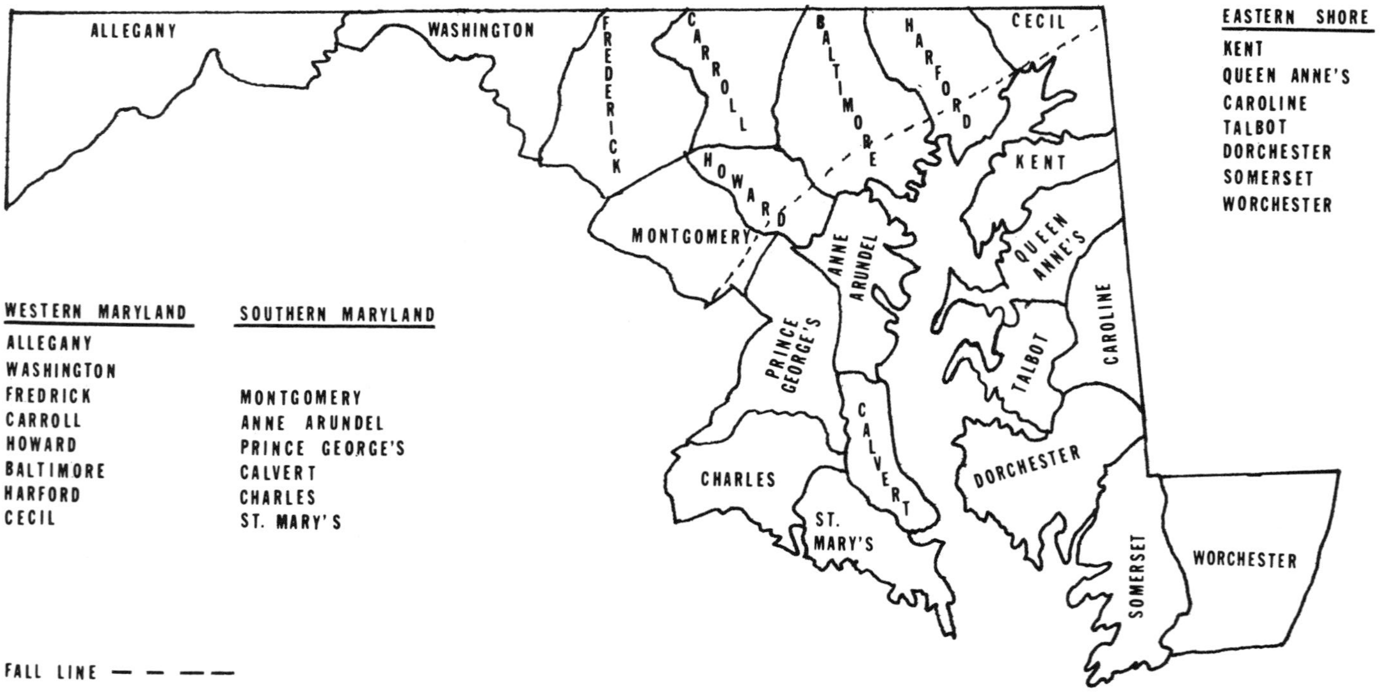
ALLEGANY
WASHINGTON
FREDERICK
CARROLL
BALTIMORE
HARFORD
CECIL
HOWARD
MONTGOMERY
KENT
QUEEN ANNE'S
ANNE ARUNDEL
PRINCE GEORGE'S
TALBOT
CAROLINE
CALVERT
CHARLES
ST. MARY'S
DORCHESTER
SOMERSET
WORCHESTER
EASTERN SHORE
KENT
QUEEN ANNE'S
CAROLINE
TALBOT
DORCHESTER
SOMERSET
WORCHESTER
WESTERN MARYLAND
ALLEGANY
WASHINGTON
FREDRICK
CARROLL
HOWARD
BALTIMORE
HARFORD
CECIL
SOUTHERN MARYLAND
MONTGOMERY
ANNE ARUNDEL
PRINCE GEORGE'S
CALVERT
CHARLES
ST. MARY'S
FALL LINE

I

By 1850 Maryland's "old society"—descended from the original Bay settlement—had within it two further divisions, Southern Maryland and the Eastern Shore. The Bay divided the two and limited communication and cooperation between them. Nonetheless, they were quite similar.

Southern Maryland epitomized the old society—slaveholding and rural. The entire district was tidewater flats; it was not swampy, but was surrounded by the Bay and the Potomac River and was cut by numerous streams. Tobacco had lost its stranglehold on the land by 1850, but it remained a major influence. Wheat and corn grew on the hills away from the river bottoms. Portions of Southern Maryland could be mistaken for deep South black belt. A traveler in 1844 met only two white persons in a fourteen-mile ride; everything he saw there fit the plantation stereotype—extensive fields worked by slaves, scattered stately homes, and the dominance of the land by one famliy.[14] Fifty-four percent of Southern Maryland's population was Negro. These six counties housed 14.9 percent of the state's rural white population and 36.2 percent of the rural slaveowners. One white in nine, on the average, was a slaveowner.[15] The effect of this social and agricultural pattern was often dismal. The area was described in 1819 as "dreary and uncultivated wastes, a barren . . . soil, half-clothed Negroes, lean and hungry stock, a puny race of horses . . . houses falling to decay."[16] Southern Maryland roads were muddy tracks through field and forest, a source of constant complaint.[17] An agricultural revival after 1850 brightened but did not substantially change this picture of the region. The heritage of tobacco culture was dispersion, slavery, and eroded soil. Southern Maryland actually lost part of its white population between 1800 and 1850; the area attracted few outsiders.

Southern Maryland was a colonial world grown old and beginning to decay. Annapolis, the only town of any size,[18] stirred busily during meetings of the General Assembly, but usually it lay quietly by the

14 "A Maryland Tour in 1844: Diary of Isaac Van Bibber," *Maryland Historical Magazine*, 39 (1944): 263.

15 U.S., Bureau of the Census, *Seventh Census of the United States* (Washington, D.C.: GPO, 1850), p. 220. The figures on slaveownership are taken from U.S., Bureau of the Census, *Eighth Census of the United States* (Washington, D.C.: GPO, 1860), p. 231; such figures are not available for 1850. "Rural" here means outside Baltimore City.

16 Craven, *op. cit.*, p. 84.

17 See, for example, *Upper Marlboro Gazette* (Upper Marlboro, Md.), January 5 and March 30, 1853.

18 In 1850 the population of Annapolis was 3,011. Bureau of the Census, *Seventh Census*, p. 214.

Severn River.[19] Even the genteel, coffee-house cosmopolitanism that had once marked the town was gone. "This town," sniffed a Western Maryland editor, "which was in by-gone days the seat of fashion of the Union, has degenerated into one of the most dreary, dull, and monotonous places in the state."[20] "Annapolis is always asleep," admitted one Southern Marylander.[21] The six counties of Southern Maryland represented Southern values in a Southern economy.

The Eastern Shore, although a part of the old society, retained a certain distinctiveness. Mostly it was a backwater. Cut off by the Delaware River on the northeast and by the Chesapeake Bay on the west, people of the Delaware-Maryland-Virginia peninsula kept largely to themselves.[22] One of the consequences of this isolation was a keen interest in the internal improvements necessary to build links to the outside world. Also, although descended from the original old society of the Bay, the people of the Eastern Shore developed in time a spirit of separateness and self-conscious identity. One citizen, for example, urged parents to educate their children at local academies to ensure their virtue and happiness; he described himself as "an Eastern Shoreman by birth and education, in spirit and feeling."[23] In their aloofness and jealousy of the "western shore," the Easterners sometimes overlooked the common origin of the Bay society. On several occasions before 1850, the region threatened to secede from the state. Everyone on the Shore was near water—the Bay, the ocean, or one of the many rivers. To this day the term "waterman" in Maryland parlance refers to that breed of Eastern Shore native who follows any one of the livings provided by the abundant marine life. Farming east of the Bay was more diversified than that in Southern Maryland. Tobacco did not do well in the sandy soil of the peninsula, and by 1850 almost none was grown there. Truck, potato, and corn farming sufficed in its place. The decline of tobacco culture on the Eastern Shore led directly to the erosion of slavery as a profitable labor system. Consequently, almost half of the blacks on the Eastern Shore were free by

[19] See John C. French, "Poe's Literary Baltimore," *Maryland Historical Magazine*, 32 (1937): 101–12; see also "St. John's College, Annapolis, 1789–1849," *ibid.*, 29 (1934): 305–10.

[20] *Herald and Torch Light*, February 22, 1854.

[21] *Planters' Advocate* (Upper Marlboro, Md.), September 20, 1852.

[22] Abraham Lincoln told a story of an old farmer in court who gave his age as "sixty." The judge admonished him that he, the judge, knew the farmer to be much older than that. "Oh," was the reply, "you're thinking about that fifteen years that I lived down on the Eastern Shore of Maryland; that was so much lost time and don't count." Willard L. King, *Lincoln's Manager, David Davis* (Cambridge, Mass.: Harvard University Press, 1960), p. 168. I have also seen this story attributed to Senator Thomas Corwin of Ohio.

[23] *Cambridge Democrat* (Cambridge, Md.), May 2, 1853.

mid-century, and that trend continued until the death of the institution of slavery itself.[24] In 1850, approximately one Eastern Shore white in every seventeen owned a slave.[25]

II

The active growth and prosperity of the region above the Fall Line—the new society—sharply contrasted the lethargic pace of the Bay settlements. Usually called "Western Maryland" for convenience, this region actually reached the Delaware border in northeastern Cecil County. Diversity was the area's hallmark. The land included rolling Piedmont , deep valleys, and the timbered ridges of the Allegheny and Blue Ridge ranges. The people, nearly two-thirds of Maryland's rural population, had varied ethnic and national backgrounds. The farms produced a wide assortment of crops. Agricultural methods were far more progressive there than in the lower counties.[26] One visitor reported that lime to enrich the soil was "pouring" into Cecil County in the spring of 1850,[27] and conditions were the same elsewhere in Western Maryland. Farming acreage there was consequently the most valuable in the state.[28] Washington County claimed to be the third-largest wheat-producing county in the United States.[29] Towns were numerous and active. Boonsboro, sixty miles west of Baltimore on the National Road, did a very heavy "mercantile business," the *Baltimore Sun* reported: "The streets are constantly jammed with wagons, carts, and vehicles of all sorts, hauling goods to the country. It is a busy town, full of life and energy."[30] The population of Cumberland, Maryland, jumped from 2,428 people in 1840 to over 6,000 in 1850.[31] That part of Maryland's manufacturing which was not located in Baltimore was scattered throughout Western Maryland. Allegany County coal was a highly esteemed variety of anthracite, and was in great demand nationally. Once the Chesapeake and Ohio Canal permitted volume shipments from the region, the George's Creek Coal Company obtained supply contracts with the Government, Cunard Steamship Line, and the Royal Mail Steamship Company.[32] While Eastern and Southern

[24] In the 1850 census these seven counties recorded 46.6 percent of the colored population as free; by 1860, 48.7 percent were living out of bondage.

[25] Again, 1860 figures were used for slaveownership.

[26] See Craven, *op. cit., passim.*

[27] *Baltimore Sun,* April 15, 1850.

[28] Bureau of the Census, *Seventh Census,* p. 226.

[29] *Baltimore Sun,* April 5, 1860.

[30] *Ibid.,* April 26, 1850.

[31] US., Bureau of the Census, *Sixth Census of the United States* (Washington, D.C.: GPO,1840); *idem, Seventh Census.*

[32] *Baltimore Sun,* August 1, 1853.

Maryland were largely isolated by geography and habit, Western Maryland looked outward—north and south through the valleys, and west to the Ohio River and beyond. Western Maryland's need for a marketing and a storage port called Baltimore into being. Baltimore, in turn, reached westward to tap the trade of the interior. This was the "new society," alert, mobile, diversified, and well integrated into the national economy. This was essentially a Northern culture with a marginal dose of slavery.[33]

Baltimore, the center of the new society, was a striking schizophrenic city. The Chesapeake Bay cuts very close to the Fall Line at Baltimore. This geographical quirk made the city a seaport with manufacturing potential, an uplands center on the water. Located on the Bay, Baltimore was nonetheless a Piedmont, not a Tidewater, city. Unlike the other major East Coast seaports—Boston, New York, Philadelphia, Charleston—Baltimore did not develop with the initial settlement of the colony; it was a product of the growth of the interior. The city was not even created until 1729. Furthermore, it was an artificial creation specifically designed as an outlet for the western counties; there was no town on that spot.[34] Baltimore remained small until after the American Revolution. In 1765 the city boasted only fifty houses.[35] By 1850, however, it was the third-largest metropolis in the Union. Animated by a hustling commercialism, Baltimore was built on a Northern pattern. Immigrants swelled the population, as they had in other Northern cities. Yet, pleased though they might have been at having their commerce compared with New York's, Baltimoreans would have been outraged by the idea that anyone thought of them as Northerners. This ambivalence between a Northern life style and Southern sentiment always plagued Baltimore—and Maryland as a whole—whenever the sectional crisis became acute.[36]

Baltimore was essentially trade oriented. Manufacturing grew in and around it, using the power generated by the falls, but the heart of the city was involved in foreign and domestic trade. It was a leading center for commerce to South America.[37] It was an entrepôt

[33] In Western Maryland one white in fifty-eight owned a slave in 1860.

[34] Matthew Page Andrews, *History of Maryland, Province and State* (Hatboro, Pa.: Tradition Press, 1965), p. 226.

[35] *Niles Register* (Baltimore), September 18, 1812.

[36] For comment on Baltimore's sectional ambivalence, see M. Ray Della, Jr., "An Analysis of Baltimore's Population in 1850," *Maryland Historical Magazine,* 68 (1973): 20.

[37] For Baltimore's trade patterns, especially with South America, see William B. Catton, "The Baltimore Business Community and the Secession Crisis, 1860–1861" (Master's thesis, University of Maryland, 1952); and Laura Bornholdt, *Baltimore and Early Pan-Americanism,* Smith College Studies in History, vol. 34 (Northampton, Mass.: Smith College, 1949).

of the internal trade between North and South. The archetype of a Baltimore businessman was the commission merchant who had salesmen in the West and South.[38] Enoch Pratt, future benefactor of Baltimore's free library system, made his money as a commission merchant. The Baltimore and Ohio Railroad was doubly the creation of trade; trading needs dictated its construction, and trading money—notably, that of the Garrett family—financed it.[39] This trading emphasis in Baltimore's economy exerted a strong influence in keeping Maryland in the Union in 1861.[40]

Because the balance between parties and sections in Maryland was so delicate, the politics of the state sensitively recorded changes in attitudes, tempers, and loyalties. Maryland's voters were a diverse lot, and were affected by many issues. As Marylanders reacted to immigration, urbanization, sectional strain, and economic and social change, the state's political balance bobbed back and forth. Masses of people completely switched their allegiances, parties died, new organizations and new leaders emerged—all with bewildering speed. Extreme solutions, such as nativism, were improbably paired with a desperate search for national compromise and quiet. To examine Maryland, especially its politics, in the 1850s is to appreciate the confusion that preceded the Civil War.

III

Maryland's politics seemed orderly enough in 1850. When the second American party system took shape in the Jacksonian era, Maryland was one of the first states to exhibit a strong two-party organization.[41] By 1850 Marylanders had experienced twenty years of lively campaigns and close elections featuring very stable alignments. In presidential contests from 1832 through 1848, Maryland was a safe Whig enclave—close but safe. Clay defeated Jackson in 1832 by fifty-two votes, and that election set the pattern.[42] The elections after

38 The *Seventh Census* (1850) lists 55 Baltimore commission merchants. The *Eighth Census* (1860) lists 114.

39 Another good source for trade patterns is the John W. Garrett Papers, Library of Congress, Washington, D.C.

40 See Chapter V.

41 Two good accounts exist of early party politics in Maryland. See Mark H. Haller, "The Rise of the Jackson Party in Maryland, 1820–1829," *Journal of Southern History,* 28 (1962): 309–26; and Richard P. McCormick, *The Second American Party System* (Chapel Hill: The University of North Carolina Press, 1966), pp. 154–73.

42 Despite the closeness of the popular vote, Clay received seven out of ten electoral votes. Maryland had a districted system of electoral votes, and the anti-Jacksonians had carefully arranged them in Clay's favor during the last redistricting.

1832 were alike, not only in being close, but also in the party-county alignments they projected (see Table 1 and Map 2). Maryland's

TABLE 1. PARTY-COUNTY ALIGNMENTS IN PRESIDENTIAL ELECTIONS IN MARYLAND, 1836–1848

County	Party Winning Presidential Election				Average Whig Margin (%)[a]
	1836	1840	1844	1848	
Allegany	Whig	Whig	Dem.	Whig	51.8
Anne Arundel	Whig	Whig	Whig	Whig	54.0
Baltimore City	Dem.	Dem.	Dem.	Dem.	49.1
Baltimore County	Dem.	Dem.	Dem.	Dem.	45.7
Calvert	Whig	Whig	Whig	Whig	57.5
Caroline	Whig	Whig	Whig	Dem.	53.0
Carroll	[b]	Dem.	Whig	Whig	50.6
Cecil	Dem.	Whig	Whig	Whig	50.6
Charles	Whig	Whig	Whig	Whig	63.5
Dorchester	Whig	Whig	Whig	Whig	60.6
Frederick	Whig	Whig	Whig	Whig	51.7
Harford	Whig	Whig	Whig	Whig	53.9
Kent	Whig	Whig	Whig	Whig	59.2
Montgomery	Whig	Whig	Whig	Whig	59.9
Prince Georges	Whig	Whig	Whig	Whig	61.0
Queen Anne's	Whig	Whig	Whig	Whig	53.5
St. Mary's	Whig	Whig	Whig	Whig	67.5
Somerset	Whig	Whig	Whig	Whig	62.3
Talbot	Whig	Whig	Whig	Dem.	52.8
Washington	Whig	Whig	Whig	Dem.	51.6
Worcester	Whig	Whig	Whig	Whig	62.0
Maryland	Whig	Whig	Whig	Whig	53.9

[a] That is, the average percentage polled by Whig presidential candidates in each county for the four elections listed.

[b] Carroll County was not created until after the 1836 election.

counties were almost uniformly Whig in presidential elections, but the Democrats piled up large majorities in Baltimore City and surrounding Baltimore County.[43] Only five times in the four presidential elections preceding 1850 did any of Maryland's counties vote Democratic, if Baltimore and Baltimore County are excluded. The Baltimore area, on the other hand, consistently went against the Whigs. The results were always the same. Maryland could be counted on to be safely Whig in presidential elections by a vote of roughly 53 percent—until 1850. This pattern of Whig dominance foreshadowed two striking developments of the 1850s. If anything should split the counties—and we have seen how potentially divisable they were—the balance would

[43] Baltimore City and Baltimore County are always counted separately, although they were not technically separated by law until 1850.

Map 2. Average Whig Dominance in Presidential Elections in Maryland, 1836–1848

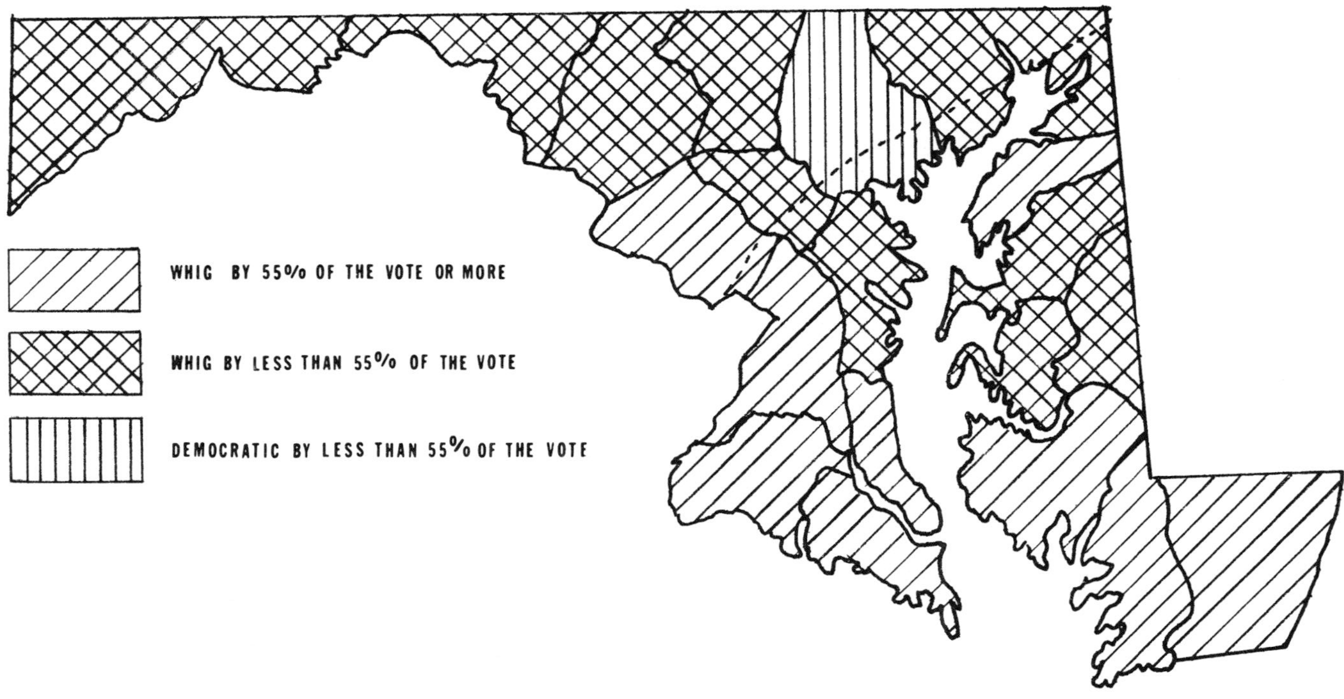

be wrecked. Also, should anything happen to the Whig party, major changes in political alignment would be necessary.

If Maryland's politics were predictable, however, they were still not simple. Beneath the surface solidity of the predictable presidential voting lurked a tangle of various allegiances based on economic, geographic, and historical peculiarities. One hint of the complexity of Maryland politics was that, while the Whigs swept the presidential races in the 1830s and 1840s, they captured the governorship only once, in 1844. Why Maryland went Whig on one level and Democratic on another can be suggested but not proved. Most likely, different issues operated in the different kinds of elections. As noted below, the Whigs advanced a national economic program which was agreeable to many Marylanders. At the state level, however, the counties of Western Maryland were concerned with reform of the state government and particularly with a more equitable legislative apportionment, and the Democrats were the consistent champions of constitutional reform. In this way the Democrats captured the allegiance of marginal Whig voters in the state elections and swung certain counties out of the Whig presidential column and into the Democratic gubernatorial camp (see Table 2 and Map 3). Perhaps federal patronage strengthened the Democratic party organization as well. The Democrats held

TABLE 2. PRESIDENTIAL AND GUBERNATORIAL ELECTION RESULTS IN MARYLAND, 1836–1848

County	Presidential Elections (4): Winning Party and Average Percentage of Vote	Gubernatorial Elections (4): Winning Party and Average Percentage of Vote
Allegany	Whig—51.8	Dem.—51.4
Anne Arundel	Whig—54.0	Dem.—50.3
Baltimore County [a]	Dem.—54.3	Dem.—59.6
Calvert	Whig—57.5	Whig—53.9
Caroline	Whig—53.0	Whig—50.4
Carroll	Whig—50.6	Dem.—52.7
Cecil	Whig—50.6	Dem.—51.7
Charles	Whig—63.5	Whig—56.8
Dorchester	Whig—60.6	Whig—58.1
Frederick	Whig—51.7	Dem.—50.5
Harford	Whig—53.9	Dem.—50.5
Kent	Whig—59.2	Whig—54.5
Montgomery	Whig—59.9	Whig—58.1
Prince Georges	Whig—61.0	Whig—55.5
Queen Anne's	Whig—53.5	Whig—50.3
St. Mary's	Whig—67.5	Whig—62.5
Somerset	Whig—62.3	Whig—56.5
Talbot	Whig—52.8	Dem.—52.1
Washington	Whig—51.6	Whig—50.1
Worcester	Whig—62.0	Whig—58.3

[a] Baltimore City not included.

Map 3. The Pattern of State Elections: Average Whig and Democratic Vote for Governor in Maryland, 1836–1848

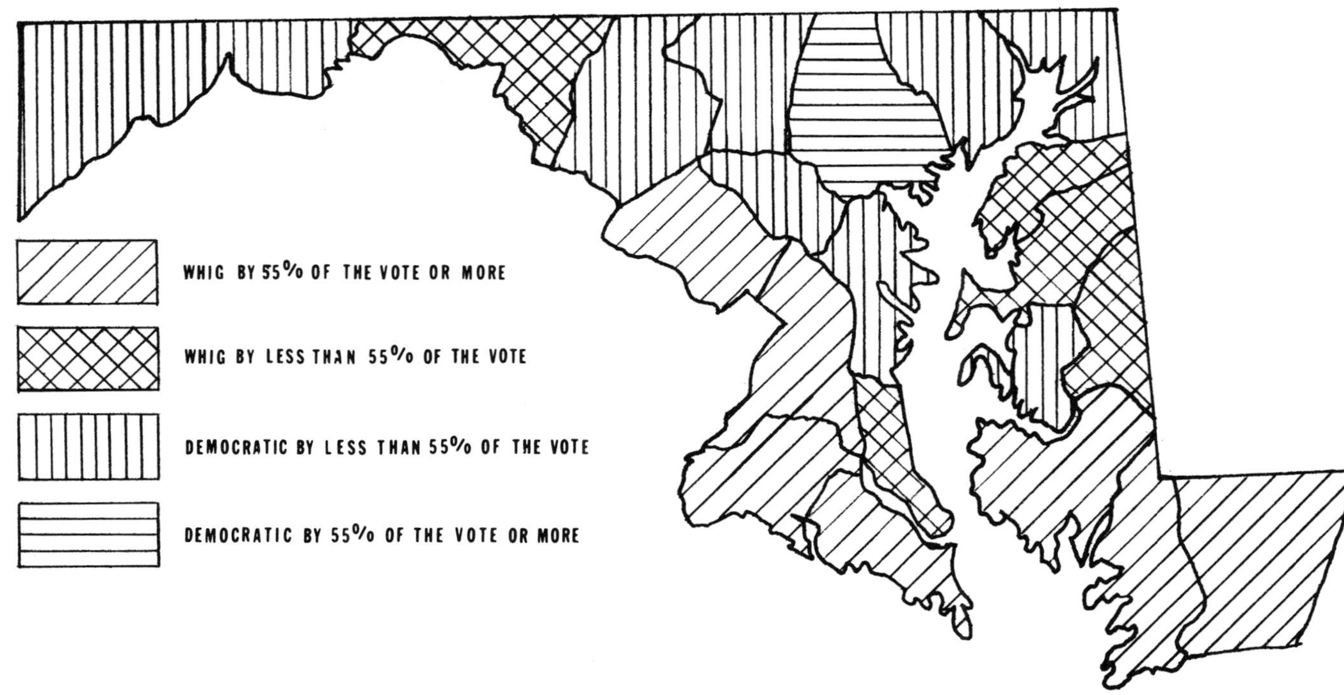

the presidency for most of the years from 1828 through 1848, and the lone Whig gubernatorial victory in Maryland came in 1844, at the end of the only Whig presidency before Zachary Taylor. One thing about the gubernatorial contests is clear, however; although the results were directly the reverse of the presidential canvasses, the patterns of allegiance in the two elections were quite similar. Baltimore and Baltimore County led the Democratic effort at both levels. The strongest Whig counties in the presidential elections from 1836 through 1848—St. Mary's, Charles, Somerset, and Worcester—were the strongest Whig counties in gubernatorial contests, though by a smaller margin. The counties which showed the weakest Whig allegiance at the presidential level—Cecil, Carroll, Frederick, and Washington—slipped to the Democratic column in gubernatorial races. In fact, there was a high correlation between the voting behavior of Marylanders in the two types of elections, but the Democrats did better by a small but significant margin in the state elections.[44]

The Whig presidential victories in Maryland through 1848 were founded on a fortuitous combination of geography, economics, and tradition. The simple fact that Whigs carried the state in four presi-

[44] In this study I have employed a statistical device called the coefficient of correlation, and it requires considerable explanation. When two different phenomena—such as the Whig vote and the extent of slaveholding among whites, for example—can be precisely measured in many different cases—in the counties of a state, for example—it is possible to compare these phenomena statistically. One statistical measure is called the "coefficient of correlation." This coefficient is an abstract number which measures the tendency of the two phenomena (or variables, if you prefer) to fluctuate together from case to case. The two variables may have a "positive correlation;" that is, if one goes up or down, the other tends to go up or down in like manner. If the Whig vote increases from county to county as the percentage of whites owning slaves increases in those counties, then a positive correlation is said to exist between those two variables. If one variable tends to fall as the other rises, and vice versa, then the correlation between the two is said to be negative. The strength and direction (positive or negative) of the correlation is expressed by the coefficient of correlation. This coefficient is a number ranging from plus 1.000 through 0 to minus 1.000. A plus coefficient indicates a positive correlation and a minus coefficient indicates a negative correlation. This coefficient can be calculated by a number of formulas; coefficients of correlation in this study were calculated by a computer, using the Pearson "product-moment" formula. Generally, if two variables are compared to find their coefficient of correlation, that coefficient must be greater than +0.5000 or −0.5000 in order to register as a significant tendency toward correlation—that is, a notable tendency for the two variables to change together in a predictable way.

It should be noted that any coefficient of correlation indicates *only* that two variables move together in a predictable way from case to case. The coefficient says nothing about cause and effect, and does not in itself prove any relationship between the two phenomena.

The coefficient of correlation between Democratic voting in presidential elections in Maryland from 1836 through 1848 and Democratic voting in gubernatorial elections in Maryland during the same period is a high, positive one, +0.874.

dential elections using the same voting pattern produced an illusion of monolithic solidarity, but it was only an illusion. For example, the strength of the attachment to Whiggery varied sharply from place to place in Maryland.[45] In the thirteen counties of Southern and Eastern Maryland the average aggregate Whig presidential vote from 1836 through 1848 was 58.98 percent. In Western Maryland it was only 51.70 percent, even excluding heavily Democratic Baltimore County. In only one county above the Fall Line did the Whigs poll better than 53 percent on the average from 1836 through 1848.[46] In only one county of the old society did they receive less than 53 percent in those same elections.[47]

Some Marylanders were attached to the Whig party because of its economic policy—notably, federal internal improvement spending and tariffs, which the Whigs favored and the Democrats denounced. Marylanders were particularly interested in federal funding for transportation. Baltimore merchants wanted good trade connections with the Ohio Valley. Western Maryland was a natural crossroads for trade north and south through the Shenandoah Valley and west from Baltimore by whatever means could be found to cross the mountains. Like Baltimore, Western Maryland profited from such projects as the National Road. The Eastern Shore always showed an interest in transportation of any kind as a means to overcome their geographic isolation. Southern Marylanders were the least interested in internal improvements, although it is true they complained constantly about bad roads and often protested that some of the money lavished on Western Maryland ought to be spent on them.[48]

Marylanders' internal improvement mania dated from the structuring of the new party system in the late 1820s. On July 4, 1828, President John Quincy Adams broke ground for the Chesapeake and Ohio Canal in Washington, and old Charles Carroll, the last living signer of the Declaration of Independence, turned the first shovel for the Baltimore and Ohio Railroad in Baltimore.[49] In the 1825-1826 session the General Assembly pledged an initial 1.7 million dollars for the canal, a branch canal to Baltimore, and the Baltimore and Ohio Railroad. The federal government contributed an even one million dollars in 1828.[50] Both the canal and the railroad neared completion in 1850,

45 See Table 1, col. 5.

46 That one county was Harford, and the percentage was 53.9.

47 That one county was Talbot, and the percentage was 52.8.

48 See, for example, *Worcester County Shield* (Snow Hill, Md.), February 8, 1853.

49 Haller, *op. cit.*, p. 314. See also Sanderlin, *The Great National Project;* and Hungerford, *op. cit.*

50 Haller, *op. cit.*, p. 314.

having in the meantime consumed the money and attention of Marylanders for twenty years.

At first both political parties in Maryland seemed anxious to support internal improvement projects. The National Republican followers of John Quincy Adams and Henry Clay accused the Jacksonians of being opposed to improvements, but the Jacksonians hotly denied it.[51] Several influential members of the Baltimore and Ohio's leadership were Democrats, including arch-Jacksonian Roger Brooke Taney. But by 1830 the federal Democratic administration had established itself on a states'-rights, hard-money position, and was hostile to federal spending in local matters. First came Jackson's famous Maysville Road veto, in 1830, in which he refused to use federal funds for a local road in Kentucky. Then, shortly afterward, Jackson vetoed funds for a Washington, D.C.-Frederick, Maryland turnpike. Jackson's stock in Maryland had been high, but this veto ruined it. All but one of Maryland's congressmen voted to override the veto.[52] The anti-Jackson coalition swept the state elections in the fall of 1830. Many influential Jacksonians left the president's banner over this internal improvements issue and became Whigs; one of these was John Pendleton Kennedy, who later became Maryland's leading Whig and who will be important to this narrative. Maryland's presidential loyalties, then, went to the Whigs partly because of the economic stand of the two major parties; the Whigs favored internal improvements and aid to commerce.

Most historians have focused on this commercial aspect of Maryland Whiggery. "The interests of Maryland were so largely commercial," reasoned Arthur C. Cole, "that we can only expect to find her offering a strong support . . . for . . . [Henry] Clay's measures,"—meaning a federal bank, tariffs, and internal improvement spending.[53] Charles G. Sellers differed with Cole on the nature of Southern Whiggery, but he nonetheless agreed that in Maryland the party "was simply National Republicanism continued under a new name."[54] Wilfred E. Binkley noted significantly that Marylanders were heavy subscribers to the stock of the Second Bank of the United States.[55]

52 *Ibid.*, p. 324.

51 *Ibid.*, pp. 321–23.

53 Arthur C. Cole, *The Whig Party in the South* (Washington, D.C.: American Historical Association, 1913), pp. 3–4.

54 Charles Grier Sellers, "Who Were the Southern Whigs?" *American Historical Review*, 58 (1954): 344.

55 Wilfred E. Binkley, *American Political Parties: Their Natural History* (New York: Alfred A. Knopf, 1965), p. 173.

This emphasis on "Clay's measures" and commerce was important for many Marylanders but, as a complete explanation for Whiggery, it falls short. The inadequacy of the economic approach can be seen clearly by referring again to Table 1. If the various sections of Maryland were ranked according to their interest in internal improvements, Baltimore and its environs would lead the list. Railroad and canal fever consumed that city. Manufacturers on the Fall Line near Baltimore were candidates for tariff protection. Next on the interest list would be Western Maryland, followed by the Eastern Shore. Southern Maryland would rate last in terms of a natural affection for Whig economic programs. In other words, the area most likely to favor Whig economic policies was, in fact, the most Democratic area of Maryland, and the tendency to vote for the Whig party grew as the logical attraction to economic policies advocated by the Whigs declined. Obviously, something beyond commercial policy was necessary, though not sufficient, to explain Maryland's voting.

Whiggery was strongest in the old society; the reasons for this were historical. From 1800 to 1821 Marylanders were divided politically along the Fall Line, in a rough way. The Jeffersonian Democrats had solid support in Annapolis, Baltimore, and the new society of the North and West. The Federalists controlled the old society, especially Southern Maryland, and often did not contest Baltimore or Allegany County.[56] After 1821 the Federalists vanished as a party, but leaders and followers still formed a distinct faction within the Democratic-Republican party in Maryland. Old Federalist chieftains still retained control of their counties. Furthermore, because Maryland held all its elections by districts and counties and did not hold a statewide election until 1836, local control was both significant and satisfying. So local pockets of Federalists survived and flourished. Most of these Federalist voters became Whigs, according to contemporary testimony. Virgil Maxcy, a Calhoun supporter who fell in with Jackson in 1828, noted that some Maryland ex-Federalist leaders had become Jacksonians, but "the majority of that party i.e., the Federalist . . . went with John Quincy Adams," while most former "democratic" voters stayed with Jackson.[57]

Whiggery in Southern and Eastern Maryland, then, may best be ascribed to tradition or less charitably, to inertia. These areas of old settlement, with their overwhelmingly English stock and negligible new immigration, went from Federalist in the first party system to

[56] See Haller, *op. cit.;* and McCormick, *op. cit.*
[57] Haller, *op. cit.*, p. 324.

anti-Jacksonian in the second party system.[58] Family ties and tradition exerted a very strong pull in this direction. Governor Philip Francis Thomas (1848–1851) upset his Eastern Shore family when he became a Democrat. His father was a Federalist-Whig, as were the rest of the family and most of his neighbors. Thomas's apostasy caused much shame and regret in this situation; he violated regional and social canons.[59] Tradition was better served by Henry Winter Davis, scion of an old Maryland family from Anne Arundel; he never forgot his Federalist father's stern injunction: "My son, beware of follies of Jacksonism!"[60] John Dennis, for another example, was a Federalist representative from Worcester County; his son John went to Congress almost forty years later as a Whig, and his nephew, Littleton P. Dennis, also was a Whig congressman from the same area.[61]

This kind of Whiggery was the antithesis of the commercial variety that appealed to voters in Western Maryland. This was the old-fashioned concept of the Whig as defined by Arthur Cole, a Whiggery based on a plantation system. This Whiggery correlated strongly with slavery and the number of Negroes in the community.[62] Subjective opinions about class also were clearly involved. Whigs tended to see themselves as upper class, and they regarded Democrats as "locofoco" and parvenu. Since the Revolution, the conservatives of Eastern and Southern Maryland had been fighting a rear-guard action against the burgeoning West, and the Federalist and Whig parties were their vehicle. These agricultural Whigs lived in uneasy alliance with commercial Whigs from the new society.

58 Haller and McCormick both support this observation, based on their own researches into voting results. Also, a check of the members of the House of Representatives from Maryland confirms the generalization that the Federalist areas of the first party system later favored the Whigs. In the Sixth through the Seventeenth Congresses the counties of Eastern and Southern Maryland sent twelve Federalists and eight Democrats to the House of Representatives. (These Congresses were chosen because the party system was firmly established during their period. I have counted only individuals, not number of times elected.) When parties realigned themselves in the Jacksonian era, the former Federalist areas sent eleven Whigs and only two Democrats to the Twenty-fifth through the Thirtieth Congresses, while the old Jeffersonian area of Maryland sent thirteen Democrats and five Whigs. Information on Congressional membership and party affiliation was derived from *The Biographical Directory of American Congresses* (Washington, D.C.: GPO, 1961).

59 Heinrich E. Buchholz, *Governors of Maryland* (Baltimore: Williams & Wilkins, 1908), p. 151.

60 Bernard C. Steiner, *Life of Henry Winter Davis* (Baltimore: John Murphy Co., 1916), p. 9. This portion of the work is autobiographical. Davis made his political and legal career in Baltimore, but his family was from the Annapolis area.

61 *Biographical Directory of American Congresses.*

62 The coefficient of correlation between the percentage of the Whig presidential vote, 1836–1848, and the number of slaves in a county is +0.696. The coefficient of correlation between the percentage of the Whig vote and the percentage of Negroes living in a county is +0.730.

The Democrats were stronger in Baltimore and the West because the mass of workers and farmers found it easier to identify with the party of Jefferson and, later, Jackson. Where the Whigs advanced a concrete economic platform and combined it with a vague snob appeal, the Jacksonians relied on the personal charisma of the Tennessean himself and on rhetoric which extolled the "common" man and his governmental champions.[63] This appeal created a following largely composed of slaveless farmers and urban labor. In addition, the Democratic party in Maryland led the Westerners' fight against the old society for governmental reform and fairer representation, and this was especially true in the early years of party formation, before the reforms of 1837. Before that date Baltimore was allowed one senatorial elector, for example, while each county had two, although Baltimore was several times larger than any county.[64] Baltimore was seriously slighted in the House of Delegates, too, and, since the legislature chose the governor and other leading state officers until 1837, Baltimore was nowhere represented in a degree commensurate with its size.[65] In Charles Sellers's description of the Southern Whigs, urban areas were supposed to go Whig, as, say, Richmond, Virginia, did in this period.[66] But Baltimore followed the pattern set by Northern cities, such as Philadelphia and New York, and went Democratic.

From the formation of the second American party system down to 1850 the Whig coalition functioned well enough to control Maryland, at least at the presidential level. The period showed striking political stability. Election results could be regularly predicted from past performance. Similarly, Maryland enjoyed a stable existence, growing steadily and prosperously on the whole. But by 1850 this pattern was breaking and would not be repeated. The society and the economy began to change rapidly after 1850, and politics quickly followed suit. The year 1850 was a significant watershed for Maryland and the Union, for in that year the forces of change built up enough pressure to tip Maryland over the edge of stability, downhill from 1850 into confusion and corruption. As mid-century turned, Maryland began a decade of dramatic transformation.

[63] McCormick, *op. cit.*, p. 165n.

[64] Baltimore in 1820 had a population of 62,700. Maryland's state senators were chosen indirectly before 1837 by "electors," who were popularly elected, as in the federal Electoral College.

[65] It is worth noting that Annapolis also was slighted in representation, and also was Democratic.

[66] See Sellers, *op. cit.*

II

"AS THOUGH THE WORLD WAS BUT BEGINNING"

PERIODS OF CHANGE, such as the years 1850 to 1854 in Maryland, are exciting times, but they can be threatening, too. Opportunity for one person becomes a perceived menace for another. Marylanders reacted differently to the significant alterations in their world at mid-century. Some responded with the ebullient energy of the Baltimore and Ohio magnates, others became alarmed. All seemed to agree, however, that they were in the midst of swift transformations. An approving Marylander noted "the onward tendencies of this progressive age,"[1] but he spoke mainly for the growing new society. In the old society of the South and East, change meant more than mere adjustment; it threatened a way of life. "If there is a tendency in this age more dangerous than another," complained a Southern Maryland editor, "it is that morbid love of change which has seized upon our people everywhere. . . . Change suggests change as rapidly and as recklessly as though the world was but beginning."[2]

Between 1850 and 1854 the rush of events left old values, old institutions, and old allegiances littered in its wake. The population itself was changed by the flood of European immigrants that crested in the early fifties. The Chesapeake and Ohio Canal was completed in 1850, and linked Western Maryland's coal fields with the world market. The Baltimore and Ohio Railroad's main line to the Ohio River was finished by 1853. Trade and personal fortunes grew enormously. Steam navigation on the Bay cut into the Eastern Shore's cherished isolation. Labor unrest disrupted the Baltimore commercial complex and threatened the operation of the B. & O. The problem of what to do

1 "Blunderer" to *Baltimore County Advocate* (Towson, Md.), July 3, 1852.
2 *Planters' Advocate* (Upper Marlboro, Md.), November 5, 1851.

with Maryland's huge and still growing free Negro population reached acute proportions and forced slaveowners to look to their interest.

Change came from within and without the state. It came from old festering grievances and unexpected new troubles. It was social, economic, and political. Section was pitted against section, Baltimore challenged the rural counties, and the whole state was squeezed tighter and tighter by national sectional antagonisms. Most important, national and local problems became entangled through the medium of politics so that each reacted on the other. Maryland began to lead a double life—one as the conservative broker in national quarrels, and one as a state torn by internal divisions. The years 1850-1854 were a Marylanders, was a politicians' sham, a conflict among "ultraists,"

I

Marylanders would have had trouble enough keeping their house in order without pressure from outside, but national issues refused to leave them alone. As a border state, Maryland was very vulnerable to sectional excitement. Any threat to the harmony of the Union was a threat to Maryland's very existence. Whenever the controversy between North and South became intense, no one in Maryland could afford to ignore the possibility of disunion and civil war. Calculating the value of the Union became a popular local pastime.

Most Marylanders were sure that they lived in a Southern state, but they were much less certain about what this meant in practice.[3] When the protracted crisis of 1850 forced the sectional question upon them in its most serious form, Marylanders quickly developed a response that became standard for them down to the outbreak of the Civil War. They were as neutral as their geographic position, Southern sentiment notwithstanding. The agitation over slavery, said most Marylanders, was a politicians' sham, a conflict among "ultraists," "fanatics," and "extremists" only.[4] Maryland behaved consistently in

[3] While most Marylanders habitually referred to Maryland as a Southern state, they seldom called themselves Southerners. Most Northerners thought that Baltimore was Southern. On a southward journey, after all, Baltimore was the first major city where a Northerner would encounter slavery and a large black population. See, for example, the reaction of Ralph Waldo Emerson as examined in George E. Bell, "Emerson and Baltimore: A Biographical Study," *Maryland Historical Magazine*, 65 (1970): 331–68.

[4] Most historical interpretations of the causes of the Civil War are not entirely new, but existed in some form among those who were involved with the sectional crisis itself. See Thomas J. Pressly, *Americans Interpret Their Civil War* (New York: The Free Press, 1962), p. 146. In this sense, modern "revisionism" could have been cribbed from Marylanders in the 1850s. Ninety years before historical revisionism reached the same conclusion, the notion was commonly held by Marylanders that crises and conflict were the artificial creations of political leaders and fanaticism, and that no meaningful or insoluble differences divided the North from the South.

the border-state tradition of compromise, a tradition best represented by Whigs like Henry Clay and John J. Crittenden, two national leaders who were highly respected in Maryland. Marylanders refused to take a stance with either the North or the South. Even if an occasional reference to "Southern rights" escaped the lips of a Marylander in the early fifties, it was certain to be part of a prescription for saving the Union, and not at all intended to advance Southern sectionalism. Marylanders valued the Union; more, they loved and needed it, and could not conceive of existence without it. Yet they clearly perceived the threat of federal dissolution. They therefore faced a double crisis: to preserve the Union while preparing themselves to make a choice if they failed.

Maryland's test of allegiances began in 1850. Agitation erupted over the admission of California, the territorial organization of New Mexico and Utah, the border dispute in Texas, the renewed attempt to enact Wilmot's Proviso, and the demands of slaveowners that their human property be protected throughout the Union. The two major parties were each split into Northern and Southern wings, and the simple chore of organizing the Thirty-first Congress and selecting a Speaker of the House became a bitter contest of wills that resisted compromise and held up national business for weeks.[5] Fears for the Union seemed especially justified when Southern secessionists called for a summer convention of slave states in Nashville, Tennessee. Hope temporarily replaced fear when Henry Clay, the old hero of previous compromises, came forth with his Omnibus Bill. Daniel Webster's dramatic, Union-preserving speech of March 7 made it seem for a time that the grand old tradition of American statesmanship was reviving. But fear returned when the Omnibus Bill met defeat after defeat. Many Americans believed the presidency lost stature and leadership when soldier-hero Zachary Taylor died on July 9 and was replaced by Millard Fillmore. By the end of the summer Clay was exhausted and over-shadowed, Calhoun was dead, and Webster left the legislature for Fillmore's cabinet. In place of Clay's grand measure, Congress enacted a conglomerate of separate bills that fully satisfied no one. The threat of immediate Southern secession was beaten off but by no means killed. As future Maryland Congressman Henry Winter Davis warned: "The day of final collision is adjourned, it is not gotten rid of. Emancipation or disunion may be the only alternatives."[6] Faith in the American future has seldom been so badly shaken as it was in 1850.

[5] The selection of a Speaker required sixty-three ballots.

[6] Bernard C. Steiner, *Life of Henry Winter Davis* (Baltimore: John Murphy Co., 1916), p. 74.

As a general reaction to the crisis, Marylanders expressed shock and scorn. The major Baltimore newspapers, which carried the load of national news reporting, were full of events from Washington. The *Baltimore Sun,* largest and most influential paper in the state, reported daily the progress of various bills, the state of disunion in the South, and the full text of the great speeches of the session. The *Sun,* the *Baltimore American,* and other papers reported that fanatics and scheming politicians were endangering the Union.[7] "The cry of disunion," fumed the *Sun,* is "sounded by the factions of party; the great mass of the people are united in heart."[8] The speakership crisis was greeted with editorial catcalls. One of the *Sun's* regular Washington correspondents concluded, "it is better for the House to have no organization at all than that it should be organized on sectional grounds, or for purposes of sectional legislation," and added that organization would probably come when the representatives got tired of waiting for their pay.[9] Northern and Southern extremists alike were criticized. Compromise in any form was welcome. "The murder of the Compromise Bill," which so deeply depressed many Marylanders, was laid to "a combination of the Northern and Southern abstractionists."[10] The papers praised Henry Clay, Daniel Webster,[11] and John Crittenden.[12] The villains were men like John C. Calhoun,[13] Robert Barnwell Rhett,[14] Henry S. Foote, Jeremiah Clemens,[15] and even Lewis Cass.[16] It was not enough to struggle for compromise; public men were also expected to refrain from mere expression of concern, for that sapped the strength of Union loyalty and made the "extremists" into plausible politicians with a following.

Public opinion, so far as it can be traced, followed the lead of the metropolitan newspapers. The *Rockville Journal* reported that in Montgomery county "there is not . . . an individual . . . who does not

[7] The *Baltimore Sun* was politically independent, while the *American* tended to support the Whig party.

[8] February 22, 1850.

[9] "X" to the *Baltimore Sun,* December 22, 1849. The *American* agreed on January 7, 1850.

[10] *Baltimore Sun,* August 3 and 1, 1850.

[11] *Ibid.,* February 25, 1850. The paper even reprinted the climax of Webster's famous reply to South Carolina Senator Robert Y. Hayne in 1830.

[12] *Ibid.,* January 19, 1850.

[13] *Ibid.,* March 5, 1850; see both editorial and correspondent "Ion."

[14] *Ibid.,* July 26, 1850. R. B. Rhett was a South Carolina Democrat and a Southern extremist.

[15] *Ibid.,* March 1, 1850. Henry Foote was Democratic senator from Mississippi from 1847 to 1852. Jeremiah Clemens was Democratic senator from Alabama, later an elector for Buchanan in 1856, and for John C. Breckinridge in 1860.

[16] *Ibid.,* January 2, 1850. Lewis Cass, after losing the 1848 presidential race to Zachary Taylor, served as Democratic senator from Michigan from 1849 to 1857, then moved to be secretary of state under President Buchanan.

scout the idea of disunion, and condemn the ultraism which has marked the course of the few factionists in Congress from both North and South."[17] In Baltimore, a bipartisan group met in late February to call a massive Union demonstration at the Monument Square by City Hall on March 4.[18] Despite extremely damp, cold weather, five thousand persons gathered there to hear various orators perform under a banner reading "The Union Must and Shall be Preserved."[19] A similar rally occurred in June, this time in response to a bipartisan call signed by over two hundred leading Baltimore businessmen.[20] Henry Winter Davis spoke for many Marylanders when he lamented that the "North is filled with the fanatics of liberty, as the South is with the Quixotes of slavery."[21] There was not a dissenting voice in the state, Whig or Democratic. Maryland stood foursquare for compromise and quiet.

In the state legislature, where simple sentiment had to be replaced by hard decisions and recorded votes, Maryland's middle-of-the-road position remained intact. The state Senate voted unanimously that the Maryland stone in the Washington Monument should record the state's "cordial, habitual, and immovable attachment to the American Union."[22] The Whig-dominated legislature was notable throughout the spring session for its conservative approach.[23] Democratic Governor Philip F. Thomas did dare to stray a little from the orthodox neutrality in his annual message for 1850. His heresy was in suggesting that, if the Union split, Maryland should "make common cause with the South."[24] But this cautiously phrased advice was predicated upon the passage of the Wilmot Proviso, a very unlikely prospect by 1850. Reaction to the message was quick and unfriendly. The legislature received it unenthusiastically, and the *Baltimore Sun* objected to "expressions indicative of a partial alienation from the great, paramount idea of the indissolubleness of the Union."[25] "The Governor is in pursuit of a crisis," scoffed the *Baltimore American;* it predicted

17 Reprinted in *ibid.,* February 27, 1850.

18 John Pendleton Kennedy, Journal, February 27, March 1, and March 2, 1850, John Pendleton Kennedy Papers, Peabody Institute Library, Baltimore.

19 *Ibid.,* March 4, 1850; see also *Baltimore Sun,* March 6, 1850.

20 *Baltimore Sun,* June 19, 1850. The specific object of the meeting was to support Henry Clay's Omnibus Bill.

21 Steiner, *Life of Henry Winter Davis,* p. 73.

22 Maryland, Senate, *Journal,* 1850, p. 255. The words "cordial, habitual, and immovable attachment to the American Union" also appear in the Whig national platform for 1852. Kirk H. Porter and Donald Bruce Johnson, eds., *National Party Platforms, 1840–1956* (Urbana: The University of Illinois Press, 1956), p. 20.

23 Arthur C. Cole, *The Whig Party in the South* (Washington, D.C.: American Historical Association, 1913), p. 151.

24 Maryland, Senate, *Journal,* 1850, app., p. 34.

25 January 2, 1850.

that "the people of Maryland . . . have too much sense and too much patriotism" ever to consider secession.[26]

The legislature had many opportunities to demonstrate its attachment to the Union. From the Deep South and far North it received petitions and resolutions passed by other states, resolutions defining the extreme positions in the sectional crisis. Foremost was an invitation to send representatives to the Southern convention in Nashville in June. An Annapolis observer reported that the legislature was flatly hostile to the idea of the convention.[27] The invitation was tabled, and available comment on that action was unanimously favorable.[28] Resolutions from Mississippi, Rhode Island, Georgia, New Hampshire, Florida, Missouri, Virginia, and South Carolina were referred to the committee on "Federal Relations," and there they languished, never to be reported to the floor.[29] The one communication from another state which elicited a response from the General Assembly was a strong antislavery document forwarded by the legislature of Vermont. The Maryland legislature denounced it, not alone on the grounds of its attack on one of Maryland's domestic institutions, but also because, "firmly attached to the Union of the States, we will not entertain or consider resolutions . . . having for their palpable object to provoke a dissolution of the Union."[30]

In Washington, meanwhile, Maryland's representatives went into the fierce congressional skirmishes of 1850 bearing the flag of compromise. "The adjustment-minded Marylanders," as Holman Hamilton has called them, were to a man members of the forces of sectional conciliation.[31] Maryland votes in the Thirty-first Congress upheld first the Omnibus Bill and then the separate measures which replaced it. Joel H. Silbey's elaborate analysis of congressional voting behavior in 1850 gives all Marylanders a solid "pro-Compromise" rating.[32] On the five different bills that replaced Clay's Omnibus measure to become "the Compromise of 1850," Marylanders were solidly in favor of all except the bill to prohibit the slave trade in the neighboring District of Colum-

26 January 7, 1850.

27 Unknown correspondent to *Baltimore Sun,* March 26, 1850.

28 See, for example, *National Intelligencer* (Washington, D.C.), January 25, February 2, and March 3, 1850; *Baltimore Clipper,* February 26, March 5, and March 15, 1850.

29 See Maryland, House of Delegates, *Journal,* 1850; and Senate, *Journal,* 1850.

30 Maryland, House of Delegates, *Journal,* 1850, p. 127.

31 Holman Hamilton, *Prologue to Conflict: The Crisis and Compromise of 1850* (Lexington: University of Kentucky Press, 1964), p. 110.

32 Joel Silbey, *The Shrine of Party: Congressional Voting Behavior, 1841–1852* (Pittsburgh: University of Pittsburgh Press, 1967), pp. 112, 192–93. Further evidence of the conservatism of Maryland congressmen can be found in W. Wayne Smith, "The Dilemma of the Maryland Whigs in the Sectional Crisis" (Paper presented to the annual meeting of the Southern Historical Association, October 31, 1969, Washington, D.C.)

bia.[33] If the D.C. question is omitted, and the votes on the remaining four enactments of the Compromise are totalled, Marylanders in the House and Senate voted for the compromise measures twenty-one times; in only two instances did a Maryland legislator vote against any of these four bills; on fifteen occasions, Marylanders did not vote one way or the other.[34] And the very form of the Compromise as separate bills rather than the Omnibus was in large part due to the workings of a Maryland senator, who thus became one of the major figures in the shaping of the sectional adjustment.

Senator James Alfred Pearce was a wealthy Whig lawyer from Chestertown, on the Eastern Shore. He brought eight years of senatorial experience into the Compromise controversy, and he counted the great Clay among his personal and political friends. Pearce watched with growing dismay as neither parties nor sections were able to mobilize on behalf of the Omnibus. The death of President Taylor in July 1850, however, put Pearce's old friend Millard Fillmore in the White House, and the possibility of a veto of any form of compromise except the Omnibus diminished. Under these changed conditions, and animated by a desire to secure compromise whatever the cost, Pearce led the move to dismantle the Omnibus. He used the most vulnerable issue—the settlement of the western boundary of Texas—to begin the breakup of the legislative logjam. His approach worked, and he took all but five voting Whigs with him when he deserted Clay.[35] He realized, he said later, that the Omnibus format had been "Mr. Clay's one blunder."[36] Whether Pearce was acting as President Fillmore's agent in this matter is doubtful. Fillmore's biographer, Robert Rayback, says that Fillmore and Pearce worked out the strategy jointly.[37] Holman Hamilton rightly questions this assessment, despite Pearce's long friendship with the chief executive.[38] Most probably

[33] The four bills of the Compromise besides the D.C. slave-trade prohibition, in order of their final passage, were: (1) the admission of California as a free state; (2) the Texas and New Mexico Boundary Act, which established New Mexico as a territory and provided for popular sovereignty in determining the status of slavery, and which gave Texas a $10 million settlement for relinquishing boundary claims against New Mexico; (3) the Utah Territorial Bill, which also provided for popular sovereignty; (4) a Fugitive Slave Law (much more stringent than existing statutes) which put the federal government directly into the business of returning runaway slaves.

[34] The voting records of all members of Congress on the Compromise measures are summarized in Hamilton, *op. cit.*, pp. 191–192, 195–200.

[35] Hamilton, *op. cit.*, p. 111.

[36] James Alfred Pearce to "My Dear Sir," 1850, manuscript, James Alfred Pearce Papers, Maryland Historical Society, Baltimore.

[37] For comment on the Pearce-Fillmore friendship and possible collaboration, see Robert Rayback, *Millard Fillmore: Biography of a President* (Buffalo, N.Y.: Buffalo Historical Society, 1959).

[38] Hamilton, *op. cit.*, p. 113.

Pearce counted on Fillmore's support, but there is no hard evidence that the break with Clay was anything but his own idea. For certain, Pearce was acting out of concern for successful completion of the Compromise, even though it produced a bitter rift between himself and his old hero, Clay. Pearce's "valiant effort," as Hamilton has called it, was made "in the spirit of border-state adjustment."[39] He represented his state well.

The Compromise was applauded in Maryland, but few people seemed to appreciate the importance of the heated debates. The conflict had raised questions of slavery and Southern rights to a shrill pitch throughout the nation, and having once been put forth so violently they would never again be far out of mind. The very vehemence with which Marylanders tried to push aside these questions is an index of just how uneasy they were. Also, it was in 1850 that the gradual identification of the Democratic party in Maryland with the cause of Southern rights began to occur.[40] The leading Southern rights spokesmen in Congress were Democrats, as were the majority of movers for the Nashville convention. The Maryland governor who asked for a "common cause with the South" was a Democrat. His successor in office, Democrat Enoch Louis Lowe, voiced similar sentiments a year later.[41]

Perhaps most significantly, the crisis of 1850 splintered the Whig party very badly. The Northern wing of the party held too many antislavery partisans like William H. Seward to be acceptable to the Southern wing. The Whig president, Taylor, by siding generally with the Northern wing and relying heavily on such people as Seward's ally Thurlow Weed, further helped to alienate the Southern Whigs and to divide the party. Fillmore was not strong enough to put it back together again; indeed, Fillmore lost control of the Whig organization in his own state in 1851. An unlikely coalition at best, the national Whig party began to come apart after 1850. What this meant for Maryland was that the state Whigs would be robbed of the support of a united national party should they need it. And, thanks to a volatile local issue, Maryland's Whigs would very soon need all the outside help they could get.

II

Every so often a political party manages to appropriate a hot issue as its own special cause. It is a proved political gambit. Maryland's

39 *Ibid.*, pp. 110–11.

40 Cole, *op. cit.*, p. 151; see also editorials in the *Baltimore Clipper*, January 1, 3, and 7, 1850.

41 *Republican Citizen* (Frederick, Md.), January 10, 1851; see also *Baltimore American*, January 7, 1851.

Democrats did exactly this in 1850 and afterward, when they adopted as their own the cause of constitutional reform. The effect on Maryland's Whig party was devastating.

An old issue, constitutional reform was certainly overdue.[42] Until 1837 the Maryland Constitution was virtually unchanged from that adopted in 1776. Even the revised document was still seriously out of date, especially in its pyramiding structure of government, which elected the state Senate indirectly and made the governor a legislative appointee. Since its adoption, Baltimore and Western Maryland had grown enormously, while Southern and Eastern Maryland had stagnated. What began in 1776 as a cautious compromise between the Eastern Shore and the rest of the state became a nightmare of inequitable apportionment. The situation was explosive as early as 1820, when the Federalists fought off the first concerted attempts at structural reform. In 1836 and 1837 the agitation reached a climax. The Democratic members of the state Senate created a crisis by refusing to make a quorum, thereby preventing the election of a new governor. Reform leaders made plans for a popular convention. The Eastern Shore threatened to secede rather than submit to a loss of its unequal share in the state government. Maryland nearly had its own Dorr's Rebellion, and only long overdue amendments to the state constitution prevented it.[43] These amendments, the first major alterations in the organic law in sixty-one years made the governor a popularly elected official and adjusted legislative apportionment so that it corresponded more closely to the actual distribution of the population.[44] These alterations relieved for a while the pressure for reform, but fundamental dissatisfaction with the old constitution remained. Agitation continued to build throughout the 1840s.

Democrats identified their party with the movement for constitu-

[42] Charles James Rohr, *The Governor of Maryland: A Constitutional Study,* The Johns Hopkins University Studies in Historical and Political Science, ser. 40 (Baltimore: The Johns Hopkins Press, 1932), pp. 67–68.

[43] In Rhode Island in 1841 and 1842, friction over an antiquated state constitution and a very restricted franchise led to an extralegal "People's Convention," which wrote its own constitution. Some citizens clung to the old charter and the regular government; others supported the new, liberalized constitution. This led to two elections in 1842, two complete sets of state legislators, and two state governments, each claiming legitimacy. The regular state legislature declared the liberals, under Thomas W. Dorr, to be in rebellion and instituted martial law. President John Tyler stood ready to intervene against Dorr should the need arise, but Dorr's followers were defeated while trying to capture the state arsenal. Dorr was sentenced to life imprisonment, but was pardoned in 1845. Meanwhile, the state modernized its constitution and franchise. A search-and-seizure case arising from "Dorr's Rebellion" reached the Supreme Court in 1849 as *Luther v. Borden.*

[44] See A. Clark Hagensick, "Revolution or Reform in 1836: Maryland's Preface to Dorr's Rebellion," *Maryland Historical Magazine,* 57 (1962): 346–66.

tional reform. The natural and historical alignment of the Democrats with reform was not, of course, exact; reform-minded Whigs existed, too. Most Baltimoreans of both parties favored reform, as did a majority in Frederick and other populous western areas. Baltimore, however, was both the center of Maryland's Democratic strength and the area most afflicted by under-representation. Leading reform advocates of the thirties and forties were conspicuously Democratic. In 1847, Democrat Philip F. Thomas won the governorship on a platform of "Reform, Retrenchment, and Convention," while his Whig opponent, William W. Goldsborough, railed against politicians who would "pander to the prejudice and interest of the larger counties in hope of lucre."[45] Thomas won handily. When the reform effort reached a climax in 1850, the Democrats rode it hard and successfully. The result was increased sectional tension within the state and a disastrous weakening of the local Whig organization at precisely the same time that the national party was reeling from the Compromise crisis.

The forces of opposition to reform were Whig. Simple geography shows that clearly. The Whig bastion was in the old society, whose citizens feared and fought all moves to strip them of the unequal privilege they enjoyed under the old constitution. The slavery issue had not yet driven these people away from Whiggery. The crux of the dispute was representation; a strict population basis or anything like it meant disaster for the declining sector of Maryland society. Tidewater Marylanders could picture the horrors of rule by the Baltimore masses, the foreign-born miners, and the slaveless, German-descended farmers of Western Maryland.

Several forces came together to push reform through in 1850. The most important and obvious grievance was apportionment, but in addition, there was great concern over the debt-making power of the legislature; an orgy of internal improvement spending in the thirties left Maryland with a sixteen-million-dollar state debt. Payment of interest on the debt was suspended from 1841 to 1848 and resumed only under heavy taxation.[46] This experience left a legacy of fear about state spending, especially in the old society, which found itself taxed for the roads, canals, and railroads that were helping Western Maryland to become even more commercially powerful and populous. This debt issue finally diluted the traditional hostility of Southern and Eastern Maryland to a new constitution; if the convention could

[45] James Warner Harry, *The Maryland Constitution of 1851*, The Johns Hopkins University Studies in Historical and Political Science, ser. 20 (Baltimore: The Johns Hopkins Press, 1902), p. 24.

[46] L. E. Blauch, "Education and the Maryland Constitutional Convention, 1850–1851," *Maryland Historical Magazine*, 25 (1920): 170–71.

be controlled, it could produce solid benefits for them, too. In addition, the prospect of judicial reform had universal appeal. Maryland, it was believed, had the most cumbersome and expensive state court system in the Union.[47] It was possible, therefore, to find considerable reform enthusiasm in every county by 1850. Even Worcester County, on the Eastern Shore, held a reform meeting to complain of excessive taxes and the want of a check on the state debt.[48]

The opponents of reform were of two types. The first type would consider reform, but only through amending, not rewriting, the existing charter. Constitutional scruples were exhumed for the occasion; since Articles 42 and 59 of the 1776 document forbade alteration of the organic law except through the specified amendment procedure, a convention called to form a new constitution was, in effect, unconstitutional.[49] Perhaps the argument over legitimacy was something more than a smoke screen for other interests, yet a heightened sense of constitutional exactness usually appeared in those who had something to lose in the convention proposal. Everyone realized that if the regular amending process were utilized, the malapportioned legislature itself would handle the question of reform. In this way the old-society representatives might permit minimal changes, secure a limit on state spending, reduce court costs, and still avoid the hazards of reapportionment.

Other enemies of reform simply wanted nothing to do with alteration of the historic and time-honored charter.[50] Conservative Kent County Judge Ezekiel F. Chambers, for example, complained bitterly of "the destructive sweep which is leveling all the valuable institutions of the State."[51] Such fear of change was prevalent in the areas of heavy slavery. The excitement generated by the Compromise debates in Washington only heightened the slaveowners' sensitivity. Elaborate safeguards over the institution had been written into the old constitution in 1836. The threat of losing this protection was a primary cause for resisting reform.[52] In the referendum on calling a convention, held May 8, 1850, the six counties in which reform was voted down

[47] In 1842 Governor Francis Thomas declared that Maryland's annual $36,000 expenditure was the largest judicial salary bill in all the states. In fact, it was not, but most Marylanders took the governor's estimate as gospel. Carroll T. Bond, *The Court of Appeals of Maryland: A History* (Baltimore: Barton-Gillet Co., 1928), p. 148.

[48] *Baltimore Sun,* July 16, 1849.

[49] Charles J. M. Gwinn to the *Baltimore Argus,* April 15 and 16, 1850.

[50] Harry, *The Maryland Constitution,* pp. 10–11.

[51] Ezekiel F. Chambers to James Alfred Pearce, July 25, 1850, Pearce Papers.

[52] Harry, *The Maryland Constitution,* pp. 20–21, 44.

were all areas of heavy slaveowning.[53] The anti-reform areas were therefore the traditional Whig regions, and the leading individual opponents of reform were Whig leaders like Judge Chambers. "There is not a . . . Whig reformer in this district," reported a Southern Maryland newspaper.[54]

When the Maryland General Assembly met in 1850, everyone knew that the calling of a reform convention would be the major issue and that it had a better chance of passing than ever before.[55] In 1845 such a bill had been defeated by a tie vote, and reform organizers had been building strength ever since.[56] Proreform mass meetings became commonplace in Baltimore. Petitions rained on the legislature. Hagerstown held a huge meeting on December 14, 1849, in preparation for the coming session.[57] The influential Baltimore press hammered on the topic almost daily. The expectation was that all Democrats and some Whigs would vote for the measure.[58] On February 5, 1850, the Whig legislative caucus decided to let each member pick his own course on reform.[59] A bill to send the convention plan to referendum passed the Maryland House of Delegates on February 16 and the Senate on February 27. The vote in both cases was essentially sectional. Since the Whigs possessed a majority in both branches, votes from that party were necessary for passage. In the House these came mostly from Western Maryland. In the Senate the support of some Eastern Shore members assured success—a cooperation which no doubt was attributable to the desire to curb legislative spending. Fear may also have had something to do with it. The *Baltimore Sun* credited a movement to call an extralegal convention, independently of the legislature, with forcing the General Assembly's hand. The legislature approved the referendum, argued the paper, in order to prevent popular enthusiasm from taking reform out of legislative control.[60] Reform had gained too much momentum to be stopped. The issue finally went to a popular vote.

The referendum of May 8 was anticlimactic. The measure would

[53] In the 1860 census figures on slaveownership, the six counties which recorded majorities against calling a convention ranked first, second, third, fourth, sixth, and eighth in density of slaveholders among the white population. Also, the Eastern Shore county with the heaviest proconvention vote was Caroline County, which had the lowest slaveholding ratio in the region.

[54] *Rockville Journal*, reprinted in the *Baltimore Sun*, July 31, 1849.

[55] Annapolis correspondent to the *Baltimore Sun*, January 14, 1850.

[56] Harry, *The Maryland Constitution*, p. 23.

[57] *Baltimore Sun*, December 15, 1849.

[58] *Ibid.*, January 28, 1850.

[59] *Ibid.*, February 6, 1850.

[60] *Ibid.*, May 7, 1850.

so obviously pass a straight popular vote that the turnout was very light; many opponents of the measure simply stayed home. The referendum carried in Baltimore and in fourteen of Maryland's twenty counties; a convention was called by a majority of 18,883 votes.[61]

The canvass for governor in 1850 quickly developed into a debate over which candidate was the better reformer. Once the Democrats succeeded in phrasing the issue in these terms, they were in absolute control of the situation. The Democratic nominee was Enoch Louis Lowe of Frederick, a dynamic young man who was campaigning hard as a reformer fully two months before the convention nominated him.[62] His campaign paper was conspicuously titled *The Maryland Reformer*. On the stump, Lowe always hammered at the reform issue, particularly when he was in joint debate with his Whig opponent, William B. Clarke of Washington County.[63] Clark himself tried to appear to be as good a reformer as Lowe was, but the Democrats persistently, in Lowe's own words, "linked him [Clarke] to the fortunes of the anti-reform leaders of the Whig party and . . . held him responsible for their opposition to reform."[64] In truth, Lowe and Clarke were personally on friendly terms, but Lowe had a lively issue to exploit and he knew it. In November, Lowe was easily elected.

Running consecutively with the gubernatorial contest was the canvass for delegates to the constitutional convention. After the overwhelming statewide call for a convention, the reform battle moved down to the county level, where voters would choose the men to shape the new organic law. With the convention already called, and the gubernatorial race predictably going in favor of reformer Lowe, these local contests became the last refuge of the conservatives. They also proved to be an acute embarrassment to many local Whig organizations.

The Whigs of the old society succeeded in electing as delegates to the convention many persons who were openly hostile to its purposes, even to its existence. Judge Chambers, of Kent County, whose distaste for the convention was notorious, headed his local delegation. As soon as the convention was called, the Whig *Easton Gazette* called for "conservative men" to take charge, while the *Centreville*

61 Harry, *The Maryland Constitution*, p. 32.

62 *Baltimore County Advocate*, March 23, 1850. Lowe just barely reached the minimum age of thirty when he was inaugurated.

63 A good account of one such debate in Baltimore can be found in the *Baltimore Sun*, September 19, 1850. There were at least five such joint encounters throughout the state.

64 Enoch Louis Lowe to the *Baltimore Sun*, August 16, 1850. See also the *Maryland Free Press* (Annapolis, Md.), July 27, 1850; and the *Worcester County Shield* (Snow Hill, Md.), August 20, 1850. Unfortunately, no copies of Lowe's campaign paper exist.

Times pleaded for "men who are conservative in their views" and who would not "betray [our] interests by truckling to the influence of Baltimore City."[65] The Whig convention in Queen Anne's County nominated as delegates men who were totally opposed to the idea of convention.[66] The *Worcester County Shield* editorially exhumed the warning of John Randolph that "every change is not a Reform," adding morosely that "good may be done—let us trust."[67] In seeking to do good, the Southern and Eastern counties sent forty-four Whigs and only fifteen Democrats to the convention; eight of the thirteen county delegations were solidly Whig. One foe of reform gleefully predicted that, even if "the foul serpent" of reform got past the referendum to the convention, "it will be with a broken back."[68]

Above the Fall Line, however, the desire for a sweeping change in the state constitution left the county Whig organizations in an acute dilemma. Whig gubernatorial candidate William Clarke had been stuck with the antireform label because of his party; the Whig convention delegates suffered the same stigma. The Harford County Whig nominees, for example, went on record as opposing the election of judges and, most disastrously, as opposing a strict population basis for legislative representation.[69] Predictably, the Democratic ticket defeated the Whigs soundly. No county above the Fall Line elected a solidly Whig delegation.

In desperation the reform Whigs tried to pull reform out of party politics and secure a temporary fusion with the Democrats against the common enemy, the conservatives who opposed reform. The Democrats, in most cases, refused to share the benefits of a proreform position. When the Baltimore County Whigs offered a fusion, denying that reform was a party issue, the Democrats scorned their friendship and went ahead to elect five of the six county delegates.[70] In strongly Democratic Baltimore City, the Whigs likewise failed of fusion and without it found the situation so hopeless that they declined to nominate anyone.[71] The Carroll County Whigs, thanks to the long advocacy of reform by local leader Andrew Ege, were in a position to secure a fusion ticket.[72] At that, three of the five places went to

65 Both reprinted in the *Worcester County Shield,* May 21, 1850.

66 *Centreville Times,* reprinted in the *Baltimore Sun,* August 16, 1850.

67 May 21, 1850.

68 Unknown Correspondent to John Pendleton Kennedy, March 25, 1850, Kennedy Papers.

69 *Baltimore Sun,* August 1, 1850.

70 *Ibid.,* August 14, 1850.

71 *Ibid.,* August 6 and September 3, 1850.

72 *Ibid.,* April 14 and 16, 1850. Ege's advocacy of reform at first made it appear that he had left his party, and he took great pains to deny this charge. Actually, Carroll County Whigs, under Ege's direction, were encouraging a reform convention at least as early as the summer of 1849. *Ibid.,* August 16, 1849.

Democrats. Fusion was also achieved in Frederick County, which sent an evenly split six-man delegation. In Allegany County, however, a "Union" ticket lost to the regular Democratic nominees. Fusion was clearly the only hope for Whigs in Western Maryland and was useful then only if the individual nominees were known friends of reform. Of the forty-four delegates elected from this region, all ten Whigs were fusion candidates.

The hopes of the constitutional reformers were dashed by the composition of the convention. The conservatives had the numbers to dilute or even discard much of what the reformers wanted. In order to secure passage of the original enabling bill through the General Assembly the reform leaders had had to agree to use existing legislative representation as the basis for delegate representation. Of 103 delegates, fifty-four were Whigs; forty-four of these, from Southern and Eastern Maryland were certain to be timid, if not downright hostile, about modernizing the state charter. Fifteen of the Democratic delegates were likewise questionable reformers who represented old-society constituencies. Passage of any measure, therefore, depended on cooperation between rival sections, or rival parties, or usually both.

The convention encountered difficulty as soon as it opened; permanent organization of the meeting was delayed a week because of party and sectional jealousies. The Democratic delegates could not unite to support one man for convention president. The Whig caucus nominated John G. Chapman, a Charles County conservative. They were unable to elect Chapman right away, however, despite their slim majority in the convention. Three of the Western Whigs, elected on fusion tickets, could not support him, and neither would any of the Southern and Eastern Democrats.[73] So, for the first week of the convention the balloting for president found Chapman just short of election but unable to reach the necessary fifty-two votes. Finally Chapman was elected when the weary delegates agreed to settle the vote by plurality. Leadership of the convention therefore fell to an avowed opponent of reform, who freely admitted his "doubts and misgivings" about the whole idea of a convention and who later "witnessed with profound regret" all the major features of the new constitution and vowed to vote against its ratification.[74]

73 The three fusion Whigs who could not support Chapman also split among themselves; one voted for a Democrat, and the other two wasted their vote on a Whig who had no chance of being elected.

74 *Proceedings of the Maryland State Convention to Frame a New Constitution* (Annapolis: Riley & Davis, 1850), p. 783. Since publication of the proceedings had to wait at least until the convention was finished, the publication date given in the volume is in error, and should most probably be 1851.

From Chapman's election to the final adjournment the delegates bickered and argued until finally they produced a document which fully satisfied no one. Neither reformers nor conservatives secured more than a portion of what they wanted. The conservatives managed to get a limit on state spending. The reformers did gain some concessions. The offices of judge of the orphans' court, court clerk, register of wills, states attorney, justice of the peace, and constable were changed from appointive to elective. Entirely new were the offices of county commissioner, state comptroller, commissioner of public works, and lottery commissioner. State Senators faced reelection every four years instead of six. The conservatives managed to thwart reformers' attempts to put representation on a strict population basis; many reformers were bitter over this defeat. The representation question, in fact, resisted four different compromise plans before being settled by a forty-three to forty vote on a day of low attendance. Voting on the representation issue was split between the Western counties, which would gain population, and the counties of the old society, which would hold their present levels or lose representation. The new plan apportioned the House of Delegates on a population basis, with the limitation that Baltimore City could have a maximum of four delegates more than the most populous county. No county was to have fewer than two members. The Senate was put on a geographic basis: one senator per county and one from Baltimore City. Overall, Baltimore increased its share in the General Assembly from one-sixteenth under the old system to one-eighth under the new system.[75]

Public reaction mirrored the divisions in the convention; no one seemed to like the new constitution. The conservative *Planters' Advocate,* of Prince George's County, for example, complained that the new constitution was "entirely different from the old."[76] For the reformers of Baltimore and the Western counties, on the other hand, the changes were too meager. The *Republican Citizen,* of Frederick, voiced the frustration of the populous areas: "We want a man in Frederick County to be acknowledged and recognized under the constitution as the equal of any other man in any other section of the state." "Why," they asked plaintively, "shall not a majority of the people rule?"[77]

Marylanders were not only disappointed in the document itself, but they were also disgusted with the behavior of the convention that drafted it. The time-consuming argument over the presidency of the convention strongly resembled the struggle for Speaker of the House

75 Harry, *The Maryland Constitution,* pp. 46–47.
76 December 24, 1851.
77 March 14, 1850.

that had immobilized the Thirty-first Congress and earned the scorn of Marylanders of both parties. Halfway through the convention a *Republican Citizen* correspondent reported sourly on the conduct of the delegates.[78] The editors concluded: "The people are beginning to give up all hope of the fruits they expected."[79] The *Baltimore Sun* summed up the general disgust of Marylanders: "Instead of a convention of men acting under an exalted sense of great responsibility, we have seen . . . a constant display of factious opposition, originating in sectional interest and party prejudices."[80] Averaging the total cost of the six-month session into the length of its product, one Cumberland, Maryland, man figured out that the new constitution cost better than a dollar and a half per word, and, considering the quality of the goods, concluded that it was "about the hardest bargain of modern times."[81]

That the new constitution was adopted by popular vote was simply an index of how inadequate the old one had become. John Pendleton Kennedy, Baltimore Whig, felt that, although the convention was of dubious legality, "Nothing can be worse than our present collection of scattered laws which are called the Constitution of Maryland."[82] A group of prominent citizens in Frederick urged ratification on the discouraging grounds that "the most that could be expected would be that the new constitution, as a whole, would be entitled to a preference" over the old.[83] In a modest turnout, the document was ratified by 61 percent of the votes cast in the election of June 4, 1851.[84] Eight counties voted against ratification; all were from the South and East, and all but one stood to lose legislative representation under the new instrument.[85] The *Baltimore Sun* reported that 48 of the 103 convention delegates were opposed to ratification.[86]

The ultimate effects of the Maryland Constitution of 1851 went beyond simple structural changes in state government, important as those were. By making more offices elective the document increased the tempo of electoral activity and stimulated a sense of popular in-

[78] *Ibid.*, January 17, 1851.

[79] *Ibid.*

[80] May 7, 1851.

[81] *Baltimore American*, June 2, 1851.

[82] John Pendleton Kennedy, Journal, April 20, 1850, Kennedy Papers.

[83] *Republican Citizen*, May 16, 1951.

[84] Harry, *The Maryland Constitution*, p. 86.

[85] The one county that opposed ratification and did not stand to lose representation was St. Mary's, whose delegation was already the minimum—two.

[86] May 14, 1851. The Constitution of 1851 remained in effect only thirteen years, being replaced in 1864. The replacement itself was overturned but three years later, in 1867. This plethora of constitutions in the fifties and sixties is one indication of the unsettled condition of the state at this time.

volvement with government. "This is the entering wedge to the future," said Lowe in his inaugural. "This is the key to the treasury of popular rights."[87] Second, the dissatisfaction over the new constitution and the convention that created it helped to galvanize a growing dissatisfaction with the current condition of politics.[88] Third, the whole issue of constitutional reform beset the state Whig organization just when that party was already under considerable strain at the national level. Fourth, the new constitution rearranged Maryland's elective offices, creating several new posts, at a time when the Democrats were in a position of strength.

The autumn elections of 1851 tested the new constitutional system for the first time. At stake were three offices which had never existed before—comptroller, lottery commissioner, and land commissioner—as well as the entire House of Delegates, eight places in the state Senate, all six congressional seats, and a swarm of local offices. This wealth of voting opportunities was an exciting prospect, but it was confusing. "We are in a fog," confessed the Frederick Democratic organ.[89] The Whigs, too, as the *Worcester County Shield* reported, were "in a dilemma [*sic*] about making calculations."[90]

The Democrats virtually swept the 1851 elections. Although a serious local split in Baltimore's Democratic machine cost them a congressional seat they usually held, the party more than made up for it elsewhere. In the five remaining congressional districts the Democrats carried two by greater majorities than they had in 1849. The Democrats carried the three new statewide offices by comfortable margins. Democrats seized control of the House of Delegates, forty-two to thirty-one, and achieved parity in the Senate by capturing seven of eight seats there.

For the Whigs the 1851 elections were a bitter blow, and they demonstrated the debilitating effects of the reform encounter. Western Maryland's Whigs were in the most serious trouble. The reform issue cost them dearly in popular support and party unity. The betrayal of reform by the fusion Whigs, who voted with the conservative majority of their party in the constitutional convention, lost the party votes in Western Maryland.[91] The fusion movement also split the party in many localities. Many Whig candidates for local and congressional offices in Western Maryland ran independently, without a tightly knit

87 Harry, *The Maryland Constitution*, pp. 71–72.

88 See pp. 42–48.

89 *Republican Citizen*, June 27, 1851.

90 September 24, 1851.

91 Seven of the ten fusion Whigs sent to the constitutional convention from Western Maryland voted for Southern conservative Chapman, for example.

party nominating convention behind them.[92] Whig papers like the *Herald* and *Examiner* of Frederick tried to make the best of it by denouncing party solidarity as somehow undemocratic and subversive.[93] A Whig nominating convention at Hagerstown, which was called to select a congressional candidate for the far-western district, dissolved in despair when only one of the three counties sent delegates.[94] Even on the fringes of Southern Maryland, in Montgomery County, the Whig *Rockville Journal* pleaded for the dispersed party faithful to act in unison or face "certain defeat."[95] The Whigs' situation was scarcely better in Southern and Eastern Maryland. An "independent Whig" defeated the regular party nominee on the lower Eastern Shore; another "independent Whig" gave the regular party congressional nominee a tough battle in Southern Maryland. Individual Whigs often found that the only way to succeed was to run with disaffected Democrats on some variety of fusion ticket, like the one which captured several offices in Frederick in 1851.[96] The *Catoctin Whig*, of Hagerstown, denounced fusion as "this political abortion," but practical office seekers could hardly ignore that promising course.[97]

For the Whig party the lesson of the 1851 elections was a grim one. Fusion, independent candidates, and the breakdown of many of their local conventions showed the party to be in disarray. Before 1851 the only statewide office open to popular election was the governorship, and the Whigs had been able to win that office only once since 1837. Now, under the new constitution, many more state offices existed, and the Democrats had swept these, too. The legislature was Democratic, and the new apportionment plan could very well keep it that way for the forseeable future. Since the Whig national party was painfully divided after the 1850 Compromise, Maryland Whigs' earliest hope for a comeback would be in 1852, when they could try to reassert their traditional mastery over the state's presidential vote; if they failed there, the party would be in very deep trouble.

III

By 1851 many Marylanders were turning away from politics altogether, in disgust and dismay. This disaffection was the result of at least twenty years of disturbing change in the conduct of Maryland politics. Ever since the elections of Andrew Jackson the election

92 *Republican Citizen*, August 22, 1851.
93 *Ibid.*
94 *Ibid.*, August 8, 1851.
95 Reprinted in *ibid.*, August 22, 1851.
96 *Ibid.*, November 6 and 13, 1851.
97 *Ibid.*, October 17, 1851.

process had been growing increasingly rougher and cruder and more taxing to its participants. The noise, the shouting, the emotional stump appeals,[98] the underhanded maneuvering, and the sporadic violence that characterized Maryland elections by 1850 were in sharp contrast to the orderly pre-Jacksonian polls that many people could remember clearly.[99] By 1850 the aversion to politics surfaced into something tangible and became a sentiment that it is possible to measure from over a century away.

Maryland politics was originally for "gentlemen," as Roger Brooke Taney of Maryland, Chief Justice of the United States in 1850, could vividly remember. Taney was the younger son of a Calvert County planter, raised to a world of slaves and to riding to hounds; he had a college education when that was a rarity. As a younger son he was not slated for any sizable inheritance, so his father sent him to read law in what Taney called "the highly polished and educated society" of Annapolis, where many of his professional colleagues were also his "fox hunting friends."[100] As the son of a prominent Federalist politician, Taney stepped naturally into Calvert County politics when he returned home, running as a Federalist for a seat in the House of Delegates. Despite youth and inexperience, he was elected, and he made no pretense that this success was due to anything but the influence of his family name and connections.[101] The polling required several days, and was done *viva voce,* in the presence of the candidates, who were on hand to greet the voters personally. Perhaps some candidates would buy drinks for their adherents; even the drinking was done under the personal auspices of the gentlemen office seekers. Nor was this paternalistic, almost patrician political style entirely restricted to the old society. When Taney transferred to Frederick in 1801 to further his law practice, he still moved in an atmosphere of established leadership. In Frederick lived former Governor Thomas Johnson (a friend of Taney's father) and Judge Richard Potts, who was known to Taney from his Annapolis days. Taney re-entered Federalist politics with the aid of his friend John Hanson Thomas, scion of a venerable Maryland family.[102] The urban life of Frederick

98 As Roy F. Nichols said of 1850-style politics, "This was a romantic age which had inherited little of the rationalism of the founders of the Republic." *The Invention of the American Political Parties* (New York: Macmillan, 1967), p. 375.

99 Even when the elections in the rest of the state were orderly, however, Baltimore could be counted on for rough elections.

100 Samuel Tyler, *Memoir of Roger Brooke Taney* (Baltimore: John Murphy Co., 1872), p. 59.

101 *Ibid.*, pp. 80–84.

102 Carl Brent Swisher, *Roger B. Taney* (New York: Macmillan, 1936), pp. 40–44.

made politics there a bit rougher than Taney was used to, but the major campaign technique seems to have been the informal barbecue and picnic held in some rural grove.

A generation later such scenes were becoming obsolete; by 1850 politics had developed a new style altogether. Politics became a regular profession, and thousands of officeholders and subsidiary placemen lived by that trade.[103] State legislatures had at hand an enormous amount of largess in the form of charters, special contracts, and internal improvement grants. Conventions of elected delegates chose the candidates in heated, often bitter contests; gone were the caucuses of party dignitaries. Party divisions cleaved through all levels of politics, from Washington to ward, as Taney remembered they had not done in his youth.[104] Thousands clustered into Monument Square, Baltimore, for political rallies. Politics became a mass entertainment as much as it was a means of carrying on the public business.[105]

Baltimore, for one thing, had given elections a bad name. Although the depths of degradation at the polls were not reached until the Know-Nothing reign of the middle fifties, election violence in Maryland's metropolis was a long-standing source of scandal and shame in 1850.[106] Repeated attempts to prevent fraud and to institute effective voter registration there had come to nothing.[107] Election reform was a persistent theme at the constitutional convention of 1851. A second probable influence which was thought to be debasing politics was the institution in the 1830s of an effective national two-party system, which split the nation's politically active citizens into warring camps all the way down to the local level. When politics was a matter of social and personal identification, a friends-and-neighbors kind of alignment, contests were more orderly, more predictable, less inclined to vilification between individual opponents. One cannot picture a Roger B. Taney in old Calvert County treating his opponents to the kind of abuse that was common among politicians by 1850. Finally, the simple growth of the state's population had ushered in the beginnings of an impersonal mass society, especially in Balti-

[103] For the historical development of the elaborate machinery that marked the professionalization of politics by "parties, institutionalized and permanently organized," see Nichols, *op. cit.*, esp. chap. 23, "The Machine is Completed," pp. 359–77.

[104] Tyler, *Memoir of Roger Brooke Taney*, p. 82.

[105] W. Wayne Smith, "Jacksonian Democracy on the Chesapeake," *Maryland Historical Magazine*, 62 (1967): 388–89.

[106] See Chapter IV for an analysis of Know-Nothing violence in Baltimore.

[107] Bernard C. Steiner, *Citizenship and Suffrage in Maryland* (Baltimore: Cushing & Co., 1895), pp. 33–34, 37, 38.

more. Of the Maryland electorate and their representatives the Whig *Baltimore American* said in 1851:

> The average grade of intelligence and of moral elevation that characterize this whole indiscriminate mass must necessarily be much below that which distinguished the political world in the last century. . . . Yet the average grade in our day of extended and extending Democracy, must be taken as the standard of estimation; the political representatives are according to the sort of their constituencies; you cannot have great men as the representatives of small men any more than you can shoot cannon balls from a blunderbuss.[108]

Adverse reactions to politics, like the *American*'s, became more and more evident as politics grew more and more raucous. By 1850 many men were repelled by political life, and "politician" became to many minds a term of opprobrium. The dangerous and seemingly pointless disruption in Congress in 1849-1850, followed quickly by the shabby conduct of the Maryland state reform convention, brought the public estimation of elected statesmanship to a new low.

Disillusionment became evident in both the public at large and in those prominent individuals who would be expected to offer leadership to political organizations. Popular moods are difficult to discern, but, when even the party press becomes jaded, it is safe to assume that a larger disillusionment is abroad. The Whig *Baltimore Clipper* complained that "controversy is continued not for measures, but for men—not for the public good, but for the public offices."[109] The *Worcester County Shield,* although a rabid Whig party sheet, nonetheless asked that the delegates selected for the constitutional convention be better than "such representatives as we generally have at Annapolis," who were almost all Whigs.[110] The *Baltimore Sun,* noting the "corruption, selfishness, and gross audacity that belong to the modern system of politics," concluded that "political wire-working is, beyond doubt, one of the meanest employments that men can lay their hands to."[111] A correspondent to the *Patriot* protested that, when gentlemen's names come up in political contests, "even without their consent, [they] are thereby divested of their private rights, and become fair game."[112]

Perhaps it was a debasing effect of politics on sensitive men that

108 September 12, 1851.
109 January 6, 1851.
110 May 21, 1850.
111 October 23, 1850.
112 "Veritas" to the *Patriot* (Baltimore), 1852, from a clipping in the Pearce Papers.

most seriously hurt the quality of mid-century statesmanship. John Pendleton Kennedy is a clear case of political disillusionment in a community leader. Kennedy was a wealthy lawyer and prominent author, a Baltimorean who numbered among his personal friends many of the leading literary and political figures of his time.[113] He had served his neighbors often before 1850, in the General Assembly and in Congress, and had been a leader of the Maryland Whig party for decades. Then, in 1850, he announced he was through with public office. "I am done with public elections," he confided to his diary; "I prefer my books." A man in public life could expect that "envy, detraction, and malice are to be his only rewards." Unloading his wrath at length, he continued:

> I have half a mind to employ my pen . . . in exhibiting the miserable inferiority into which we have fallen. . . . Nothing can be more contemptible than the state politics and management of Maryland. We have not a man in public service above mediocrity, and the whole machinery of our politics is moved by the smallest, narrowest, most ignorant and corrupt men in the State. The result is something even below a shaky mediocrity in every department of affairs.[114]

Kennedy was not just a bitter, out-of-office Whig. On the contrary, in 1850 he was in a vigorous state of physical and political health (he would live eighteen more years), and his friends in the Whig-controlled General Assembly suggested him as a candidate for U.S. senator. But Kennedy's distaste extended even to the senatorship and to the party leaders who were "disgracing as well as ruining the Whig party in Maryland" by their handling of the election.[115] Active in any kind of informal civic enterprise, and willing to lend his energy and talent to the organization of the nonpartisan Union rallies of 1850, he nonetheless chose never to run for office again.[116] Furthermore, he

[113] The range of Kennedy's correspondence is astonishing. Many of the leading political and literary figures of the time were his close personal friends. Kennedy's irritation at the speakership crisis of 1849 was attributable in part to his friendship with Robert Winthrop of Massachusetts, a leading candidate for Speaker until the political impasse ruined his chances.

[114] John Pendleton Kennedy, Journal, April 20, 1850, Kennedy Papers.

[115] John Pendleton Kennedy to Joseph Grinnell, January 8, 1850, *ibid.*

[116] Kennedy's only noteworthy ventures into politics until 1860 were limited to serving his old friend and fellow Whig Millard Fillmore. Kennedy was Fillmore's secretary of the navy from July 1852, to March 1853. He also worked for Fillmore's presidential candidacy in 1856. Kennedy did not run again himself, however, and spent most of his energy as a supporter of the fledgling Maryland Historical Society and as a trustee of the Peabody estate. The best and most recent biography of Kennedy is Charles H. Bohner, *John Pendleton Kennedy, Gentleman from Baltimore* (Baltimore: The Johns Hopkins Press, 1961). Most biographies of Kennedy unfortunately concentrate on his literary career and slight the political.

knew he was not alone. "There is a sentiment of universal disgust prevailing amongst the better class of Whigs," he wrote, "and the result is almost certain to be a total indifference thenceforth to every thing that belongs to our state politics." And, he added to a friend, "I don't think you are much better off in Washington."[117]

Others felt Kennedy's despair. "Politics," said a former Eastern Shore congressman, "is now become a complete trade, and what is worse, every fellow follows it, fool or knave, and aspires to the best jobs."[118] Baltimore merchant Brantz Mayer had the spoils system in mind when he objected that a "blind submission to the tyranny of majorities is rapidly producing a state of things in our Union that was never contemplated by the authors of our constitution."[119] And, he might have added, that had been unthinkable thirty years earlier. The growing aversion to contemporary political conduct was not, by any means, limited to snobbish Whigs, though Whigs were most vocal on the subject; newspapers and individuals of all political stripes joined in the complaint. Defenses of the political system simply were not to be found. A Democrat reacted to Benjamin C. Howard's request for aid by refusing to participate in "the dirty competition" of politics.[120] Judge Chambers, of Chestertown, loftily observed that, if the public wished him to serve as an elective judge under the new state constitution of 1851, they would have to draft him. "I expect to be excused from the indelicacy of 'taking the stump.' "[121] Such an attitude was out of step with the times; delicacy was outmoded, and Chambers was defeated.

Two significant results were to be expected from the view of politics as a mean, degrading business—a view held by many old officeholders and members of Maryland's elite. The process was circular, cumulative in its effects. As certain kinds of persons shunned the pursuit of politics, others less offended by the new brusqueness took their place. Once politics earned a dubious reputation, many who might have redeemed its honor were driven away, or held back. The more that sensitive people—whatever their class or party—backed off from politics, the less likely it was that Maryland would find the disinterested leadership it needed in troubled times.

117 John Pendleton Kennedy to Joseph Grinnell, January 8, 1850, Kennedy Papers.

118 John Leeds Kerr, quoted in Smith, *op. cit.*, p. 381.

119 Manuscript essay, "False Ambitions," Brantz Mayer Papers, Maryland Historical Society, Baltimore.

120 Unknown correspondent to Benjamin C. Howard, May 11, 1850, Benjamin C. Howard Papers, Maryland Historical Society, Baltimore.

121 Ezekiel F. Chambers to James A. Pearce, January 12, 1851, Pearce Papers.

Withdrawal from politics seems to have affected the Whigs more than the Democrats. Kennedy, Chambers, Mayer, and the Eastern Shore congressman just quoted all were Whigs. Mostly the upper class was turning away, and in Maryland that class tended to be Whig. Democratic journals constantly sought to pin an aristocratic label on the Whig party, a label which Whig journals seemed partly willing to accept, denouncing the opposition party as "locofoco," in the sense of being the organization of the rabble. Clearly there was a fuzzy class line between parties, at least in the consciousness of those involved, if not in the reality of the polling booth. The alienation of the self-proclaimed social elite from politics damaged the tone of politics in general; in terms of party labels, it seems to have been most ennervating for the Whig organization.

IV

The Presidential campaign of 1852 was marked, in Maryland, by a peculiar sense of lethargy.[122] Instead of damning rowdyism, as usual, newspapers began to complain of a dearth of excitement. "We had rather, fifty times over, see the mania of forty and forty-four re-acted," complained the *Planters' Advocate,* "than the still but contemptible canvassing of fifty-two."[123] Other parts of the state reported the same lack of enthusiasm.[124] Maryland voters felt as unaroused as did the editors; the increase in voter turnout in 1852 over the presidential election of 1848 was the smallest such increase recorded in any anti-bellum election.[125] This apathetic tone can be

[122] One analyst of the campaign of 1852 has called it "issueless, spiritless, and hopelessly dull." Eugene Roseboom, *A History of Presidential Elections* (New York: Macmillan, 1957), p. 147. Another commentary called 1852 "a campaign chiefly fought over personalities," with "enthusiasm lagging, isolated, and sporadic, the public . . . uninterested." Roy Nichols and Jeannette Nichols, "Election of 1852," in *History of American Presidential Elections,* ed. Arthur M. Schlesinger, Jr., and Fred L. Israel, 4 vols. (New York, Toronto, London, Sydney: McGraw-Hill, 1971), 2: 944, 947.

[123] October 13, 1852.

[124] *Ibid.,* September 20, 1852.

[125] Lack of enthusiasm for the candidates in 1852 shows up in the relatively low increase in turnout for 1852 over 1848. The increase in the total vote cast in Maryland was:

1836–1840, 29.0%
1840–1844, 10.3%
1844–1848, 5.3%
1848–1852, 3.9%
1852–1856, 15.6%
1856–1860, 6.5%

These percentages were computed from W. Dean Burnham, *Presidential Ballots, 1836–1892* (Baltimore: The Johns Hopkins Press, 1955), p. 504.

traced to three causes—the lack of a sense of important issues, dissatisfaction with the nominees, and the increasing weakness of the Whig party.

No one seemed excited about the issues in 1852. The lack of differences between the Democrats and the Whigs supported the current notion that politics had become simply a personal struggle for office and spoils. The reason for the "remarkably quiet" campaign, explained the *Baltimore County Advocate,* was that, after watching both parties in office, people could not tell them apart. "Let either win that may," the editor concluded; "we have nothing at stake."[126] The *Baltimore American* agreed that with both parties standing squarely on the Compromise of 1850, there was little to choose between them.[127] "The result is of but little moment," yawned one paper.[128]

The personalities of Winfield Scott, "Old Fuss and Feathers," and Franklin Pierce aroused as little enthusiasm as the issues. Neither candidate was the first choice of Maryland politicians. Both men were chosen at bickering, bargaining conventions. Pierce was a dark horse from distant New Hampshire, and one Marylander complained that if Pierce were a bad choice, "the Whigs are equally mortified."[129] Certainly it was not a contest to reawaken popular faith in the political process.

The Maryland Whigs had hopes that at least the campaign would reawaken their party. The national convention was held in Baltimore that year, and perhaps the excitement would be contagious, many reasoned.[130] But the choice of Scott was disastrous to them. Maryland Whigs wanted to make the Compromise of 1850 the key to the presidential campaign; accordingly, they favored Millard Fillmore as the candidate. The Maryland delegates to the national convention were pledged to Fillmore and under orders to switch only to a candidate who openly endorsed the Compromise.[131] At the national convention, however, the party split into Northern and Southern wings, both over the candidate and the platform.[132] The Southerners managed to

126 September 4, 1852.

127 September 12, 1851; see also the *Republican Citizen,* January 10, 1851. Also compare the Democratic platform for 1852, third resolve, with the Whig platform of the same year, point eight. Porter and Johnson, *op. cit.,* pp. 16, 21. These platforms were ratified by the state party organizations.

128 *Baltimore County Advocate,* November 13, 1852.

129 "Rambler" to *ibid.,* November 13, 1852.

130 Smith, *op. cit.,* pp. 6–7.

131 *Baltimore American,* May 21, 1852.

132 Charles R. Schultz, "The Last Great Conclave of the Whigs," *Maryland Historical Magazine,* 63 (1968): 379–400, has a competent account of the 1852 Whig convention, as do the works of Roseboom and Schlesinger and Israel, cited in note 122 above.

have the Compromise accepted as the basis of the platform—even the Fugitive Slave Law—but the price they paid was that Scott headed the ticket. He was not acceptable to many Marylanders. The Maryland delegates rated him a distant third behind their favorites, Fillmore and Daniel Webster. Scott was regarded as unsafe on the Compromise issue, especially the Fugitive Slave Law, and all of the sixty-six convention delegates who voted against endorsing the Compromise Bill were Northern supporters of the general. Many Southern Whig delegates simply refused to support Scott, fearing that the Free-Soilers in the party would dominate him as they had dominated the previous general-candidate, Zachary Taylor.[133] A life-long Whig from Southern Maryland, Daniel Jenifer, spoke for many when he specifically cited Scott's nomination as the reason he bolted the party. He criticized Scott because Scott equivocated about upholding the Compromise of 1850, and because "his nomination has given encouragement to the Free-Soilers and Abolitionists." "Political party ties, of long standing, are amongst . . . the most difficult to break," Jenifer lamented. "No one feels this more than I do."[134] But break them he did, and so did others.

The resurgent Democrats and their unoffensive candidate carried Maryland in 1852; perhaps it is more correct to say that the Whigs lost the state. This marked the first Democratic victory in a presidential election in Maryland since the formation of the second American party system. Several counties which had been Whig by less than 55 percent in 1848 switched to the Democratic column. Compared to 1848, the Whigs in 1852 lost strength in every county but one; although all the counties which went Whig were in the old society, even there the party was declining (see Table 3 and Map 4). The election that was supposed to salvage the party was instead a debacle.

V

After the 1852 election the Whig party in Maryland, as elsewhere, was headed for extinction. Nationally, it was pulled apart by the slavery issue. Locally, the Whigs were bludgeoned with their opposition to reform. The combination was disastrous.

In Maryland's new society the old attraction of the Whig party, its economic program, was no longer a fighting issue and could not sustain the party. The bank, the tariff, and internal improvements all

133 For one good summary of the reaction to Scott's nomination, see Schlesinger and Israel, *op. cit.*, pp. 944–45.

134 Daniel Jenifer to the *Planters' Advocate*, September 22, 1852.

TABLE 3. THE DECLINE OF MARYLAND'S WHIGS: COMPARISON OF THE PRESIDENTIAL ELECTIONS OF 1848 AND 1852

County	Whig Percentage of the Vote		Change (%)
	1848	1852	
Allegany	50.6	42.4	−8.2
Anne Arundel	53.2	48.4	−4.8
Baltimore City[a]	48.8	40.5	−8.3
Baltimore County[a]	48.6	39.3	−9.3
Calvert	56.3	50.1	−6.2
Caroline	45.9	52.6	+6.7
Carroll	51.3	46.8	−4.5
Cecil	51.0	49.1	−1.9
Charles	65.9	61.5	−4.5
Dorchester	62.5	57.0	−7.0
Frederick	51.5	48.9	−2.6
Harford	54.8	49.5	−5.3
Kent	59.1	54.6	−4.5
Montgomery	57.8	55.8	−2.0
Prince George's	58.9	55.8	−3.1
Queen Anne's	54.2	49.6	−4.6
St. Mary's	65.1	60.7	−4.4
Somerset	58.4	56.4	−2.0
Talbot	49.5	48.2	−1.3
Washington	52.2	49.5	−3.0
Worcester	54.5	51.5	−3.0
Maryland	52.3	46.7	−5.6

[a] Note that Baltimore City and Baltimore County are counted separately.

declined as political drawing cards.[135] The C. & O. Canal had been completed and the B. & O. Railroad was almost built; the problem by 1852 was not to construct new things but to pay for the old ones.

What did excite voters in the more populous part of the state was reform and reapportionment, and the Whigs were in a minority on that question. Their opposition to modernization of the state government and equalization of legislative apportionment ruined the party above the Fall Line. That individual Whigs favored reform was of no importance; the party as a group was on the wrong side of the question. Reform was the focal issue of the state elections in 1850 and 1851, and the Whigs were driven from office over that issue.

In the Southern and Eastern counties the Whigs were severely damaged by the presence of antislavery sentiments in their party at the national level. The radical antislavery voices in Congress were embarrassingly Whig. The Democrats, on the other hand, were becoming increasingly identified as the champions of Southern rights.

135 See, for example, Cole, *op. cit.*, p. 219.

Map 4. A Disastrous Setback for the Whigs: Scott Loses to Pierce in Maryland, 1852

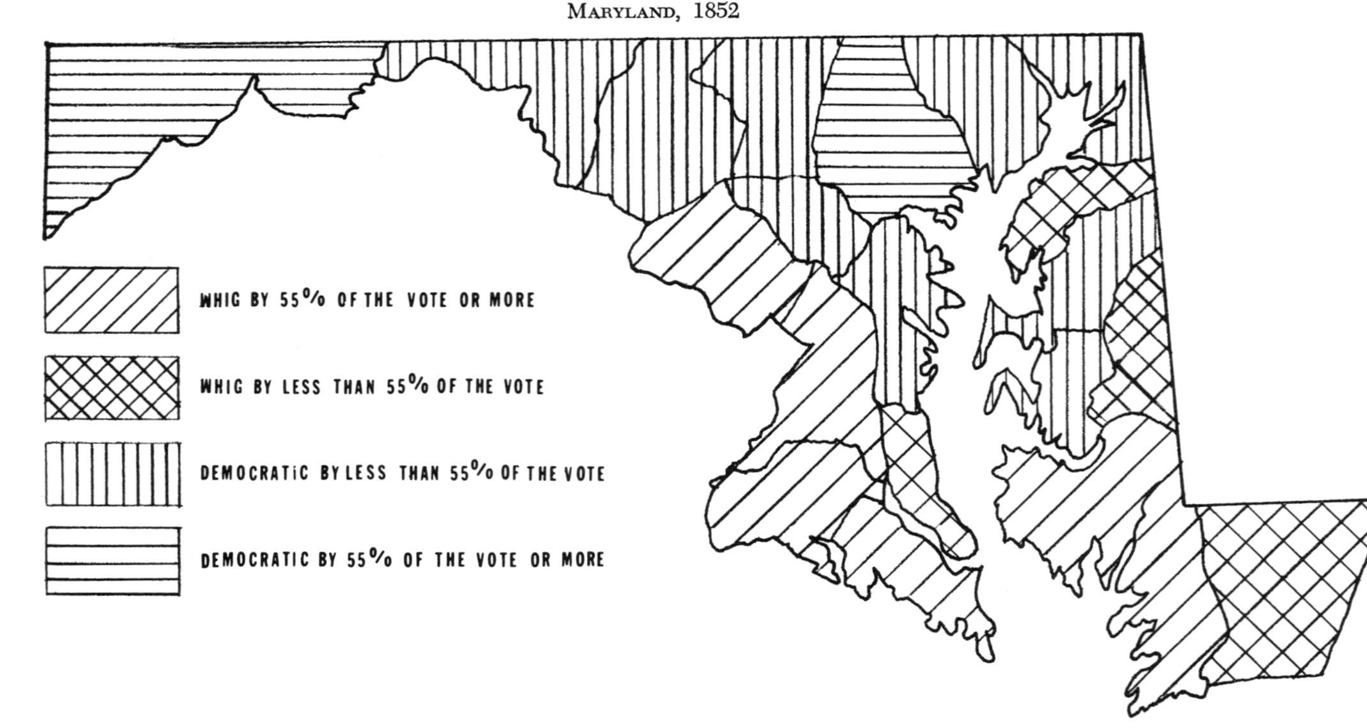

The disunion speeches of men like John C. Calhoun, Henry S. Foote, Jeremiah Clemens, and others may not have been well received in Maryland in 1850, but by 1852 slaveowners were bitter over Northern defiance of the Fugitive Slave Law. When a mob killed a Maryland slaveowner who was trying to retrieve a runaway in Pennsylvania, many Maryland slaveowners became much more susceptible to the blandishments of the "Southern rights" advocates.[136] Then, when the Whig party put up Winfield Scott for president in 1852, that was the final affront to many Southern and Eastern Shore Marylanders.

The Whig party lingered for a few years after 1850, but progressively and surely it withered. The *Worcester County Shield,* an ardent Whig sheet, provided a good running index of the party's decay. For years the *Shield* had fought a rear-guard action against Baltimore, foreigners, taxes, and reform. After the 1852 defeat the *Shield* declared in an overexcited editorial that, despite the late losses, the Whig party could never die—at least not in spirit.[137] Hopefully, the paper reprinted the opinion of a Washington journal that feuds within the opposition might permit a Whig comeback.[138] Frantically, the editors strove to keep the patient alive and his spirits up. Editorials were signed "nil desperandum."[139] Election time brought fervent, almost tearful pleas to "wake up, Whigs," but a month before the 1853 congressional vote no organization had yet appeared in once solidly Whig Worcester County.[140] By the end of 1854 the subtitle that had been carried so long and so proudly by the paper—"Spirit of the Whig Press"— disappeared from the masthead. The party sank out of sight just as quietly.

The party which had been such a significant factor in Maryland life was finished by 1853, or 1854 at the latest. It lost the allegiance of Maryland voters because new issues supplanted the old; increases in urbanization, wealth, sectional tension, and immigration were beginning to mount up. The rush of events passed the Whig party by. New arrangements, new responses, and new allegiances would have to be made.

[136] In September 1851 a mob killed and mutilated the body of Marylander Edward Gorsuch in Christiana, Lancaster County, Pa. Gorsuch's son was seriously injured.

[137] May 10, 1853.

[138] *Ibid.*, August 9, 1853.

[139] *Ibid.*, September 6, 1853.

[140] *Ibid.*, September 13, 1853.

III

THE POLITICS OF CHANGE

THE FORCES SET IN MOTION in 1850 controlled events in Maryland to the end of 1853. The issues dividing the North and South continued to grow, while Maryland's own regions provided ever sharper contrasts between frenetic growth and baneful stagnation. The Whigs sickened and grew weaker. Their imminent passing, combined with the higher pitch of electoral activity which the new constitution had created, produced confusion and imbalance in the machinery which had been designed to settle issues and preserve equilibrium.

Change came faster and faster. "The law of change is written upon almost everything," marvelled one Maryland editor, "upon Nature and Art in one direction, upon Theology, Physic, Jurisprudence, Chemistry, Philosophy in another."[1] With the old familiar patterns going to pieces around them, many Marylanders became jittery. Nostalgia broke out into editorials lamenting the meagerness of Independence Day celebrations, or into sad eulogies on the passing away of many old heroes from the War of 1812.[2] One Maryland paper—the same one that expressed the alarm over change noted above—rediscovered its old files and proudly reprinted news from fifty years past, commenting all the while that things were not the same.

Indeed, things were becoming less and less familiar every day. Immigrants entered the Baltimore port in numbers that alarmed many Marylanders. Labor militancy erupted into unusual violence.[3] The long-term erosion of slavery as a labor system also frightened

1 *Herald and Torch Light* (Hagerstown, Md.), September 6, 1854.

2 See *ibid.*, July 4 and September 20, 1854.

3 See Richard B. Morris, "Labor Controls in Maryland in the Nineteenth Century," *Journal of Southern History,* 14 (August 1948): 335–400.

some people.[4] Prosperity reached a heady peak in 1853, but for many it merely sharpened the contrast between the very rich and the very poor. For some, prosperity was just another excuse to become nervous about the future.[5] Economic activity was frantic. Railroad building became a mania; every little town wanted to be connected to the commercial centers. If no railroad existed, subscription lists to build one were filled with no trouble.[6] The spreading telegraphic network brought increased contact– but not necessarily increased understanding–between Maryland's small towns and the rest of the state and nation. By 1854 the forces of change again put too much strain on the existing balance of allegiances. The cracks in the new, post-1850 facade began to appear in 1853.

I

Though prosperity was general throughout the state,[7] labor was beginning an attempt to cash in on the boom. Coal miners in Allegany County struck for a raise in March 1853, just as spring trade was due to begin over the Chesapeake and Ohio Canal. The strike dragged on through June.[8] In April Baltimore County limestone quarriers struck successfully for a substantial raise.[9] In August the Western Maryland iron puddlers staged a walkout.[10] That same month the Elk River Mills textile workers of Harford County achieved a ten-hour day.[11] The ten-hour day was also the object of a massive walkout in Baltimore County manufacturing plants in December.[12] Baltimore was rapidly becoming one of the nation's most unionized towns.[13] The big city's politicians began to advertise themselves as being from working-class backgrounds or emphasized that they were the "workingman's friend."[14] Baltimore unions actively advertised for members, justifying association as a necessary weapon in the war of "Capital arrayed against Labor."[15]

4 James M. Wright, *The Free Negro in Maryland, 1639–1860,* Columbia University Series in History, Economics, and Public Law, vol. 97, no. 3 (New York: Columbia University, 1921), pp. 306–10. See also *Port Tobacco Times,* December 15, 1853; and *Upper Marlboro Gazette* (Upper Marlboro, Md.), May 18, 1853.

5 *Upper Marlboro Gazette,* January 19, 1853.

6 *Baltimore County Advocate* (Towson, Md.), April 2, 1853; and *Upper Marlboro Gazette,* March 2, 1853.

7 *Baltimore Sun,* September 11, 19, and October 6, 1853.

8 The miners wanted an increase in pay from thirty cents a ton dug to thirty-six cents, but settled for thirty-three. *Ibid.,* March 16 and June 25, 1853.

9 *Baltimore County Advocate,* April 16, 1853.

10 *Baltimore Sun,* August 1, 1853.

11 *Ibid.,* August 29, 1853.

12 *Baltimore County Advocate,* December 19, 1853.

13 Morris, *op. cit.,* pp. 285–86.

14 *Baltimore Sun,* July 1–7, 1853. Note especially the cards for Martin F. Conway.

15 *Ibid.,* September 5, 19, and October 4, 1853.

This sense of mutual hostility between money and the masses was certainly not eased by the newspapers' discovery of the names and estimated fortunes of the state's richest men. The Maryland nabobs, all Baltimoreans, each claimed a net worth conservatively estimated at anywhere from $200,000 to $800,000; their real fortunes may have been considerably larger.[16] That the rising level of wealth brought with it an increase in labor dissatisfaction proved again that general prosperity does not necessarily breed general contentment.

In 1853 an imbalance in the strength of the political parties in Maryland produced confusion in the political system. Both parties were victims of a rash of independent candidates. Some Whigs ran as independents in order to be free of the declining party's label; others did so because the party was too feeble to make nominations in their area. Some Democrats ran as independents because that party did not have enough nominations to accommodate all the aspiring campaigners. Too much success led the Democrats into intraparty fights over spoils and office. The Democratic nominating convention of 1853, for example, ground on through an unusual thirty-three ballots before selecting a gubernatorial candidate. Bitter factional feuds were also common at local party gatherings.

In Baltimore the Democrats used a primary election system for the first time in 1853. Democrats violently attacked other Democrats in the local papers and created a harvest of ill-feeling which often took the practical form of an independent candidacy for the primary's losers. John P. Kennedy feared the ballot would be so long that it would take an extra day or two to tally the results.[17] After William P. Preston lost the Democratic congressional nomination in the Third District to Joshua Vasant, he ran instead as an "independent Democrat." Vasant was a veteran of Maryland politics, but no Whig had ever set upon him with the viciousness of his fellow Democrat, Preston. "The candidate . . . is degraded in such a contest," Vasant complained bitterly, and then announced his withdrawal from the race.[18] The party refused his resignation because the election was so near that a substitute could not be chosen. In fact, Vasant ultimately won the election, but the hard feelings lingered. "Angry contention has

[16] *Ibid.*, October 5, 1853; *Herald and Torch Light*, February 15, 1854. Maryland's richest men were George Brown, John Ridgley, Johns Hopkins, John S. Gittings, and Jacob Albert. Their interests included banking, wholesale and retail trade, and manufacturing.

[17] John Pendleton Kennedy, Journal, November 3, 1853, John Pendleton Kennedy Papers, Peabody Institute Library, Baltimore.

[18] *Baltimore Sun*, October 17, 1853. In 1853 the Third Congressional District contained Baltimore County and Baltimore City, Wards 13–20, on the northern side of the city.

arisen in . . . Baltimore among Democrats," observed a card in the *Baltimore Sun*, "which threatens disaster to our cause."[19]

The situation in the counties that fall of 1853 was little different. With Whiggery weakened, the Democrats divided over certain spoils, and the ballot cluttered with independents, some incumbents chose not to run at all. In Southern Maryland, independents ran well against regular nominees for the House of Delegates, state Senate, and even Congress itself.[20] In St. Mary's and Anne Arundel counties, several prominent men declined to participate in the canvass, despite popular movements on their behalf. Richard J. Bowie, congressman from Southern Maryland's Sixth District, refused renomination.[21] Refusals to run became so regular that the *Port Tobacco Times* simply headed such items "more declensions." Referring to the custom of plying voters with strong drink, one Baltimore County man refused to run for political office because it was "without profit, and worse still, without honor," to engage in a "wholesale whiskey business."[22] The Democrats of Dorchester County gave up trying to make party nominations; instead interested individuals simply announced themselves.[23] In Frederick County, the Democratic congressional nominating convention selected William T. Hamilton; at this, the supporters of former Governor Francis Thomas walked out. Thomas ran as an independent, and the enfeebled Whigs supported him rather than send one of their own out to certain defeat.[24] In all, four of Maryland's six congressional races had independents in them. All four mavericks lost, but they all made respectable showings.[25] The situation was unprecedented.

[19] See card signed "Hundreds of Democrats," in the *Baltimore Sun*, July 13, 1853; see also William H. Hope to Robert J. Brent, *ibid.*

[20] *Port Tobacco Times*, November 11, 1853.

[21] *Ibid.*, September 22, October 13, and August 25, 1853.

[22] *Baltimore County Advocate*, April 15, 1854.

[23] *Baltimore Sun*, October 1, 1853.

[24] *Baltimore County Advocate*, September 24, 1853.

[25] The results of the 1853 Maryland congressional races were as follows:

District I—the lower Eastern Shore	
Franklin, Whig	5,815
Stevens, independent	5,127
District II—the head of the Bay and north-central Maryland	
Shower, Democrat	7,246
Wethered, Whig	6,330
District III—Baltimore County and eight city wards	
Vasant, Democrat	5,876
Preston, independent	5,661
District IV—twelve wards in Baltimore	
May, Democrat	6,792
Walsh, Whig	6,440

Maryland in the early 1850s had no political machines of any size to provide order in the face of the wide-open political situation. Though Baltimorean Henry Winter Davis wrote angrily to a friend about a "court house clique," the general level of political association never rose above just that —a clique.[26] Factions in Maryland politics tended to be highly personal under the second party system; nothing like Van Buren's Albany Regency ever appeared in Maryland. The diversity of the state, and its close political balance, threw insuperable obstacles in the way of any would-be statewide machine. Whigs for example, were actually divided into the commercial Whigs of the new society and the planter Whigs of the old. The regular rotation of the governorship to the various subdivisions of the state, established in the 1837 reorganization, limited the power of any potential king-makers and encouraged sectional factions to hold aloof and await their turn. Even in Baltimore, where the Democrats had been well entrenched since the 1830s, the party machinery was relatively simple and out in the open. This may in part be accounted for by the city's newness; almost all of its growth occurred in the nineteenth century, and the town was in a considerable state of flux most of the time. From a relatively small base the city had rapidly increased in size, diversity, and wealth. The formal party structure existed to nominate candidates, turn out the faithful, and support the state and national organization, but open mass meetings and a changing population thwarted any plans for a smooth-running urban machine, and no one group could claim control of Baltimore.

The new flexibility of politics and the absence of powerful machines did not, however, restore the tarnished reputation that politics had earned by the early fifties. The General Assembly of 1853 was the most laggard, long-winded, and expensive in memory. The session, which normally adjourned in March, dragged on into May. Delegates continued to draw *per diem* salary while on pleasure junkets to Virginia and Pennsylvania. The press alternately mocked and excoriated

---

District V—the three westernmost counties	
Hamilton, Democrat	7,545
Thomas, independent	6,429
District VI—Southern Maryland	
Sollers, Whig	3,820
Jenifer, independent	2,438

Note: In the Fifth District, independent Thomas had Whig endorsement. The Sixth District returns are not complete, no returns being available for Calvert County, but Sollers was the victor, nonetheless.

26 Henry Winter Davis to Samuel F. DuPont, March 13, 1850, Samuel F. DuPont Papers, Eleutherian Mills Historical Library, Greenville, Del.

the legislators.[27] The *Baltimore Clipper* concluded that "condemnation is universal."[28]

The *Baltimore Sun* claimed to find hope in all this political confusion. A Hagerstown correspondent to that paper noted approvingly that "people are getting tired in these parts of party organizations, and will in the future select the best men," instead of slavishly voting a party ticket.[29] The *Sun* editors themselves concluded that, with differences in party platforms reduced to invisibility, "we have the promise of a civil and social millenium."[30] Henry Winter Davis, who would profit enormously from the upheaval in Maryland politics, likewise cheered "this great breaking up of parties," which would bury forever the "old fogy" politics of the past.[31] The condition of politics, in short, had sunk so low that any change, even one which in fact reflected the diseased state of things, was greeted with some cheers.

If the editors of the *Sun* and other political observers had had the benefit of hindsight, they might have seen that, even as 1854 began, Maryland was stumbling through a transitional phase toward a startling new alignment. People were dissatisfied both with the condition of society and with the shape of politics. Social unrest provided the impetus for change while political confusion gave it an opening through which to express itself. Reform was in the air; the years after 1853 were full of the strivings of Marylanders to regain their poise, equilibrium, and sense of values. Reform struck out in many directions, most notably in the fields of temperance and nativism, which were related much more closely than most contemporaries or historians have realized. The editors of the *Sun* may be forgiven for not seeing, in late 1853, the astonishing times that were coming to Maryland.

II

The temperance movement of the 1850s was a symptom of the concern with social ills that marked that decade. True, the great era of reform that characterized America in the thirties and forties had lost momentum by mid-century. Yet temperance reform, and nativism too, can be understood as attempts to check the evil course of Ameri-

27 *Cambridge Democrat* (Cambridge, Md.), May 11, 1853; *Worcester County Shield* (Snow Hill, Md.), May 31, 1853; *Upper Marlboro Gazette,* June 1, 1853.

28 May 18, 1853.

29 September 6, 1853.

30 *Ibid.,* August 18, 1853.

31 Henry Winter Davis to Samuel F. DuPont, October 1854, DuPont Papers.

can politics and society as perceived by Marylanders in the middle fifties.

Antisaloon agitation had been a fairly constant product of the American moralist mentality since at least the 1830s. Like many towns, Baltimore had a "Temperance Hall," a venerable structure used for many political conventions and other gatherings. The sudden and signal success of temperance in the early fifties, however, was one more proof that people were becoming socially concerned. The antisaloon gospel had finally found a large audience.

By the summer of 1853 the temperance movement had built both momentum and a program. The great object of the crusaders was passage in Maryland of a "Maine Law," an act to ban the manufacture and sale of spirits except for medicinal purposes. The act took its name from the New England state which first passed such a prohibition. Following glowing reports of its successful operation in Maine and elsewhere, the law became the cherished goal of those who wished to stem the flow of corruption in Maryland.

Maine Law advocates attributed all sorts of evils to strong drink. A stabbing death in Southern Maryland was said to be an object lesson on the need for prohibition.[32] Close readers of the *Baltimore Sun* could note that, while Allegany County lacked skilled and industrious laborers, it did have twenty-nine public houses, only two of which bothered to serve food.[33] Furthermore, temperance was a return to the glorious past, for Maryland's laws of 1639 had contained a stiff prohibition statute. Several newspapers editorialized for a Maine Law on the basis of this hoary precedent.[34] Religion rallied to temperance, pulpit and street-corner preachers alike.[35] To its adherents, the Maine Law was the answer to pauperism, sloth, broken homes, and, of course, crime.[36] Maine Law proponents in this respect did not sound conspicuously different from previous or subsequent temperance advocates. What was unique about the Maine Law program was its strength.

Virtually every county in Maryland had a temperance organization by the end of the summer of 1853. The prohibition outbreak became very prominent in August and September, when local and state temperance conventions made a striking display of enthusiasm and numbers. Here at last, outside the tainted arena of formal party

[32] *Port Tobacco Times,* November 18, 1853.

[33] August 1 and October 8, 1853.

[34] *Port Tobacco Times,* December 1, 1853; see also reprint from *Baltimore Clipper, ibid.,* November 24, 1853.

[35] *Baltimore Sun,* July 26–August 1, 1853.

[36] *Baltimore County Advocate,* February 18, 1854.

politics, was a movement which recognized a prime social sickness and presented a program to cure it.

The 1853 Maine Law meetings did not create a political party, but rather sought to influence elections and to work through political channels without becoming too directly involved. Activity was limited to the county or municipal level; state conventions stayed on the lofty plane of exhortation and rhetoric. The standard procedure at local meetings was to urge a Maine Law for Maryland and to promise to vote for anyone, of either party, who agreed to work for that end. Where the movement had the requisite strength and confidence, Maine Law conventions would also threaten to nominate their own ticket if neither party slate was acceptable. This alternative was used in Howard, Prince George's, Montgomery, and Anne Arundel Counties, and with complete success in Baltimore City. The organizers of these meetings and the candidates they put forth—when they did so—were usually political nonentities and newcomers. The reluctance of the Maine Law men to field many nominations, plus their unfamiliarity with state politics, pointed to the essentially nonpartisan orientation of the movement. Furthermore, in no Maryland county was the Maine Law movement able to elect one of its own nominees.[37]

In Baltimore, the situation was different; Baltimore offered a set of conditions that were uniquely ripe for exploitation by the new movement. Unlike rural politics, Baltimore's urban alignments were potentially less stable, more open to change, surprise, and manipulation. Here 170,000 people lived in close proximity.[38] Rumor traveled quickly; the press was daily and active. Mass meetings were easily called and easily filled. Popular excitements traveled much faster and reached far more people than was ever possible in a rural environment. Additionally, in the fall of 1853 the Baltimore Whigs were feeble and the Democrats were quarreling among themselves. The Maine Law forces in the city aimed at the House of Delegates seats because hope for passage of a Maine Law centered on the state legislature. They also coveted the sheriff's office because the incumbent was notoriously lax in enforcing the Sunday Liquor Law. Although the city Maine Law convention decided not to split its ticket, five of the ten delegate

[37] Although no Maine Law candidates were elected outside Baltimore, their influence on elections may have been considerable. It is impossible, however, to gauge accurately the effect of a Maine Law endorsement of a regular party nominee, or the effect of a Maine Law candidacy on the customary party balance in a local election.

[38] U.S., Bureau of the Census, *Seventh Census of the United States* (Washington, D.C.: GPO, 1850), p. 221.

nominees were Democrats and five were Whigs.[39] Noting that they had nothing to hope for from either party, the Maine Law leaders called mass meetings and papered the city with some 30,000 tracts.[40] When the results were in, they had elected all their nominees and held the balance of power in the state House of Delegates, A well-organized, energetic, and enthusiastic group of independents, united behind a reform principle, had swept every office they contested, including the sheriff's post. The regular party professionals here received the first of many election surprises they would encounter in those changing times. (See Table 4.)

"Go it, red-eye," warned the convivial editor of the *Upper Marlboro Gazette* in January 1854, "they're gaining on you."[41] Under a barrage of petitions from all over the state, the 1854 session of the Maryland General Assembly received and debated a Maine Law.[42] For a while it seemed the forces of reform would overcome.

Ultimately, however, politics bested idealism, and the enthusiasm for temperance proved to be impotent. The temperance bill died a quiet and inglorious death on the table of the Senate finance committee. The Maine Law delegates from Baltimore, outmaneuvered in the early voting, quickly responded to the old call of party and began to split 5 to 5 on many key votes, with Democrats in one group, Whigs in the other.[43] These defeats sapped the ephemeral strength from the movement.

The short-lived Maine Law uproar did, however, expose several important truths. First, the Maine Law movement demonstrated the feasibility of launching a crusade; the popular mood was receptive to unusual nostrums and cures. Second, it showed that, if a strong crusade were to succeed, it would have to work its way into the very fabric of the political party system. The pressure-from-without approach of the Maine Law, with its optional nominations, did not exert enough coercive force. Furthermore, residual loyalty to the old parties undermined the movement. Third, the Baltimore experience showed that the imbalance of strength between the existing major parties left an opening for a third-party movement.

III

Where temperance reform failed, political nativism succeeded. It succeeded because it was better organized and because it spoke

39 *Baltimore Sun*, August 29, 1853.
40 *Ibid.*, September 13 and 20, 1853.
41 January 19, 1854.
42 *Baltimore Sun*, February 9, 1854.
43 *Upper Marlboro Gazette*, January 11 and 18, 1854.

TABLE 4. THE MAINE LAW IN BALTIMORE, 1853

	Governor's Election				Sheriff's Election				Difference in Governor's and Sheriff's Race	
Ward	Dem.	(%)	Whig	(%)	Dem.	(%)	Maine Law	(%)	Dem. Vote	(%)
1	759	(63.6)	429	(36.4)	583	(49.4)	598	(50.6)	−176	(−14.2)
2	686	(72.9)	255	(27.1)	688	(72.9)	255	(27.1)	+ 2	(+00.0)
3	795	(51.1)	749	(48.9)	685	(46.3)	793	(53.7)	−110	(− 4.8)
4	505	(47.6)	557	(52.4)	420	(40.1)	617	(59.9)	− 85	(− 7.5)
5	423	(55.7)	337	(44.3)	360	(47.9)	392	(52.1)	− 63	(− 7.8)
6	659	(57.6)	484	(42.4)	540	(47.1)	606	(52.9)	−119	(−10.5)
7	726	(60.7)	481	(39.3)	583	(49.1)	603	(50.9)	− 43	(−10.8)
8	969	(67.5)	467	(32.5)	796	(55.1)	649	(44.0)	−173	(−12.4)
9	412	(61.5)	256	(38.5)	378	(60.7)	245	(39.3)	− 34	(− 0.8)
10	327	(43.9)	431	(56.1)	284	(42.5)	397	(57.5)	− 43	(− 1.4)
11	488	(57.8)	532	(52.2)	433	(47.9)	471	(52.1)	− 55	(− 0.1)
12	615	(49.8)	622	(50.2)	504	(43.5)	664	(56.5)	−109	(− 6.4)
13	323	(43.6)	417	(56.4)	261	(37.6)	433	(62.4)	− 62	(− 6.0)
14	513	(46.7)	596	(53.3)	433	(41.3)	615	(58.7)	− 80	(− 5.4)
15	681	(52.1)	620	(47.9)	570	(45.7)	677	(54.3)	−111	(− 6.4)
16	507	(57.2)	381	(42.8)	382	(43.9)	488	(56.1)	−125	(−13.3)
17	825	(70.5)	346	(29.5)	613	(52.8)	547	(47.2)	−212	(−17.7)
18	1,291	(58.0)	935	(42.0)	856	(38.6)	1,333	(61.4)	−435	(−19.4)
19	684	(56.9)	518	(43.1)	490	(42.2)	670	(57.8)	−194	(−14.7)
20	698	(60.4)	463	(39.6)	491	(47.1)	551	(52.9)	−207	(−13.3)
City Total	12,886	(56.7)	9,846	(43.3)	10,293	(46.8)	11,688	(53.2)	−2,593	(− 9.9)

NOTE: This table shows two things about Maine Law strength in the Baltimore wards in 1853. First, it paralleled Whig strength in the simultaneous gubernatorial contest. This is natural; since the Whigs made no nominations for local office, their voters had the alternative of voting only for the Maine Law candidate. Second, however, note that many Democrats voted for the Maine Law sheriff, too. Not only did the Whigs lose while Maine Law won, but also in every case except Ward 2—the most heavily Democratic ward in the city at this election—the Democratic sheriff's candidate ran considerably behind his gubernatorial party mate, both in the number of votes and in the percentage of the vote.

more directly to the concerns which agitated Marylanders in a time of change. Political nativism promised solutions to the problems of immigration, sectionalism, political corruption, and national purpose. Nativism was as colorful and crusading as temperance reform and seemingly a good deal more relevant to contemporary problems.

Maryland's nativist tradition dated from the 1830s.[44] Despite an early colonial history of religious toleration and a continuing high proportion of Catholics in the population,[45] Maryland proved to be no more immune to religious and national prejudice than any other state. Nativism—best defined as "intense opposition to an internal minority on grounds of its foreign connections"[46]—erupted into a "Native American" party in Baltimore in 1844 and 1845. After a signal lack of success in these years, nativism left politics and went underground.[47] Between 1845 and 1853 the nativist faith was kept alive by fraternal orders carrying names like the United Sons of America, the Order of United Americans, and the Union of American Mechanics. Because their lodges were secret societies, complete with grips, passwords, and oaths, no accurate estimate of their strength exists.[48] By the early fifties, however, these societies were certainly well attended. Furthermore, conditions were right for their shift into politics.

By 1853 the nativist societies had changed their policy; their numbers and influence warranted a more active pursuit of their principles. First, the various Maryland nativist societies merged into one large body called the Order of the Star Spangled Banner or, more commonly,

44 Mary St. Patrick McConville, *Political Nativism in the State of Maryland* (Washington, D.C.: The Catholic University of America, 1928), is the best compact reference to Maryland nativism prior to 1850. Bernard C. Steiner, in *Citizenship and Suffrage in Maryland* (Baltimore: Cushing & Co., 1895), traces anti-foreign sentiment back to 1820.

45 According to the best available statistics, which record not church members but church seating capacity, 12 percent of Maryland's population was Catholic in 1850. See Joseph C. G. Kennedy, *Historical Account of Maryland* (Washington, D.C.: Gideon & Co., 1852); and U.S., Bureau of the Census, *Eighth Census of the United States* (Washington, D.C.: GPO, 1860), p. 542.

46 John Higham, *Strangers in the Land* (New Brunswick: Rutgers University Press, 1955), p. 4.

47 In 1845 the Native American party received 9 percent of the vote in Baltimore.

48 No membership lists for nativist lodges in Maryland exist, and they are equally scarce in other states. In her first-rate analysis of nativist leadership, "Dark Lantern Crusade: An Analysis of the Know-Nothing Party in Maryland" (Master's thesis, The Johns Hopkins University, 1965), Jean H. Baker had to limit her investigation of party leadership to the period after nativism had abandoned secrecy and made its membership a matter of public record. In all probability, nativist leadership in the non-secret, party phase of the movement was similar to the leadership of the lodges, but this is not necessarily so.

the Know-Nothing Order.[49] The amalgamated Order retained secrecy and had three degrees of membership—a novice degree, an intermediate degree, and a third degree reserved for those with a distinguished record of service to the Order and high standing in the community. Members swore oaths to protect the American nation and the ideals it stood for from all subversion. In August of 1853 the Order finally staged its first public demonstration, an effort to influence the House of Delegates election in Baltimore.[50] Then, in the spring of 1854, the Order scored its first clear political victories when all the candidates which it had secretly endorsed won in local elections in Hagerstown and Cumberland.[51]

Still, the Order remained a mystery to most uninitiated Marylanders until the summer of 1854. As late as two weeks before the Hagerstown elections the local papers expressed bafflement about the very existence of the group in Maryland.[52] One Baltimore County weekly showed a growing awareness of the new group that was probably typical of most Marylanders. In September 1853, its editor noticed an "American Party" in New York and discussed it as a curiosity.[53] By April 1 of the next year the paper noted that the Know-Nothings were active in Baltimore.[54] In May the paper remarked that a presumed meeting of Know-Nothings had taken place in a nearby barn loft, and that 150 persons were rumored to meet weekly in Reisterstown; however, no one was certain of this.[55] Late that month the editor said the Know-Nothings were trying to organize in Towson, but he did not believe they had done so yet.[56] By June his reaction was, "Whatever may be [their] . . . objects and principles, . . . they are certainly increasing in numbers very fast."[57] After June 1854 the paper reported often on the increasingly visible activity of the Know-Nothings.

49 The name "know-nothing" came from the practice of lodge members replying "I know nothing" or otherwise professing ignorance when asked about the organization. The exact date when the various lodges combined and began to work actively in politics is unknown. One contemporary put it in May 1853; see Anna Ella Carroll, *The Great American Battle* (New York: Miller, Orton, Mulligan, 1856).

50 See p. 000.

51 *Baltimore Sun,* May 10, 1854; and *Herald and Torch Light,* April 2, 1854. The city council selected by the nativists comprised three Democrats and two Whigs.

52 *Herald and Torch Light,* March 29, 1854.

53 *Baltimore County Advocate,* September 3, 1853. The American party and the Know-Nothing party are the same; as the nativists emerged into politics, they generally preferred to be called "Americans."

54 *Ibid.,* April 1, 1854.

55 *Ibid.,* May 6, 1854. Reisterstown is in west Baltimore County, northwest of the city.

56 *Ibid.,* May 27, 1854. Towson is in central Baltimore County, north of the city.

57 *Ibid.,* June 3, 1854.

Because of the spring elections and the suspected strength of nativism in the metropolis, Marylanders anxiously awaited the Baltimore municipal elections of October 1854. Washington, D.C., went under Know-Nothing rule in June.[58] The *Clipper*, a Baltimore daily of old nativist leanings, rallied to the new organization.[59] Several fading city and county weeklies attempted to stave off ruin by also joining the movement.[60] The nativist leaders, however, kept their own counsel until two weeks before the October 11 election. On September 26, Know-Nothing representatives from each ward in Baltimore gathered in a secret city convention. The next morning the *Clipper* carried the name of Samuel Hinks as the American party candidate for mayor.[61] Except that it was probably considerable, exact nativist strength remained a matter of mystery and conjecture until the election was over. In an election marred by violence, the Know-Nothings carried the mayoralty and a majority of the city council seats. A new party could now be said to be well launched.

The details of the Maryland Know-Nothings' transformation from clandestine order to political party are fogged by nativist secrecy, but the party obviously owed much to its underground origins.[62] The movement passed its vulnerable period sheltered by silence and buttressed by oath-bound loyalty. When nativism emerged into the light it was, furthermore, already tightly organized. Local clubs had councils to lead them; interestingly enough, in Baltimore these clubs were organized by existing political wards. Above the local councils were district and state councils. This machinery shifted without a pause from running the Order to providing a party organization. At the base of the system, all members could influence their local councils, and nativists bragged of this highly "democratic" method of member participation. The difficulty with the Know-Nothings' organizational arrangement came when political success brought the true nativist brotherhood into contact with the populace as a whole. At first all ranking members of the American party were most probably members of the Order. But certainly not all of the persons who voted

[58] Laurence Frederick Schmeckebier, *History of the Know Nothing Party in Maryland* (Baltimore: N. Murray, 1899), p. 17.

[59] The *Baltimore Clipper* had been the official spokesman for the Maryland National American party in 1844–1845.

[60] *Baltimore County Advocate*, June 17, 1854.

[61] September 27, 1854. Samuel Hinks was a wealthy flour merchant, formerly a Democrat, and had not been active in Baltimore politics before this time.

[62] Baker, *op. cit.*, pp. 59–75, contains a very thorough and valuable analysis of the nativist organization and its transformation in the 1850s. My work owes much to her clear and energetic explanation of the Know-Nothings—who they were and how they were organized. Her as yet unpublished master's thesis is the best detailed study of the nativists that I know of.

for the party's candidates were. This broadening of the Order into a party proved temporarily awkward, as Samuel Hinks discovered when he tried to appoint several nonmembers to city posts in late 1854. He had to compromise with the nativists on the city council and he eventually gave some of the jobs to members of the Order instead. But after such early embarrassments the nativists steadily became a routine party which enjoyed mass support and operated by the usual pyramiding structure of local-state-national conventions. The official policy of secrecy was recognized as dead by the Order's national council meeting of June 1855. After that the distinction between members and general public quickly disappeared. The council of the Order lingered on as the refuge of the ideological diehards, while the party functioned separately, as a party.

Thanks to their earlier, apolitical existence, the nativists had a tightly structured organization in a time of political confusion. The Democrats were caught fighting among themselves, and the Whigs were collapsing. Organization and surprise, then, account partly for the remarkable initial successes of the Know-Nothings—but only partly. The most important key to the creation of the powerful American party was the depth of discontent which was building among Marylanders. When this discontent with the changing times reached the necessary intensity, the well disciplined American party emerged with a program designed to meet it.

IV

Immigration was one of the sources of discontent. Maryland was caught up in the rush of immigrants who came to America in the 1840s and early 1850s.[63] Most of these were Irish and German and came in response to famine and political unrest in their homelands. In 1842, 4,662 immigrants landed in Baltimore; in 1844 that number

[63] U.S., Bureau of the Census, *Historical Statistics of the United States, Colonial Times to 1957* (Washington, D.C.: GPO, 1960), p. 57.

Year	Number of Immigrants
1844	78,615
1847	234,968
1848	226,527
1849	297,024
1850	369,980
1851	379,466
1852	371,603
1853	368,645
1854	427,833

Immigration began to taper off in 1855.

climbed to 6,001; by 1846 it was 12,009.[64] Not all of those who landed stayed in Maryland, of course, but many did; the *Baltimore Sun* estimated that at least 25 percent of the new arrivals remained in the state.[65] The foreign-born population of Maryland increased from 7 percent in 1840 to 12 percent in 1850 and kept going up.[66] In 1854 the courts in Maryland granted 907 naturalization papers; in 1856 that figure rose to 2,235, and 1,531 more immigrants filed declarations of intent to become citizens.[67] One estimate in 1854 put Baltimore's foreign-born population at 40,000.[68]

The problem of the immigrants went beyond their numbers to their behavior. The new immigrants did not assimilate quickly. Being a large community, the Irish or German newcomers could band together and form an extensive network of churches, social clubs, and protective societies.[69] They clung together, retaining their alien language and identity. Most of these new arrivals were laborers, tradesmen, or mechanics, and remained clustered in Baltimore.[70] Baltimore German immigrants of the forties and fifties founded clubs, athletic societies, musical societies, and German language schools and newspapers.[71] Such clannishness suggested to some Marylanders that these people did not really want to be Americans, and were not committed to cherished American ideals and institutions. One Marylander complained that, "war amidst the European powers is driving an *immense and unwilling* crowd of emigrants to our shores [who are] attuned to an antagonism of the glorious Constitution."[72] Being a haven for the grateful oppressed of the earth was fine, but the new wave of immigrants seemed hostile and aloof.

In the eyes of many Marylanders these immigrants not only were clannish but also were criminals or political radicals. The United States, said the Hagerstown *Herald of Freedom and Torch Light*,[73]

[64] Richard Swainson Fisher, *Gazeteer of the State of Maryland* (Baltimore: J. S. Waters, 1852), p. 29.

[65] January 2, 1860.

[66] In 1850, 51,209 foreign-born persons lived in Maryland, comprising 12 percent of the state's white population. In 1860, 77,529 foreign-born persons lived in the state, comprising 15 percent of the total white population.

[67] *Baltimore Sun*, December 29, 1859.

[68] *Ibid.*, September 26, 1854.

[69] Among the associations of foreign-born Baltimoreans were the Hibernian Society, the Irish Social and Benevolent Society, the German immigrant Aid Society, and the Germania Club. The Germans also founded numerous athletic and musical clubs in various neighborhoods.

[70] Dieter Cunz, *The Maryland Germans* (Princeton: Princeton University Press, 1948), p. 238.

[71] *Ibid.*, p. 281.

[72] *Baltimore Sun*, October 4, 1854.

[73] June 14, 1854.

was being "converted into a sort of Botany Bay." The paper claimed that immigrant felons were being sent to this country as a matter of deliberate European policy; behind it all lurked a plot to subvert the great democratic experiment in America.[74] German political refugees—called "forty-eighters" after the year of political uprisings in Germany—alarmed Marylanders with their radical stand against slavery.[75] The *Sozialdemokratische Turnverein* of Baltimore, an all-purpose social club, was big, influential in the German community, and outspokenly critical of slavery. In 1851 a Baltimore forty-eighter named Friedrich Schnauffer founded *Die Wecker;* the paper was bluntly abolitionist and later became the leading Republican organ in the state. The paper survived mob violence only because it was printed in German and its views were therefore not widely known.[76] Southern Marylanders became upset when a German abolitionist paper began operations in Washington, D.C.

Dislike of immigrants could easily be connected with concern about the degenerate condition of politics in Maryland. Many people feared bloc voting by ignorant naturalized citizens. Foreigners "move in a mass, they vote the same way," argued one Maryland nativist; "they think alike, and act alike, . . . [and are] the pliant instruments of subtle politicians."[77] Indeed, naturalized voters did seem to act in concert. An ad signed "Erin go Bragh" praised a candidate in the 1853 Democratic primary in Baltimore because he "did not forget his naturalized fellow-citizens."[78] In that same election a benevolent and protective association of immigrant Germans sent an open letter to all congressional aspirants in the Third District. Noting that naturalized Germans "perchance . . . hold the balance of power in the Third Congressional District," the letter asked all candidates to answer two questions. First, was the candidate "convinced of the justice and necessity" of the protective association? Second, would he openly pledge to represent naturalized citizens fairly and impartially?[79] All candidates answered affirmatively, if somewhat am-

[74] *Ibid.*, February 8, June 14, September 13, and October 4, 1854. The 1855 American party platform complained of "the transmission to our shores of felons and paupers." Schmeckebier, *op. cit.*, p. 120.

[75] According to Dieter Cunz, the "forty-eighter" immigrants were "abolitionist to the core." *Op. cit.*, p. 184.

[76] The offices of *Die Wecker* were often threatened, as after a Republican meeting in 1856 when an anti-Republican mob roamed the streets, but in an age of violence the paper remained remarkably unscathed. "*Wecker*" means "alarm" or "alarm clock" in German.

[77] Friedrich Anspach, *Sons of the Sires* (Philadelphia: Lippincott, Grambo & Co., 1855), p. 73.

[78] *Baltimore Sun,* July 6 and 7, 1853.

[79] *Ibid.*, July 4, 1853.

biguously. In response to this kind of political activity, one suspicious Marylander said: "The question of how far political organizations, founded upon national character, are advisable within the United States, is a matter of serious importance to all of us."[80]

Immigrants upset the labor market. Maryland's labor situation was turbulent in the early fifties; this was a period of rapid unionization and crusades for more pay and a sixty-hour week.[81] Already Maryland's white laborers faced stiff competition from free Negroes and hired-out slaves.[82] Now even the mechanics and skilled artisans were confronted with needy and eager immigrant competition. The Baltimore and Ohio tracks were laid largely by Irishmen. Account books from Baltimore County smelting and quarrying firms reveal a heavy proportion of Irish workers.[83] A typical Allegany County coal company employed one American-born miner in a work force of seventy-four men.[84] In 1854 the workers in the limestone quarrying district of Baltimore County struck for higher wages. On the first day of the walkout an immigrant laborer tried to break the strike and report; the strikers beat him up.[85] Coal mine owners in Western Maryland used the threat of immigrant labor to break down a strike for higher wages there.[86] The interest of American labor in nativism is further revealed by the name of one of the nativist societies active in Maryland—the Union of American Mechanics.[87] Nativist appeals to mechanics and workingmen were plentiful in Baltimore papers before each election.

80 *Ibid.*

81 See advertisements in *ibid.*, October 20, 1853, on a workingman's mass meeting held on October 15. In the early fifties the seventy-two hour week was common, but labor was having some success instituting a sixty-hour week.

82 Morris, *op. cit.*, pp. 386–88; see also Wright, *op. cit.* I am indebted to Mr. Ray Della, Jr., for giving me the benefit of his research into labor strife in the 1850s. The ship-caulking trade, Mr. Della found, was particularly disrupted by conflict between white and free Negro laborers. Mr. Della's research has appeared as "Problems of Negro Labor in the 1850's," *Maryland Historical Magazine*, 66 (1971): 14–32.

83 Manuscript Account Books of the Oregon Iron Furnace, Maryland Historical Society, Baltimore.

84 *Baltimore Sun*, September 23, 1850. This particular mine staff was composed of twenty-four Germans, twenty-one Scots, fourteen Englishmen, seven Welshmen, seven Irishmen, and one American.

85 *Baltimore County Advocate*, May 27, 1854.

86 Katherine A. Harvey, *The Best-Dressed Miners: Life and Labor in the Maryland Coal Region* (Ithaca: Cornell University Press, 1969), p. 142. The immigrant laborers were evidently imaginary, a ruse to break the strike, but to the strikers the threat was ominous.

87 This "union" was not an economic trade union, but simply a nativist association.

V

Distrust of immigrants was closely linked to fear of Catholics. Of the 1.7 million immigrants who arrived in the 1840s, an estimated 700,000 were Catholic.[88] The problem was whether Catholics could be good Americans, since they owed allegiance to a foreign heirarchy through their church. The Catholic church in America abetted nativism by becoming aggressively self-assertive in the early fifties; belligerent Catholics like Orestes Brownson, editor of the widely-circulated *Quarterly Review*, increased Protestant fears.[89] Remarks like that made by Brownson—"If the Pope directed the Roman Catholics of this country to overthrow the Constitution and to sell the nationality of their country, they would be bound to obey"—played into the hands of the nativists.[90]

In Maryland the church entered a period of rapid growth in the late forties and fifties. The First Plenary Council of the Catholic Church in America was held in Baltimore in 1852. Described by one sympathetic author as "a touch of Rome and the Middle Ages brought into a bustling American city," the council inflamed fears about the growing power of the church.[91] Added to this was the visit to the United States of Monsignor Bedini, the papal legate. His visit was unpopular because he was charged with asserting the ownership of all church property by the mother church. Anti-Catholic agitators used Bedini as a symbol of popish oppression, and riots followed the unfortunate priest around the country.[92] A Baltimore mob burned him in effigy during his visit in January 1854.[93]

The most serious Catholic-Protestant conflict in Maryland arose over the separate Catholic school system. For years past the community had been agitated over the use of the Bible in public schools. Catholic parents of public school students were naturally concerned that their children were read to from a Protestant text. They contended that either Catholic children should be permitted to use the Douai Bible, or religion should perhaps be omitted from the classroom.[94] Parallel to this intermittent debate was the question of the

[88] Robert Joseph Murphy, "The Catholic Church in the United States during the Civil War Period, 1852–1866," *Records of the American Catholic Historical Society of Philadelphia*, 39 (1928): 293–94.

[89] Ray Allen Billington, *The Protestant Crusade: 1800–1860* (Chicago: Quadrangle Books, 1964), pp. 289–314.

[90] *Ibid.*, p. 289.

[91] Murphy, *op. cit.*, pp. 278–79.

[92] *Ibid.*, pp. 300–301.

[93] *Baltimore Sun*, January 17, 1854.

[94] McConville, *op. cit.*, pp. 2–3.

Catholics' separate school system. First, separatism itself was a cause for suspicion in those who were inclined to speculate about what was taught at those Catholic schools and about why public schools were not good enough for Catholics. Second, Catholics themselves felt it unfair that they should be taxed to support a public school system which their children did not use. Catholic efforts to obtain a share of the common school fund and to divorce Protestant theology from the schools led to charges that they were seeking to destroy both the public school system and the Protestant faith of the majority of its pupils.

Mistrust mushroomed into fierce controversy in the General Assembly of 1852. Thomas Kerney, of Baltimore, introduced into the House of Delegates a bill innocuously titled "An Act to Reduce to a Uniform System the Several Laws for . . . the Public Schools of the State."[95] Ostensibly the measure would rearrange and rationalize the conglomeration of state-financed, locally administered schools. On this ground alone it met resistance. The hidden explosive in the bill, however, was the section authorizing payment to private schools from the public fund. Church schools were not specifically mentioned but were clearly included. In a very short time the entire debate over the Kerney School Bill generated into an argument over granting public funds to Catholic schools. The legislature tabled the measure in 1852, but the controversy would not go away.

The argument grew more bitter through the winter and spring of 1852-1853. A Catholic group attempted to influence the Baltimore mayoral election in 1852 by circulating an open letter to the candidates asking whether they supported the Kerney Bill. Both candidates evaded the issue. In the 1853 session of the legislature Kerney reintroduced his measure. A Baltimore meeting in April 1853, which was called to discuss the Kerney Bill, deteriorated into an anti-Catholic assembly led by Protestant clergy.[96] The legislature again ducked the issue; a special committee assigned to study the problem simply did not report.

After the adjournment of the legislature, the school funds fight moved to the Baltimore City Council. A petition from several Catholic citizens, including Archbishop Francis Kenrick, asked the council to grant a portion of the public budget to private schools. A special committee of the city council was delegated to study the

[95] *Ibid.*, pp. 21–43. McConville is biased but quite detailed in her discussion of the Kerney Bill controversy, and, unless otherwise noted, the discussion here is drawn from her account as checked against the *Journals* of the Maryland House of Delegates and Senate.

[96] *Baltimore Sun*, April 12, 1853; *Baltimore Clipper*, April 12, 1853.

question and produced in June 1853 a report which damned Kenrick and the other petitioners in strong language. The report read like a nativist tract, and was written by an incipient Know-Nothing, Councilman John McJilton.[97] The virulence of this counterattack proved how far tensions had built up over the Catholic school fund issue.

The Kerney Bill controversy was the occasion for the first public display by the Maryland nativists. A Baltimore group calling itself "Maryland Sons of America, Camp No. 1," held a huge rally in Monument Square, which was decorated with transparencies reading "The Public Schools as They Are," and "Eternal Separation of Church and State."[98] Then the nativists borrowed a gambit from the immigrants and Catholics, an open letter asking local candidates to declare themselves on the Kerney Bill. All Maine Law candidates agreed to the nativist position, all Democrats disavowed it.[99] Nativist voters undoubtedly supported the Maine Law candidates and helped them to their surprising victory.[100]

Aside from the school issue, little incidents kept raising the Catholic-Protestant tension. A Hagerstown paper thrilled its readers with an account of the "escape" of an eighteen-year-old girl from a convent in neighboring Emmitsburg.[101] Irish Catholic mobs were said to have attacked peaceful Know-Nothing demonstrations in the streets of Newark and Brooklyn.[102] An ugly incident in Annapolis further strained religious relations. A novice priest suffering from some sort of mental disorder was being transported by other priests from the capital to a Baltimore hospital for treatment. At the train he suddenly became violent, calling upon passersby to save him from kidnapping. The young man was eventually hospitalized, but the incident left an unfortunate impression on the gullible.[103]

For all this, anti-Catholic bias was not as strong in Maryland as it was in other places with a nativist tradition, such as Massachusetts or Philadelphia. Maryland was originally a Catholic settlement, and too many of the state's leading citizens and traditional heroes were

[97] McJilton was an ordained Episcopal minister, an editor of the nativist *Clipper,* and was locally renowned as a poet and literary figure.

[98] *Baltimore Sun,* August 19, 1853.

[99] Schmeckebier, *op. cit.,* p. 16.

[100] See the analysis of the Maine Law–Know-Nothing relationship below.

[101] *Herald and Torch Light,* November 29, 1854. The young lady's name was Josephine M. Bunkley, and her lurid account of her ten-month stay in the Emmitsburg convent later became a popular book entitled *The Testimony of an Escaped Novice.* Billington, *op. cit.,* pp. 310–11. Emmitsburg is in northern Frederick County.

[102] *Herald and Torch Light,* September 13, 1854; *Upper Marlboro Gazette,* June 7, 1854.

[103] *Port Tobacco Times,* May 11, 1854.

Catholic to allow widespred anti-Catholicism to take root there. At the 1845 Native American convention in Philadelphia, for example, the Maryland contingent had strongly insisted that nationality, and not religion, was to be the issue.[104] Marylanders were similarly anxious to downplay the Catholic question in the Know-Nothings' national council in 1855.[105] Anti-Catholicism in Maryland, therefore, tended to focus not simply on religious intolerance but on the question of the loyalty or patriotism of Catholics. Theological disputes were minimized. Maryland nativists often tried to distinguish between foreign-born Catholics and native Catholics.[106] In any guise, however, the relations between the state's Catholics and Protestants were badly strained, and this tension was ideal for exploitation by the nativist movement in the early fifties.

Nativism was a natural response to fears about immigrants and Catholics. The Know-Nothing Order cried out that "Americans shall rule America." No criticisms of bigotry or references to Maryland's proud history of religious toleration could hold back the rush of xenophobia. Many Marylanders, in effect, came to agree with the doctrines so long nurtured in secret by the nativist lodges. The reasons why Marylanders responded this way can only be surmised; even the extent to which American party success was built on pure nativism is open to question.[107] But the growing numbers and self-assertiveness of immigrants and Catholics undoubtedly influenced the growth of nativism. Gordon Allport, in his comprehensive study of prejudice, suggests that a number of social conditions lead to its creation; Maryland generally, and Baltimore particularly, qualified on all these counts.[108] Allport suggests that prejudice will flourish where the social structure is heterogeneous, where vertical mobility is likely, where rapid social change is in progress, where there are barriers to communication and resulting ignorance, where the size of minority groups is increasing, where direct competition between minorities and the rest of the community exists, where customs are favorable to violence, and where traditional justifications for ethnocentrism exist.

[104] McConville, *op. cit.*, p. 8.

[105] See the account in the *Baltimore Sun*, June 14, 1855.

[106] See Carroll, *op. cit.*

[107] Two studies that I have found especially useful in analyzing emotional nationalism—and, by extension, nativism—in this period are Fred A. Somkin, *Unquiet Eagle: Memory and Desire in the Idea of American Freedom, 1815–1860* (Ithaca: Cornell University Press, 1967); and Merle Curti, *The Roots of American Loyalty* (New York: Columbia University Press, 1946).

[108] Gordon W. Allport, *The Nature of Prejudice* (Garden City: Doubleday Anchor Books, 1958), pp. 215–33.

VI

Fears for the safety of the Union also continued to bother Marylanders in this period. By mid-decade Marylanders had lived through two major debates on slavery in five years, and from their exposed border-state position they looked out on the sectional conflict with deep concern. They hoped that the Compromise of 1850 would solve the problem. The Whig and Democratic parties made it a cardinal part of their presidential campaigning in Maryland in 1852.[109] One Marylander expressed the majority sentiment when he said, "In the name of God, take the Compromise of 1850 and don't let us hear any more about this matter."[110] But the Kansas-Nebraska Act of 1854 erased the old Missouri Compromise Line between slave and free territory, instituted instead the painful and confusing system of "popular sovereignty," and brought the territorial slavery debate to a boil again. The Kansas-Nebraska Act was not popular in Maryland, although it did not excite much comment.[111] Maryland's congressmen and senators voted for the bill, but apparently did so in the hope that this would lay the sectional problem to rest for good.[112] The Maryland press spent little ink on the issue, and the comments that the editors did make were unfavorable.[113] The bill was said to strengthen the hands of "fanatics."[114] When Kansas erupted into bloody war between Northern and Southern partisans later in the decade, Marylanders' worst fears were realized. The Know-Nothings tried to capitalize on the Kansas violence by blaming the administration of Democrat Franklin Pierce for the Kansas-Nebraska Act; "The Democratic administration has 'sown the wind' and must be prepared to 'reap the whirlwind.'" moralized one Maryland paper about Kansas.[115]

The American party answered concerns about the sectional crisis by taking an adamantly conservative, hands-off position on slavery

[109] For Marylanders' attitudes on the Compromise of 1850, see Chapter II.

[110] *Baltimore Sun,* January 24, 1850.

[111] W. Wayne Smith, "The Dilemma of the Maryland Whigs in the Sectional Crisis" (Paper presented at the annual meeting of the Southern Historical Association, October 31, 1969, Washington, D.C.), p. 11.

[112] Maryland Democratic Congressmen Henry May, Joshua Vasant, Jacob Shower, and William Hamilton voted yes. Whig Congressmen Augustus Sollers and William Franklin were absent. Whig Senators James A. Pearce and Thomas G. Pratt voted yes, and their hopes for the end of sectional agitation can be found in U.S., *Congressional Globe,* 33rd Cong., 1st sess., 1854, pt. 2, pp. 3101 and 3107.

[113] *Worcester County Shield,* May 20, 1854; *Baltimore County Advocate,* May 27, 1854.

[114] *Herald and Torch Light,* September 6, 1854.

[115] *Annapolis Gazette,* June 5, 1856.

and sectional issues. The national American party platform for 1855 advocated "the maintenance of the union of these United States as the paramount political good," and also demanded "the suppression of all tendencies to political division, founded on geographical discriminations, or on the belief that there is a real difference of interests and views between the various sections of the Union.[116] The Maryland Know-Nothings ratified this platform at their state meetings. A year later the national American party platform—which also was endorsed by the Maryland convention—added a condemnation of the Pierce administration for "reopening sectional agitation by the repeal of the Missouri Compromise" through the Kansas-Nebraska Act.[117] The Worcester County Americans added that they "regard[ed] the further agitation of the slavery question for any purpose in the Halls of Congress . . . as inimical to those friendly feelings which alone make the Union possible and worth preserving."[118] The Know-Nothings thus found themselves eventually in agreement with the Republicans in opposing the Kansas-Nebraska Act, but in Maryland that opposition was grounded not in hostility to slavery but in the fear that sectional skirmishing in Kansas would get out of hand.

In campaigns the Know-Nothings accused the Democrats of being Union-destroying sectionalists. "Southern Democracy," charged the *Annapolis Gazette*, "is but another name for Southern disunionists."[119] Maryland Democrats countered this charge by trying to link the Know-Nothings to Northern antislavery.[120] The presence of antislavery men in the Northern wing of the American party was consequently an embarrassment to Maryland Know-Nothings. But the antislavery "North Americans" bolted from the American party in 1856 to join the Republicans, and the official position of the party always upheld the sanctity of the Union and deliberately straddled the question of slavery in the territories. This equivocal position had a broad appeal in Maryland. Said one enraptured editor, "It is to the new party that we now look for deliverance from the parricidal hands which have been uplifted against the integrity of the Union."[121]

VII

Aside from their complaints that sectionalism specifically was undermining America, Marylanders in the early fifties were generally

[116] Schmeckebier, *op. cit.*, p. 119.

[117] *Ibid.*, p. 125.

[118] *Annapolis Gazette,* August 14, 1856.

[119] *Ibid.*, October 10, 1856.

[120] See *Port Tobacco Times,* August 23, 1855, for a report on the state Democratic convention resolutions.

[121] *Herald and Torch Light,* September 6, 1854.

distraught over the moral and social climate they saw around them. Expressions of this concern were frequent in the Maryland press, although often vague and inarticulate. One Maryland newspaper approvingly reprinted a *New York Times* editorial on "our social cancer," which turned out to be "extravagance, . . . of late origin in our society."[122] According to another authority the problem was "genteel blackguardism."[123] Observed Henry Winter Davis, "Our heart is waxing gross and our ear is dull of hearing under the deadening influence of great material and commercial prosperity."[124] Quite true, agreed a Southern Maryland editor, noting with alarm that American imports per capita had more than doubled in ten years.[125] Baltimore banker George William Brown chose as his theme for an 1853 public address, "Lawlessness, the Evil of the Day."[126] An Eastern Shore paper referred to "this age of wild and reckless fanaticism."[127]

Politics continued to be an object of scorn. The *Herald and Torch Light* complained that nobody was interested in the annual presidential message. "There was a time when this document was awaited with intense anxiety. This was in the earlier days of the Republic; but now it fails to create the slightest interest."[128] Charles B. Calvert of Riverdale, Maryland, was widely applauded in Southern Maryland for urging the formation of an agricultural party to "bring back the government to its original purity."[129]

The Know-Nothing party addressed itself to this perceived social and moral breakdown. What the party offered was a return to purer, simpler politics and the moral standards of an earlier age. Nativism aimed to be restorative, rejuvenating. This theme of return to basic principles was not new in American politics, nor was it the exclusive property of the Know-Nothings.[130] But the theme appeared with remarkable frequency in Maryland by 1855, and the Know-Nothings in particular employed it vigorously, at the propitous moment, and with great success.

In his popular Know-Nothing tract, Friedrich Anspach wisely

[122] *Ibid.*, July 26, 1854.

[123] *Upper Marlboro Gazette,* May 23, 1853, and March 22, 1854.

[124] Henry Winter Davis to Samuel F. DuPont, January 9, 1852, DuPont Papers.

[125] *Port Tobacco Times,* January 11, 1854.

[126] *Biographical Cyclopedia of Representative Men of Maryland and the District of Columbia* (Baltimore: National Biographical Publishing Co., 1879), p. 313.

[127] *Worcester County Shield,* September 13, 1853.

[128] December 13, 1854.

[129] *Port Tobacco Times,* June 28, 1855.

[130] Fred Somkin, in his *Unquiet Eagle,* sees most Americans in the middle nineteenth century engaged in a nostalgic reverence of the past, an attempt at spiritual restoration. In Maryland this nostalgia was best articulated by the nativists.

chose in his title to refer to nativists as "Sons of the Sires."[131] The one consistent theme among all the contradictory ideas and half-formed prejudices of the nativists was that they were the true heirs of the founding fathers and as such would guide America back to its proper heritage. As its fighting motto the American party chose an apocryphal phrase attributed to George Washington on the eve of the Delaware crossing, "Put none but Americans on Guard."[132] "Heed the warnings of Washington, Jefferson, Madison, Jackson," intoned the *Herald and Torch Light,* "and . . . inscribe the soul-stirring motto upon the Star-Spangled Banner–'Americans shall Rule America.' "[133] The same newspaper's choice of words was highly revealing when, in speaking of the leaders of the sectional debate, they referred to "the parricidal hands" attacking the Union.[134] Know-Nothing Congressman Henry Winter Davis joined the chorus. "Would that the people were still governed by the memory of old reverence; then would the name of Washington be a myth and an apotheosis; then indeed should we be a republic of confederated hearts where the instincts of a sublimated nature would supercede the cold calculation of reason and interest."[135] Davis's preference for instinct over "the cold calculation of reason" was typical of the emotional fifties.[136] The *Annapolis Gazette* approved as "Sound American Doctrine" a reverence for "Washington, Jefferson, Adams and the immortal patriots of the Revolution, the last 'Sons of '76' who are fast fading from our view."[137]

Involved with the return to the revolutionary era was the reawakening of a sense of America's mission as spiritual guide to a rotten Old World.[138] Anspach confidently asserted that the Catholic church was linked with "foreign despots" in a conscious plot to subvert the

131 Anspach, *op. cit.* Anspach was a Lutheran minister from Western Maryland who wrote several nativist tracts; *Sons of the Sires* was his biggest and most complete.

132 Maryland Election Ticket Collection, Maryland Historical Society, Baltimore. American party tickets often had that inscription on them, not only in Maryland but elsewhere.

133 January 10, 1855.

134 *Ibid.,* May 20, 1855, italics added.

135 Henry Winter Davis to Samuel F. DuPont, February 16, 1851, DuPont Papers.

136 On the basis of Maryland evidence I believe Roy F. Nichols was correct when he called the 1850s "years in which American imaginations were highly active; it was a romantic age." Roy F. Nichols, *Stakes of Power, 1845–1877,* Making of America Series (New York: Hill & Wang, 1961), p. 32.

137 January 24, 1856.

138 See, for example, a *Baltimore Sun* editorial on our moral influence abroad, August 15, 1853.

United States.[139] America, he contended, represented by her very existence a noble example for the masses and therefore a threat to the totalitarian governments so recently buffeted by revolution. With a curious twist of logic, Anspach concluded that America must turn away foreign immigrants in order "to execute its mission of diffusing the principles of liberal institutions throughout the world.[140]

Christianity, by which was meant Protestantism, also linked Americans to their past. "This nation is indebted to Christianity, more than to anything else, for its existence, its growth, and its prosperity."[141] In the beginning the country was "Christian"; so must it be again. One of the purposes of the Know-Nothing Order, said Anspach, was to restore Christianity in politics, to return to a presumed condition where Christian principles animated statesmen. [142] Catholics, of course, were not truly Christian or American, because they owed allegiance to a foreign organization.

It is easy to see how this cast of mind led to a suspicion of foreigners. Simply put, they were not "Americans," not imbued with our traditions. And they were "new." Of all the ominous signs of change, the immigrants were the most visible. Without too much mental effort they could be held responsible for the corrupt condition of politics. Also, in banding together against aliens, Americans made, in the words of one historian, "an agonizing . . . attempt to retain the esprit of a sacred society, a family brotherhood"; they tried to make "contact with the still-revered ideals of a past essentially communal."[143] Through the nativist lodges, and later the Know-Nothing party, disturbed Marylanders could reassert their identity, honor their heritage, and hold back for a time the terrifying sense of change and lost innocence that disturbed them.

The great reform was to be wrought through a cleansing of politics, and that, in turn, was to be accomplished by excluding immigrants or lengthening the period required for naturalization and

[139] Anspach, *op. cit.*, pp. 35–36. Nativists often referred to the democratic revolutions in Europe, and expressed sympathy for the oppressed abroad. Henry Winter Davis, for example, was quite an admirer of Louis Kossuth, the Hungarian patriot who visited America in the early fifties. Henry Winter Davis to Samuel F. DuPont, January 1, 1853, and December 24, 1854, DuPont Papers. Other Marylanders were not so enthusiastic about Kossuth, however, regarding him as a meddler who sought to soil America by involving her in European affairs. *Planters' Advocate,* December 24, 1851. The forlorn of Europe were most admired from a distance; up close they became immigrants and "foreign felons."

[140] Anspach, *op. cit.*, p. 99.

[141] From the American party's 1855 platform; see Schmeckebier, *op. cit.*, p. 121.

[142] Anspach, *op. cit.*, p. 100.

[143] Somkin, *op. cit.*, p. 7.

enfranchisement. If politics were cured of the corruption that attached to ignorant foreign-born voters, then it was assumed that political agitation for demagogic ends would cease. It also followed, argued the nativists, that the presence of model citizens in the seats of power would inevitably elevate the nation's moral tone. The American party platform of 1855 accordingly expressed "disgust for the wild hunt after office which characterizes this age," and suggested instead "imitation of the practice of the purer days of the Republic, and admiration of the maxim that 'office should seek the man.'" Playing to the contemporary disaffection with politicians, the platform also advocated "the reformation of the character of our National legislature, by elevating to that dignified and responsible position men of higher qualifications, purer morals, and more unselfish patriotism."[144] For good measure the party's 1856 statement of principle also urged "a strict economy in public expenditure."[145]

VIII

By 1855, then, the unionist-nativist programs of the American party had a very wide appeal, and the organization was ready to make its assault on the state offices. The collapse of the Whig party, of course, left a convenient vacuum opposite the Democrats. The new party also pre-empted the conservative unionism of the Whigs. But Know-Nothingism was more than Whiggery. A new alignment in Maryland politics formed around the American party.

The Americans did very well in the fall elections of 1855. Hinks won re-election as mayor in Baltimore by over 3,700 votes; in the city council the Democrats did manage to capture twelve of twenty First Branch (lower chamber) seats, but the Know-Nothings held eight of ten seats in the Second Branch (upper chamber). In November Know-Nothing William Purnell won the comptrollership, carrying twelve of Maryland's twenty-one counties plus Baltimore. The nativists elected one-half of the commissioners of public works and filled all three available judgeships. Know-Nothing Daniel McPhail won the state lottery commissioner's job. Of the six Maryland congressmen elected, four were Know-Nothings, one was an independent Whig, and one was an independent Democrat.[146] Led by a sweep of Baltimore's ten House of Delegates seats, the Know-Nothings gained

144 Schmeckebier, *op. cit.*, p. 121.

145 *Ibid.*, p. 125.

146 The members of the Maryland delegation in Washington in 1856 were: Senators James A. Pearce (Whig) and Anthony Kennedy (Am.); and Congressmen James A. Stewart (ind. Dem.), James B. Ricaud (Am.), J. Morrison Harris (Am.), Henry Winter Davis (Am.), Henry W. Hoffman (Am.), and Thomas F. Bowie (ind. Whig).

control of the state legislature.[147] The Know-Nothings had come a long way since their first cautious entry into politics as a factor in the Baltimore elections of 1853. In two years they had captured control of the state.

In the process of mastering Maryland politics the Know-Nothings wrought major changes in political allegiances and party alignment. On the surface, of course, they replaced the Whigs as the major opponent of the Democratic party. This simple fact, plus the doctrinal similarities between the two parties, has led many historians to regard the American party as Whiggery reincarnate.[148] Certainly Maryland Democrats tried to picture the Americans as Whig wolves in American sheep clothing.[149] And it must be granted that many individual Whigs did switch allegiances and become Know-Nothings. Three principal features of the new party would draw them—opposition to Democrats, sectional conservatism, and advocacy of a protective tariff.[150] Also, many Whig newspapers, such as the *Clipper*, the *Worcester County Shield*, and the *Annapolis Gazette*, supported the Know-Nothings.[151] But, beyond individual cases, the broad statistical evidence does not at all support a strong connection between Whig and American leadership or followers.

The leaders of the new party were mostly political novices who had been nurtured in the lodges of the nativist order. One Know-Nothing lodge member explained, "Members are to be educated in the ways of . . . political action by older men who are of maturer years and experience."[152] The Know-Nothing leaders were much

[147] The breakdown of seats by party was as follows:

	House	Senate		
		Holdover	New	Total
Democrat	17	2	3	5
Know-Nothing	45	0	8	8
Whig	0	9	0	9

[148] Among those who have made this oversimplification are: Schmeckebier, *op. cit.;* Wilfred E. Binkley, *American Political Parties: Their Natural History* (New York: Alfred A. Knopf, 1965); and Arthur C. Cole, *The Whig Party in the South* (Washington, D.C.: The American Historical Association, 1913).

[149] A favorite epithet of Democratic editors in the early days of the American movement was to label it a "Whig trick." See Baker, *op. cit.*, p. 33.

[150] Protective tariffs were not emphasized by the American party, but economic nationalism fit neatly into its ideological program. Foreign goods, as well as foreign people, were to be shunned. This minor theme in the American program has probably misled historians into assuming too great a Whig-American connection in Maryland. Advocacy of tariffs also reflects the presence of businessmen in the forefront of the party; see below.

[151] Of nine Whig newspapers surveyed by Jean H. Baker, eight went Know-Nothing. *Op. cit.*, p. 33.

[152] Thomas Whitney, *A Defense of the American Policy* (New York: Dewitt & Davenport, 1856), p. 260.

younger, on the average, than their Democratic counterparts and were strikingly inexperienced. Socially these men differed little from the Democratic leadership. They tended to be from upper-middle-class families; two-thirds of them were college educated.[153] A large number of Know-Nothings were Masons as well.[154] While prominent Democrats maintained the customary occupational pattern of politicians—72 percent were lawyers—the nativist leaders were often business- and professional men.[155]

The supporters of the new party were not all former Whigs by any means, either; any examination of the voting returns shows this clearly. For one thing, Baltimore was a power center for the new party, and Baltimore had formerly been Democratic. A ward-by-ward comparison of the Whig vote in the gubernatorial race of 1853 and the Know-Nothing vote in the comptroller's election of 1855 (the top of the ticket) reveals significant differences in the pattern of strength and in the level of support—that is, in the wards carried and by what margin they were carried. The statistical correlation between Whig and Know-Nothing voting in the two elections was weak. The nativists were forging a new pattern of allegiances there.

In the counties of Maryland the Know-Nothings ran best in the areas where the Whigs were traditionally weakest—in the new society of the North and East. (See Tables 5 and 6 and Map 5.) The former Whig enclaves in the old society showed up in the Democratic column by 1855. A significant positive statistical correlation existed between Know-Nothing strength in 1855 and Democratic strength in the politically stable period from 1836 through 1848.[156] Comparing Know-Nothing strength in 1855 to Whig strength in the stable period produces a negative statistical correlation. Of course, this is not proof that former Democrats were all voting Know-Nothing. But even a glance at the 1855 returns shows that many Marylanders had formed a new political allegiance.

Foreign-born and Catholic voters logically went into the Democratic ranks. A few naturalized immigrants may have voted American—the eagerness of new citizens to demonstrate their "Americanness" has often been noted—but certainly these voters were scarce. English and Protestant Irish groups that were hostile to other immigrants (a common development in some Northern cities) did not appear in Maryland. The hostility of the Catholic and foreign

[153] Baker, *op. cit.* The average age of the leading Democrats was forty-three; that of the Know-Nothings was thirty-four.

[154] Note that this refutes the often-accepted notion that the Know-Nothings were political descendents of the Anti-Masons of the 1830s.

[155] Only 38 percent of the Know-Nothing leaders studied by Jean Baker were lawyers.

[156] See the note to Table 6 for correlations.

TABLE 5. PERCENTAGE OF THE VOTE CAST BY KNOW-NOTHINGS AND WHIGS IN BALTIMORE, 1853–1855

Ward	Whig, 1853[a]	Know-Nothing, 1854[b]	Know-Nothing, 1855[c]
1	36.4	49.9	63.0
2	27.1	26.2	23.2
3	48.9	60.6	57.0
4	52.4	52.6	63.1
5	44.3	51.9	47.4
6	42.4	51.3	48.6
7	39.3	62.7	55.2
8	32.5	44.7	36.9
9	38.5	37.0	37.9
10	56.1	51.6	48.2
11	52.2	48.0	46.4
12	50.2	55.8	49.6
13	56.4	57.4	50.3
14	53.3	60.1	54.1
15	47.9	57.6	50.0
16	42.8	63.3	54.9
17	29.5	51.7	45.2
18	42.0	70.5	63.3
19	43.1	61.4	51.7
20	39.6	59.5	54.8
City Average	43.3	55.5	50.9

NOTE: Two elections are used to demonstrate Know-Nothing voting because the one in 1954 is closest in time to the election for which Whig percentages are given, and the 1855 election is the same type of election—that, for a major statewide office.

The coefficient of correlation between the Whig vote by wards in 1853 and the Know-Nothing vote by wards in 1854 is +0.267, which is not statistically significant. The coefficient of correlation between the Whig vote by wards in 1853 and the Know-Nothing vote by wards in 1855 is +0.102, which also is not significant.

[a] Gubernatorial election.

[b] Mayoral election.

[c] Comptroller's election.

language press to the Know-Nothings was pronounced and predictable.[157] The Maryland county with the highest proportion of Catholics, St. Mary's gave the Know-Nothings only 17.1 percent of the vote (see Table 6). Allegany County defied the trend in Western Maryland and voted Democratic, and this county had the largest number of Catholics outside Southern Maryland. Other areas with a

[157] One German newspaper, the conservative, business-oriented *Lait Stern* (Baltimore), supported Fillmore in 1856, but it supported him as the Whig nominee, not as the American nominee.

TABLE 6 NEW ALIGNMENTS: KNOW-NOTHING VOTES IN 1855 COMPARED WITH WHIG AND DEMOCRATIC AVERAGES FOR 1836–1848

County	Know-Nothing Vote, 1855 (%)	Average Vote (%), 1836–1848[a]	
		Whig	Democratic
Allegany	49.1	51.8	48.2
Anne Arundel	52.7	54.0	46.0
Baltimore County	55.0	45.7	54.3
Calvert	51.9	57.5	42.5
Caroline	49.9	53.0	47.0
Carroll	55.4	50.6	49.4
Cecil	55.1	50.6	49.4
Charles	37.8	63.5	36.5
Dorchester	54.0	60.6	39.4
Frederick	55.8	51.7	48.3
Harford	63.9	53.9	46.1
Kent	61.8	59.2	40.8
Montgomery	49.6	59.9	40.1
Prince George's	49.8	61.0	39.0
Queen Anne's	54.9	53.5	46.5
St. Mary's	17.1	67.5	32.5
Somerset	53.5	62.3	37.7
Talbot	43.5	52.8	47.2
Washington	50.8	51.6	48.4
Worcester	47.8	62.0	48.0
Howard	55.9	[b]	[b]

NOTE: Coefficients of correlation were calculated between the Know-Nothing vore in 1855, without Howard County, and the same twenty counties for the presidential elections. This will produce some small error because Howard was created from parts of Baltimore and Anne Arundel Counties, and so those two units will not be completely the same from the 1836–1848 period to the 1855 election. Nonetheless, this error should be quite small, and will not seriously affect the correlations over the entire state. The coefficient of correlation between the Know-Nothing vote by counties in 1855 and the Whig vote in the stable period is −0.549; between the Know-Nothing vote and the Democratic vote in the stable period, it is +0.543.

[a] From the average party vote in the Presidential elections of 1836, 1840, 1844, and 1848.

[b] Howard County did not exist until after 1850.

high Catholic population also showed a dislike for nativism; Westminster, Maryland, was a heavily Catholic town and it voted Democratic, even though surrounding Carroll County went solidly Know-Nothing. In the wards of Baltimore City, foreign voters gave evidence of voting solidly Democratic. The three wards with the highest foreign-born percentage were the three wards in which the Know-

Map 5. The American Party's Victory in the Election for Comptroller of Maryland, 1855

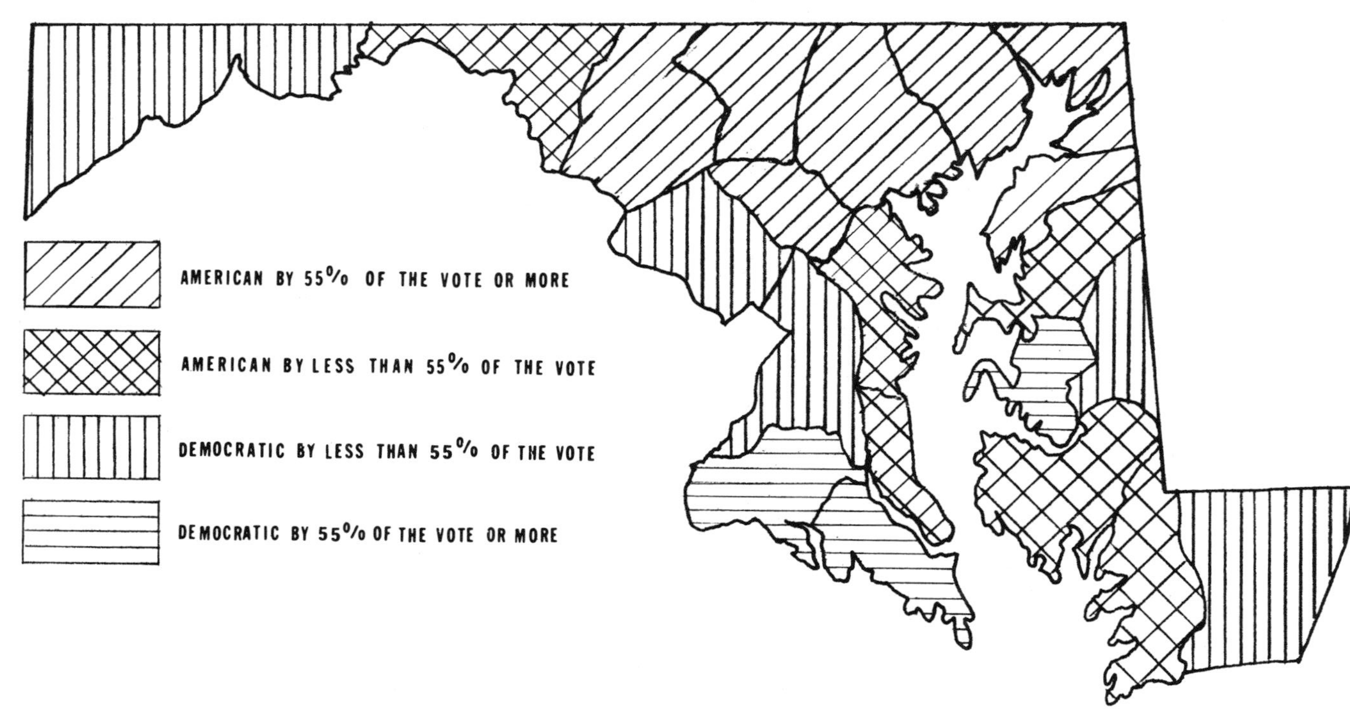

Nothings made the poorest showing—the Second, Eighth, and Ninth wards. The nativist average there was 32.7 percent of the vote.

Businessmen were evidently attracted to the Know-Nothing party. The number of businessmen in the front ranks of the party was higher than that in the Democratic party. Also, the national Know-Nothing party adopted a protectionist economic policy.[158]

Town dwellers generally showed more of a preference for the new party than did rural voters. The initial successes of the party in 1854 and early 1855 were in municipal elections. In almost every county, in all parts of the state, the larger towns gave more votes to the Americans than did the surrounding farm areas. This was true in Frostburg (Allegany County), Frederick (Frederick County), Cambridge (Dorchester County), and Annapolis (Anne Arundel County). The Know-Nothings did best in the more urbanized areas of the North and West. The reasons for this are conjectural. For one thing, the lodges of the order which spawned the party were probably located in towns; it would be difficult in a rural area to organize a secret society whose meetings were called by direct contact of members, as nativist lodge meetings usually were. In addition, not only were townspeople more likely to encounter immigrants, but also the clerks, artisans, and skilled mechanics who favored nativism would be urban. The businessmen who had an interest in the party would be town dwellers, too.

One student of the nativists has concluded that the typical American party voter was a middle-class Protestant.[159] A look at the Baltimore wards, for example, shows that the poorest wards (like the working-class, heavily immigrant Eighth Ward) and the wealthiest (like the "silk-stocking" Eleventh Ward) did not welcome nativism. Unskilled workers in the metropolis tended to be Democratic, the skilled workers split evenly, but the clerks and proprietors warmed to the new party. These statistical conclusions have the force of logic; the American party platform's stress on old American stock as the repository of virtue, the glorification of "virtuous men" in politics, criticism of commercially disruptive sectionalism, and condemnation of foreign libertarian radicals obviously appealed to those middle-class Protestant voters who felt threatened by change, immigrants, and possible disruption of the Union.

Maine Law advocates tended to support the Know-Nothings, although this assumption cannot be proved conclusively. Both crusades—temperance and nativism—stemmed from a common root of

158 Anspach, *op. cit.*, p. 112.
159 See Baker, *op. cit.*

social concern; both in a sense were reform movements. Temperance was grounded in the attitude of impatient Christian perfectionism which typified American Protestantism in the first half of the nineteenth century; Catholic social reformers were less common, and certainly the antiliquor crusade was a Protestant preserve. Also, several newspapers which supported the temperance movement in Maryland—the *Baltimore Clipper* and the *Annapolis Gazette*, for example—later supported the Know-Nothings, while Democratic papers like the *Port Tobacco Times* and the *Planters' Advocate* scoffed at temperance. Tracing the overlapping leadership of the Maine Law and nativist movements in a systematic way is, unfortunately, impossible. The leadership of the Maine Law movement was largely a group of political amateurs who left few traces on the historical record, and when Maine Law was rampant, in 1853, the Know-Nothings were still shrouded in secrecy. Interesting individual connections between the two movements did exist, however. The Maine Law sheriff who was elected in Baltimore in 1853 later ran for mayor as a Know-Nothing in 1860. One of the officers of the state Temperance Convention held in January 1854 was a Presbyterian cleric named Andrew B. Cross, who was also one of Maryland's most obdurate nativists.[160] And the nativists supported the successful Maine Law ticket for the House of Delegates in Baltimore in 1853. But there are limits to the links that can be found between temperance and political nativism. The Delegate who introduced a comprehensive Maine Law Bill into the General Assembly in 1854 was a Democrat from Harford County, William Elliott. Also, not one of the Maine Law delegates who were elected with nativist endorsement in 1853 was on the Know-Nothing delegate slate in the 1855 election.

Owners of large numbers of slaves were likely to find the nativists irrelevant or unattractive because of the slavery issue. The most "Southern" areas of Maryland—the tobacco regions and areas of extensive slaveholding—began to show up in the Democratic column in 1855. This change, from adamant Whiggery in the thirties and forties to Democratic voting by the middle fifties, had begun in 1852. As noted above, many Marylanders in the old society regarded the Whig presidential candidate, Winfield Scott, as unacceptable. In consequence Democrats and Whigs in Southern and Eastern Maryland began to merge; common sectional interests overcame old party lines.

By 1855 the fusion of Democrats and Whigs in Southern Maryland was one of the clearest features of the new party alignment. Fusion

160 See Chapter IV.

had two causes, a negative reaction to the dogma of the American party and a positive attraction to the Southern rights wing of the Democratic party. Southern Maryland Whigs began their conversion by damning the bigotry of the Know-Nothings; this area, after all, had originally been settled by Catholics and St. Mary's County had been the first English Catholic settlement in the New World. After criticizing the cant of the Know-Nothings the *Port Tobacco Times* concluded, "It appears there is a singlar unanimity between . . . the Whigs and Democrats in their opposition to the new party."[161] More than one Southern Maryland Whig agreed with William T. Merrick, a Whig who said that, since his party was gone and since he could not in good conscience join the American party, he would therefore have to go with the Democrats.[162] Fusion tickets, or Union tickets as they were often called, appeared in most Southern and Eastern Maryland counties in 1855.[163] A Whig from St. Mary's County reported to an anti-Know-Nothing newspaper that "both Whigs and Democrats in old St. Mary's, the mother of Toleration, are with you."[164] This banding together of displaced Whigs and Democrats in the old society was furthered by the charge that Know-Nothings were abolitionists.[165] These charges were supported by the antislavery beliefs of many Northern Know-Nothings, like Henry Wilson of Massachusetts, who argued vehemently for an antislavery plank at the Order's 1855 national council meeting.[166] Even after the Northern wing of the American party left to join the Republicans in 1856, Maryland Democrats accused the Know-Nothings of being an anti-Southern party—hostile, or at least dangerously indifferent, to the interests of slavery.

The new alignment that was achieved in the election of 1855—and that continued at least through 1856[167]—pitted Northern and Western Maryland, Baltimore, and some voters in Eastern Shore Maryland against the increasing Democratic strength in the Southern and Eastern counties. Formerly the anchor of Maryland's Democratic party, Baltimore was by 1855 the center of American party power. The old home of the Whigs was Democratic. A new party had risen on a wave of social discontent, and a large majority of Maryland's voters had switched political allegiance.

161 June 7, 1855.
162 *Ibid.*, October 12, 1854.
163 *Maryland Republican* (Annapolis), August 25, 1855.
164 *Ibid.*
165 *Ibid.*, September 5, 1855.
166 A full account of the convention appeared in the *Baltimore Sun*.
167 See Chapter IV.

IV

BALTIMORE AND THE POLITICS OF VIOLENCE

By 1856 THE POLITICIANS of the American party faced a classic dilemma; they had achieved power and now found themselves unsure what to do with it. Their leadership of Maryland consequently had a singular pointlessness about it. Retaining office became the ruling obsession of the Know-Nothing party. Several effects of this obsession were noticeable in the period 1856-1859. The gaudy anti-Catholic, antiforeign passions of the organizing days were overshadowed by conservative Unionism in the party programs. Some zealots still pressed antinunnery bills, or urged the General Assembly to extend the naturalization peroid to unreasonable lengths, but they were quashed by their colleagues, who obviously found them an embarrassment now that the elections had been won. When the dynamic Know-Nothing campaigners proved to be just another set of verbose politicians, the electorate began to drift away. Soon the Know-Nothings could rely only on Baltimore for votes. The outrageous means that were employed to carry large majorities there, however, alienated even more Marylanders. The disappearance of the national American organization in 1857 robbed Maryland Americans of both patronage and influence in federal councils. Finally, the American regime in Maryland collapsed under the assault of a reform movement, amid the angry hoots and jeers of many who had once seen the Know-Nothing crusade as the salvation of their society. The course of Marylanders in those four years of American rule is a study of allegiances in flux and in the pathology of an American city at mid-century.

I

In 1856, though, the American party was solidly in control of the state. The elections of November 1855 had been a complete triumph. The young party had captured Baltimore City and thirteen of twenty-one counties. American William Purnell became state comptroller with 51.4 percent of the popular vote; D. D. McPhail was elected lottery commissioner with 51.3 percent. Most of the old Whig counties went American, with some exceptions in the Southern section. The shift of the heavily slaveowning areas below Baltimore into the Democratic column continued, a shift which had begun in the presidential election of 1852. (See Table 7.)

Fresh from their victory, the Americans were ready to try out their new political strength. The ferocious partisan sentiment that marked the election of 1855 was still very much alive when the legislature met in January 1856. Many of the legislators were new to Annapolis. They were young and unassociated with the genteel political tradition of the stable period in Maryland, 1836-1850, a period which had been marked by predictable elections and long tenure in offices. Almost immediately these new assemblymen were challenged by the annual message of Democratic Governor Thomas Watkins Ligon. Ligon announced that he "would fail to discharge a public duty" if he neglected to mention the appearance of "secret political societies," whose activities "tend to the subversion of the well and dearly cherished principles of our government."[1] The governor also scored the violence of the previous elections, which he clearly linked to the existence of the secret societies.

The American legislators responded quickly and predictably. Delegate Anthony Kennedy of Baltimore, soon to be a U.S. senator, rose to challenge the governor's assertions. He moved to establish a committee of five to investigate Ligon's charges. The committee was also instructed to demand of the governor all information he had concerning the secret societies.[2] After some delay the Assembly created such a committee, consisting of three Americans and two Democrats. The three Americans consistently outvoted the minority, and they used their power ruthlessly. The committee's investigation was a sham. They called no witnesses and subpoenaed no documents.[3] In vain the Democrats supplied lists of aggrieved voters who were

[1] Maryland, *Annual Message of the Governor of Maryland,* 1856, Executive Papers, Annapolis, p. 28.

[2] Maryland, House of Delegates, *Journal,* 1856, p. 27.

[3] Laurence Frederick Schmeckebier, *History of the Know Nothing Party in Maryland,* The Johns Hopkins University Studies in Historical and Political Science, ser. 17 (Baltimore: The Johns Hopkins Press, 1899), p. 24.

TABLE 7. THE AMERICAN PARTY'S VICTORY IN 1855: THE RACE FOR COMPTROLLER

County	Percentage of Vote American
Southern Maryland	
Anne Arundel	52.7
Calvert	51.9
Charles	37.8
Montgomery	49.6
Prince George's	49.8
St. Mary's	17.1
Eastern Shore	
Caroline	49.9
Dorchester	54.0
Kent	61.8
Queen Anne's	54.9
Somerset	53.5
Talbot	43.5
Worcester	47.8
Western Maryland	
Allegany	49.1
Baltimore[a]	55.0
Carroll	55.4
Cecil	55.1
Frederick	55.8
Harford	63.9
Howard	55.9
Washington	50.8
Baltimore City	51.0
Average for Maryland	51.7

Average American percentage of the vote in counties carried in 1855 (13), 55.45
Average American percentage of the vote in counties lost in 1855 (8), 42.45

[a] Baltimore County, here as elsewhere in this study, is counted separately from Baltimore City.

eager to testify to the substance of the governor's accusations. Inevitably the majority report dismissed Ligon's charges out of hand and substituted instead a sharply worded counterattack. The Americans called the governor's speech "an unfortunate exhibition of ill-timed and undeserved discourtesy" at best, and more accurately "a breach of privilege."[4] The outmanned Democrats could only file

[4] Maryland, House of Delegates, *Majority Report of the Special Committee on Elections, House Documents,* 1856, p. 18.

a minority report containing the results of their own unofficial researches. There the matter expired.

The most startling feature of the new party in power was its abandonment of nativism. The Reverend Andrew B. Cross, Presbyterian anti-Catholic zealot from Baltimore, sent to the Assembly a stirring petition calling for the investigation of nunneries, those "priests prisons for women." Cross had been a nativist since the 1840s and no doubt reveled in what he felt was the victory of his ideals. Delegate Nelson Cullings of Baltimore County was persuaded to introduce Cross's petition on the House floor.[5] A House committee was duly appointed to look into convents, but it took little testimony and reported six weeks later—unanimously—that the existing laws afforded "ample protection . . . [and that] therefore no further legislation is necessary."[6] True nativists like Cross were stunned. One Baltimore delegate rose to protest that he could not go back to his constituents unless some action was taken. He therefore introduced, as a substitute for the committee report, a general resolution condemning convents on principle. This resolution was not even acted upon. The Senate was as reluctant as the House to be embarrassed by nativist legislation.

The Americans finally possessed the power they had been seeking, and they stoutly refused to use it for nativist purposes. The Two Hundred Fifty-first session passed hundreds of acts relating to corporations, acted to simplify Maryland's system of legal pleadings, agreed to scores of other routine bills, but made not one nativist program into law.[7] If the political composition of the General Assembly in 1856 were unknown, nothing in its legislative achievements would indicate the presence of a once-virulent nativist organization.

The desertion of nativism by the American members of the Two Hundred Fifty-first session was only the beginning of a trend. Over the next four years all the party's platforms and its allied newspapers switched the focus of party concern away from nativism. Instead, "Unionism" became the party's rallying cry. Unionism was not new to the American party, but after 1855 it dominated party policy almost completely. The flight from nativism showed up clearly in the editorials of American newspapers. In 1857 the *Annapolis Gazette*, a rabidly partisan Know-Nothing sheet, pointedly declared agitation of the north-south conflict to be a greater threat to America than foreign influence.[8] A resolution of the Sixth District (Southern Mary-

[5] *Annapolis Gazette*, February 21, 1856.

[6] *Ibid.*, March 20, 1856.

[7] Elihu S. Riley, *A History of the General Assembly of Maryland, 1635–1904* (Baltimore: n.p., 1905), pp. 361–64.

[8] July 16, 1857.

land) Americans denied that Roman Catholics were in any danger from the party, either "politically or socially."[9] The *Planters' Advocate* of Upper Marlboro reprinted a letter from a North Carolina Know-Nothing which illustrated the change from nativism to sectional conservatism. He pointed out that the American party was now no longer secret, and had largely abandoned its anti-Catholic tenets. "What remains," he asked: "Amendment of the naturalization laws[?] —forget it and band together to save the constitution."[10] The new emphasis was behind the series of stanchly Unionist editorials which the Know-Nothing *Frederick Herald* ran in 1858.[11] At the same time the *Herald* employed a German, one Jacob Ruthrauff, as its Baltimore sales representative.

The appeal to antiforeign, anti-Catholic prejudice had been vital to the rise of the party, but, once success was earned, bias became an embarrassment. In 1856 the American party ceased to be a rising mass movement. It became instead an entrenched and broad-based party that required different tactics to survive. Rather than attack, it needed, as in the case of the governor's accusations in 1856, to defend itself. For a party in power, nativism was a sterile philosophy incapable of producing results. It was suited for agitation, not action. Nativism exploited discontents but could not affect them. People were drawn to its flashy slogans and patriotic shine, but in practice nativism was useless. As holders of office the Know-Nothings could not burn convents or harass visiting monsigneurs. They now had to govern, administer, legislate. The only courses of legislation open to Maryland's nativists were either to outlaw convents and Catholic schools or to tamper with the naturalization process. The first was too obviously ludicrous, and the second stirred no real interest among Marylanders. Nativism lost its appeal after a short time because it was too glaringly irrelevant to the pressing political concerns of the age. People seemed to tire of it after a few years, just as they had in the 1840s. Horace Greeley was right when he said that a party based solely on nativist prejudice would have "as much persistance and coherence as an anti-cholera or an anti-potato-rot movement."[12]

The Americans stopped witch-hunting in 1856 and moved instead to consolidate their power. They showed off that power in the 1856 General Assembly by electing Anthony Kennedy to the U.S. Senate by an overwhelming margin. Kennedy was one of the new young

[9] *Ibid.*, February 14, 1856.

[10] *Planters' Advocate* (Upper Marlboro, Md.), April 2, 1856; Congressman T. L. Clingman of North Carolina was the author of this statement.

[11] See, for example, August 31, 1858.

[12] Carlton Beals, *Brass Knuckle Crusade* (New York: Hastings House, 1960), p. 263.

faces in the Maryland House of Delegates. He was the younger brother of John Pendleton Kennedy. He was defeated in a try for the House of Representatives as a Whig in 1844, and had never held office above the state level. Prior to the Two Hundred Fifty-first session he had not held public office in Maryland. At the age of forty-six, he was going to Washington for the first time.[13] According to his older brother, Anthony was chosen primarily for his loyalty to the nativist societies; certainly, said John P. Kennedy, the choice was not made on merit, because his brother "had never thought a thought in his life."[14] Kennedy was elected senator with only one dissenting vote; the overmatched Democrats cast blank ballots to protest their helplessness. In the face of such an impressive display of political muscle, the refusal of even the heavily American lower chamber to act on nativist programs was all the more striking. The Know-Nothings could have had what they pleased, and their choices were interestingly ordinary. They had become the establishment.

II

The Americans faced their first national election in 1856 armed with newly won offices and flushed with respectability. Symbolically, the national party held its nominating convention on Washington's birthday, in Philadelphia. This put it clearly first in the field, nine months ahead of the election and four months ahead of the Democrats. As its presidential nominee the party chose former President Millard Fillmore, a former Whig from New York who was not at all known as a nativist. They gave the second spot to Andrew Jackson Donelson, of Tennessee. Fillmore was a fine choice in the eyes of Maryland's Know-Nothings. He was a former Whig, as so many Maryland Americans were. He might also appeal to those former Whigs in Southern Maryland who showed a growing inclination to vote Democratic. He was closely identified with the Compromise of 1850, of which most Marylanders approved.[15]

[13] All of Anthony Kennedy's previous officeholding had been in Virginia. His election was challenged on the grounds that he was a member of the body that elevated him, but he resigned his seat on the last day of the session.

[14] John Pendleton Kennedy to A. Bryan, December 3, 1855, John Pendleton Kennedy Papers, Peabody Institute Library, Baltimore.

[15] See, for example, *Baltimore American*, November 17, 1856. Andrew Jackson Donelson was the nephew and namesake of Andrew Jackson, and was largely raised at President Jackson's Hermitage plantation. After serving his uncle and several other Democratic administrators in a variety of posts, Donelson broke with the Democrats over what he saw to be Southern sectional extremism in the party. He later refused to serve the Confederacy in the Civil War and died in Memphis in 1871.

The party's national platform was also very congenial to the Maryland delegation. That document denounced slavery agitation by all sides, and it stressed a florid, if vague, national patriotism. It condemned repeal of the Missouri Compromise line and called for noninterference by Congress in the slavery question. The platform denounced a great deal but proposed nothing. Furthermore, the 1856 national party platform followed the pattern being set by Maryland Know-Nothings; it reduced nativism to a clearly secondary position in the party's hierarchy of values. Altogether the 1856 platform was innocuous, and much less strident in tone and detail than the 1855 platform. One disappointed Indiana delegate admitted that, "if there was anything in it, it was so covered up with verbiage that a President would be elected before the people would find out what it was all about."[16] Many Northern delegates were outraged by what they felt to be the proslavery tone of the platform; they seceded from the convention, reassembled in June, and eventually formed an alliance with the Republicans.[17] These "North Americans" did not figure in Maryland politics, but their defection weakened the American party in a way which cast serious doubt on Fillmore's chances for election.

The Democrats waited until June to nominate their ticket, in Cincinnati. Unlike the Americans, they had little trouble with their platform. They firmly endorsed the principles and particulars of Stephen A. Douglas's Kansas-Nebraska Act.[18] Picking a candidate, on the other hand, started an intramural brawl that was settled only by Douglas's withdrawal in favor of Pennsylvania's James Buchanan. Buchanan was a Southern favorite. Maryland's delegation liked him.[19] Marylanders were also pleased with the selection of a border-state man, John Cabell Breckinridge, of Kentucky, to fill out the ticket.

In Maryland the presidential contest was between bland Fillmore and the uncontroversial American platform, on one hand, and Buchanan and the democratic platform, on the other. The Republicans were of no consequence in Maryland in 1856; their only concentrated support came from among Baltimore's Germans. Karl Heinrich Schnauffer's *Die Wecker* was the only Frèmont paper in the state. Shades of the deceased Whig party tried feebly to enter the lists, too, but their effort was futile. In mid-September the Whigs held their last national convention, in Baltimore. Only twenty-one states were represented.

16 Schmeckebier, *op. cit.*, p. 36.

17 See F. H. Harrington, *Fighting Politician, Major General N. P. Banks* (Philadelphia: University of Pennsylvania Press, 1948), p. 24.

18 Allan Nevins, *Ordeal of the Union*, 2 vols. (New York: Charles Scribner's Sons, 1947), 2: 457.

19 *Ibid.*, p. 456.

Old age was marked among the delegates. It was fitting that the last conclave of that party was held in the state which had loyally supported Whig presidential candidates for so long.[20] In 1856, however, Maryland was given over to the Americans and so were the old Whigs. They despondently endorsed Fillmore and Donelson, though they chose to draw up their own platform.[21] In Maryland the field was left to Fillmore and Buchanan.

The Fillmore forces stressed conservatism and the good old days. A meeting of Worcester County Americans praised Fillmore's "Washingtonian" reign in the White House. They also resolved "that . . . the further agitation of the slavery question for any purpose in the Halls of Congress . . . is inimical to those friendly feelings which alone make the Union possible."[22] Americans from Prince George's County echoed the same themes. They called Fillmore a "second Washington," a comparison which was as revealing as it was absurd. The tendency noted earlier,[23] to invoke the example of the golden age of the republic as a remedy for present ills, was still very prevalent among Know-Nothings in 1856. Fillmore himself stressed the need for old-fashioned "conservatism" in the face of imminent dissolution. "Buchanan," Filmore warned, "is . . . a sectional candidate, in principle."[24] Fillmore supporters also claimed that Buchanan was hostile to workingmen. It was widely believed that in an 1840 speech Buchanan had suggested that American labor should be willing to compete with European wage scales, even to ten cents a day. The *Annapolis Gazette*, for one, derided the Democrat as "Ten-Cent Jimmy," and pointed out that in his youth Buchanan had been a Federalist, and so, presumably, an elitist.[25]

The Democrats stressed most the positive protection of the Southern way of life. They focused particularly on thwarting the "Black Republican" threat. For this reason Maryland Democrats belittled the American party's chances of forming an effective opposition to the Free-Soil forces. The Americans were vulnerable to this attack on two counts: first, they would not likely win enough offices to stop the Republicans; and, second, their platform was too evasive about the rights of Southerners. Former Whig James A. Pearce, senior senator from Maryland, supported Buchanan essentially because he was the

[20] Several Maryland newspapers, including the *Baltimore Patriot* and the *Worcester County Shield* (Snow Hill, Md.), were still Whig in their politics.

[21] *Baltimore Sun*, September 18 and 19, 1856.

[22] *Annapolis Gazette*, August 14, 1856.

[23] See Chapter III.

[24] Millard Fillmore to John P. Kennedy, October 25, 1856, Kennedy Papers.

[25] September 18, 1856. See also Nevins, *op. cit.*, 2: 501. The charge that Buchanan once advocated a ten-cent-per-day wage was leveled elsewhere, too.

strongest alternative to Frémont.[26] A Whig congressman from the Eastern Shore, John W. Crisfield, also criticized the weakness of Fillmore's party. "In the House of Representatives are scarcely enough members from the free states who favor Mr. Fillmore's election to fill the Cabinet appointments," said Crisfield, "and if there is one member from those States in the Senate, Mr. Fillmore could not name him."[27] The *Maryland Republican* pleaded for former Whigs to support Buchanan. The editor argued that the issues which once divided Whigs and Democrats were now "obsolete" and completely outweighed by the Republican threat.[28] The fusion of Whigs and Democrats in Southern Maryland, which began in the 1852 campaign, was reinforced by the unattractiveness of the American alternative in 1856.

As usual, Baltimore was the focus of the election. A large majority there would overcome weakness everywhere else in the state. The Americans had a solid base of support in Baltimore, and they waged a vigorous and violent campaign.

The Baltimore municipal elections of October 8 provided practice for the presidential contest and gave an ominous warning of violence to come. Democrats and Americans harassed each other, and they both attacked the Republicans. A mob broke up a Republican rally in September; the small band of Republicans was outnumbered by as much as fifty to one.[29] That same week the election mayhem began in earnest. Three riots broke out. The tempo increased as October 8 approached. Baltimore Democrats touched off a riot on October 5 by tearing down an American banner. Then they held off the enraged Know-Nothings by barricading a house and defending it with a small cannon.[30]

The municipal election itself pitted two former railroad presidents against each other for the mayorality. American Thomas Swann, formerly of the Baltimore and Ohio, faced Democrat Robert C. Wright, previously with the Northern Central Railroad. Swann won in a flurry of bricks and blood. Every one of the city's twenty wards experienced its share of pushing, intimidation, and fights. At least two major riots erupted. The Democrats from the "Irish Eighth" drove off all American voters. The Americans counterattacked and a pitched battle raged up a steep hill along Monument Street, west of Calvert Street. Combatants used Baltimore's famous white marble

26 *Annapolis Gazette,* August 7, 1856, reprinted from the *National Intelligencer.*
27 Nevins, *op. cit.,* 2: 490.
28 *Maryland Republican* (Annapolis), April 12, 1856.
29 *Baltimore Sun,* September 12, 1856.
30 *Baltimore American,* October 6, 1856.

stoops for cover in gunfights. The Know-Nothings started the other major fracas, at the Lexington Market. This brawl featured knives, chains, bricks, clubs, and miscellaneous firearms. Similar but smaller fights broke out the day after the election as well.[31]

The official tally of the election gave Swann the mayorality by one thousand votes; the Americans also gained a majority in the city council.[32] These official returns were almost pure fiction.[33] Wherever toughs from one party controlled a polling place, they stuffed the ballot boxes and turned away opposition voters. The final human cost of the municipal election has been variously estimated. At the very least, four were killed and over fifty, in the words of one local doctor, were wounded "more or less dangerously."[34]

The Americans were ideally equipped to win such contests. Though the Democrats had their share of thugs, most of the roughnecks from the city streets seemed to be allied with the nativists. Consequently, people were outraged but not surprised when the American mayor rejected a request by concerned citizens that he take extraordinary measures to prevent November's presidential election from being "roughed"—to use the contemporary phrase. Swann turned away these requests with assurances that he had matters well in hand. He did, in fact, order the Maryland Light Division of Infantry to be in readiness the day of the election, but "ready" was as far as the troops ever got. Governor Ligon pointedly offered his services to protect law and order, but the mayor just as pointedly refused.[35] "Good citizens are anxious and apprehensive," reported the *Sun* during election week; "active partisans are serious, suspicious of wrong, and talk in a very determined tone."[36]

Astonishingly, the presidential canvass managed to be even bloodier than the local. The rioters employed at least one cannon. The casualty list was longer than before—10 dead and over 250 wounded. Electoral processes had become a mockery in Baltimore. Granted, the city had never been known for orderly campaigns, but the bloodshed of 1856 went beyond all reasonable bounds. The Americans had not invented political roughhousing, nor did they hold patent on it, but under their auspices it flourished.

[31] *Ibid.*, October 9 and 10, 1856.

[32] In the First Branch the Americans won thirteen seats, the Democrats seven; in the Second Branch it was Americans five, Democrats five.

[33] I did not use the statistical procedures applied to the returns from the counties (especially the computation of a coefficient of correlation) on the Baltimore wards, because of the clearly untrustworthy nature of city returns.

[34] Bernard C. Steiner, *Citizenship and Suffrage in Maryland* (Baltimore: Cushing & Co., 1895), p. 39.

[35] Schmeckebier, *op. cit.*, p. 39.

[36] *Baltimore Sun,* November 3, 1856.

Fillmore's brand of conservatism carried Maryland, both in Baltimore and in the counties, but Maryland's eight electoral votes were the only ones Fillmore received. American victories elsewhere in 1856 were scored only on the state or local level by the pro-Republican North Americans.[37] Maryland voters, on the other hand, responded to the Americans' appeal for peace, calm, and preservation of the Union against all agitation over the slavery question. Not even the violence in Baltimore could obscure Marylanders' endorsement of conservatism. (See Table 8, and Map 6.) Fillmore and his platform emphasized the danger of the sectional quarrel over slavery, and Maryland Americans felt the same. Congressman August R. Sollers said in the House of Representatives, for example, "Although representing the largest slaveholding interest in Maryland, I have never deemed it my duty to enter into a comparison of my state with any other or to defend the institution here or elsewhere." Sollers said his sole concern was to "uphold the unity of these states."[38] Henry Winter Davis, American congressman from Baltimore, put the case for Unionism more bluntly: "The way to settle the slavery question is to be silent on it."[39] "Unionism"—the valuing of the American federation above all issues that might divide it—was the most attractive attitude to Marylanders in 1856. Marylanders warmed to that appeal because they themselves stood badly divided. With one foot in each section, Maryland confronted the confusion of allegiances squarely. Torn thus, Marylanders prayed for peace and voted for Fillmore.

The presidential election of 1856 ruined the American party as a national political organization, despite Fillmore's victory in Maryland. Hopelessly split between the Northern and Southern branches, the Americans were barely noticed in final results. Official recognition of the Americans' dissolution came from the last national council meeting, in Louisville, Kentucky, in June 1857. The council resolved "that the American party in each State and Territory be authorized to adopt such a plan of organization as respectively may be best suited to the views of the party in their several localities."[40] Maryland's dominant political party was on its own. It had no national organization to call on, no vital federal patronage to dispense. To survive in such circumstances the Maryland Know-Nothings would have to fight for every vote they could get.

[37] North Americans scored local victories in Rhode Island, Massachusetts, and New Hampshire.

[38] U.S., *Congressional Globe,* 33rd Cong., 2nd sess., 1855, app., pp. 82–88.

[39] Henry Winter Davis, *Speeches and Addresses* (New York: Harper & Brothers, 1867), p. 158.

[40] Schmeckebier, *op. cit.,* p. 77.

TABLE 8. THE AMERICAN PARTY'S VICTORY IN 1856: THE COMPTROLLERSHIP RACE OF 1855 COMPARED WITH THE PRESIDENTIAL RACE OF 1856

	Percentage of the Vote American		
County	1855	1856	Difference
Southern Maryland			
Anne Arundel	52.7	52.9	+0.2
Calvert	51.9	53.0	+1.1
Charles	37.8	37.8	0.0
Montgomery	49.6	51.8	+2.2
Prince George's	49.8	47.3	−2.5
St. Mary's	17.1	19.0	+1.9
Eastern Shore			
Caroline	49.9	46.2	−3.7
Dorchester	54.0	56.9	+2.9
Kent	61.8	60.2	−1.6
Queen Anne's	54.9	55.0	+0.1
Somerset	53.5	54.6	+1.1
Talbot	43.5	45.1	+1.6
Worcester	47.8	46.2	−1.6
Western Maryland			
Allegany	49.1	46.3	−2.8
Baltimore	55.0	52.6	−2.4
Carroll	55.4	52.8	−2.6
Cecil	55.1	50.5	−4.6
Frederick	55.8	53.0	−2.8
Harford	63.9	59.6	−4.3
Howard	55.9	58.7	+2.8
Washington	50.8	50.4	−0.4
Baltimore City	51.0	63.1	+12.1
Average for Maryland	51.7	55.0	+3.3

Average American percentage of the vote in counties carried in 1856 (14), 54.2
Average American percentage of the vote in counties lost in 1856 (7), 41.1

III

During 1857 and 1858 Marylanders worked out the consequences of political patterns already established. The American-dominated General Assembly fought another round with Governor Ligon. American strength continued to be anchored by Baltimore while the Democrats increased their hold on the Southern counties. Violence disfigured Baltimore's elections, as it had in the past, but never again

Map 6. Fillmore's Victory in Maryland, 1856: A Know-Nothing Triumph

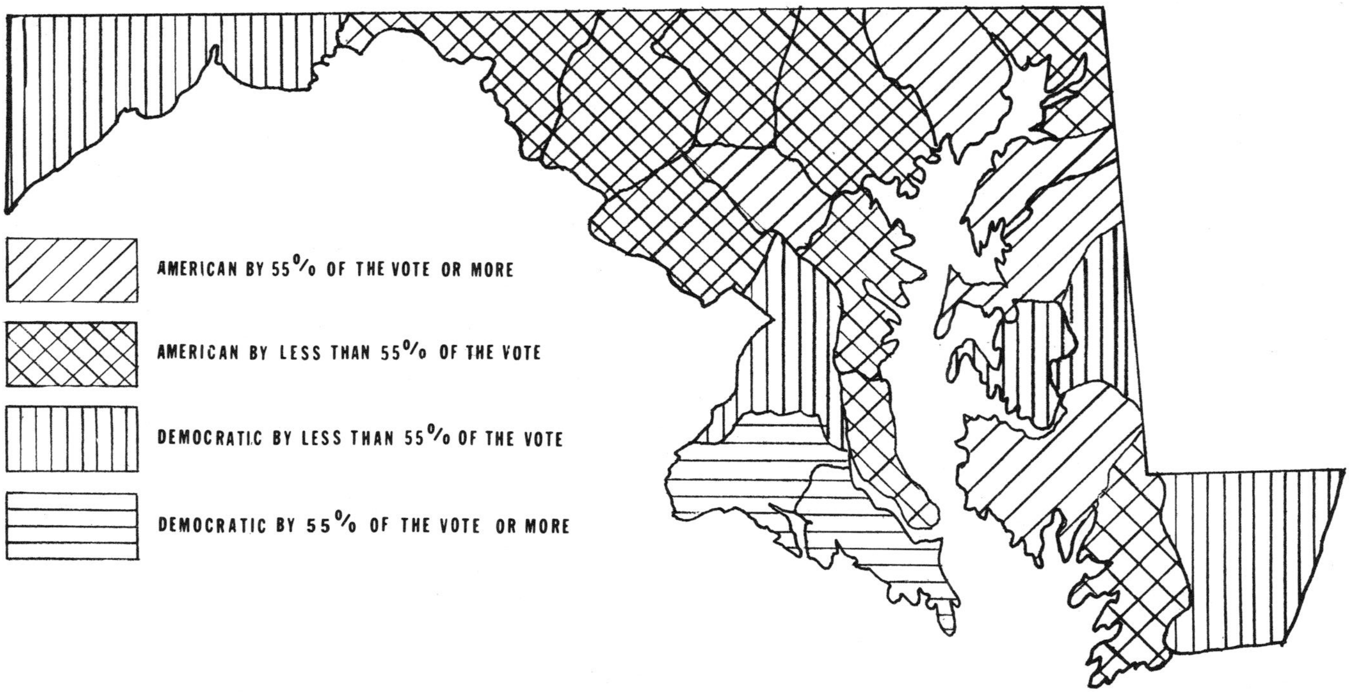

AMERICAN BY 55% OF THE VOTE OR MORE

AMERICAN BY LESS THAN 55% OF THE VOTE

DEMOCRATIC BY LESS THAN 55% OF THE VOTE

DEMOCRATIC BY 55% OF THE VOTE OR MORE

would bloodshed reach the proportions of 1856. An uneasy truce was reached in the city whereby each party avoided the strongholds of the other. This stalemate made city elections no more just, however, and only slightly less hazardous to the average citizen.

The most notable development in 1857 and 1858 was not any single, dramatic event, but rather the gradual withering of American strength in the counties. Scattered local elections in the spring of 1857 produced no great changes in the party balance; the Americans' troubles began in the fall.[41] The spoils of November promised exciting contests. At stake were the offices of governor, comptroller, lottery commissioner, land commissioner, the entire House of Delegates, and twelve of twenty-two Senate seats.

The Maryland Americans had to undergo a bitter nominating convention in July; since nominations were nearly tantamount to election, the party leaders scrapped vigorously for them. After much wrangling and compromise the party selected Thomas Hollyday Hicks, of Dorchester County, for governor, William Purnell for comptroller, D. H. McPhail for lottery commissioner, and L. W. Seabrook for land commissioner. Hicks's principal rival for the governor's nomination, James B. Ricaud, ran for Congress from the lower Eastern Shore.[42] The question of platform excited no one, so the 1856 platform remained in force. Office, not ideology, animated the Americans at this point.

Thoroughly dispirited and pessimistic, the Democrats held a dull convention one week after the Americans. They made no formal nominations but rather "recommended" candidates for various state offices. At the head of their ticket was J. C. Groome, a former Whig from Cecil County. The Baltimore Democrats were so browbeaten by this time that they did not even send a delegation to the state conclave; the party's city convention was torn by bickering and made nominations only for city council and Congress.[43] For a while it seemed that the Americans would have no opposition in the House of Delegates races in the city. Eventually, however, a group of Americans who were upset by the behavior of the party in Baltimore bolted the party and joined with some of the more determined Democrats to field independent candidates for the House of Delegates. This bipartisan action of concerned citizens was the earliest indication of the reform zeal which would unhorse the Americans.

The Americans swept the Baltimore municipal elections of October 1857. It was another violent election, though the casualty list was

[41] *Ibid.*, p. 70.
[42] Details of the convention are from the *Baltimore Sun*, July 24, 1857.
[43] Schmeckebier, *op. cit.*, p. 72; and *Baltimore Sun*, September 4, 1857.

not so long as that of 1856. One policeman was killed while attempting to suppress a riot; this may have indicated at least some effort by city forces to keep the peace.[44] On the other hand, the policeman was an agent of the American administration and he was killed in the Eighth Ward by a Democratic mob. The police also captured an astounding assortment of firearms and ammunition.[45] The election itself was no contest; the Americans retained control of the city council overwhelmingly. Voter turnout was light.

The riots of October obviously forecast more trouble for November. Since the November elections affected state offices, Governor Ligon felt he could justly use the state police power to help regulate the Baltimore polls in November, as he had tried to do in 1856. This time, however, he was determined to be firm. Citing his "constitutional duty," Ligon went to Baltimore on October 27, checked into Barnum's Hotel, and opened an exchange of cold, cutting letters with Mayor Swann.[46] Marylanders watched two leading officials who were within walking distance of each other trade formal written correspondence. Ligon first demanded to know what provisions Swann had made for supervising the coming election. Swann replied by wrapping himself in local sovereignty and bluntly denying Ligon's right to interfere. Infuriated, Ligon activated the First Light Division, Maryland State Militia, and arranged for an additional 3,600 men to be ready by noon on the Saturday before the election. To equip such a force he had to borrow 2,000 muskets from Virginia. Ligon then issued a proclamation declaring his intent to police the Baltimore election, and sent Swann a letter in which he criticized the mayor very sharply for his partisan approach to law enforcement. Swann's reply was brief and bitter. He said that, if Ligon wished to place Baltimore "under military supervision," he, Swann, could deplore but not prevent it.

The confrontation between mayor and governor seemed to be building to the point where bloodshed in the city streets might be the only possible result. The situation was finally saved because Ligon could not raise the troops he needed. The state military system simply could not mobilize that quickly, at least not for such a sensitive assignment. Many citizens were reluctant to leave home to participate in internecine warfare in the streets of Baltimore. Just as Ligon's position was being undermined, Swann also yielded a bit. At the urging of a citizens committee he agreed to appoint an extra two

44 *Baltimore Sun,* October 15, 1857.

45 *Ibid.*

46 The entire correspondence between Governor Ligon and Mayor Swann was reprinted in Maryland, House of Delegates, *House Documents,* 1858; the governor's message is there also. All references to correspondence and messages are from that source.

hundred temporary policemen, chosen from both parties.[47] He also issued a firm proclamation outlining the get-tough instructions the police force would follow.[48] Ligon then used this as an excuse to back out of his military plan, which he would have been unable to carry out in any case. The affair subsided with an exchange of hypocritically polite notes between governor and mayor. "It is a matter of extreme gratification to me," began Ligon; "It affords me pleasure to know," responded Swann.

The election was quiet in Baltimore, by contemporary standards, but it was nonetheless corrupt. Intimidation and fraud replaced open mob warfare. The fine-sounding regulations outlined in Swann's proclamation were ignored. The special police force was snubbed by the regular force; almost totally powerless, many special policemen resigned during the day.[49] Voters who were uncongenial to the gang at each polling place were turned away or beaten up. The Know-Nothings mounted a cannon at one precinct. Ballot-box stuffing was epidemic. In the Eighth Ward the Democratic vote alone was nearly twice as large as the total vote cast there in the heavily attended presidential election of 1856.[50]

All across Maryland the Americans won nearly everything. They elected the entire state slate, captured four of six congressional seats, and kept a majority in both houses of the General Assembly. Yet, buried in the statistics of their victory were the hints of trouble to come. They were too dependent on Baltimore; their power was definitely waning. Where Fillmore had won fourteen of Maryland's twenty-one counties in 1856, Hicks carried only ten in 1857. In eight of the ten counties won by Hicks, his percentage of the vote was smaller than Fillmore's. Only one of six Southern Maryland counties, Calvert, was in Hicks's column. On the Eastern Shore Hicks did not break even, losing four of seven counties there. The party's majorities in the General Assembly also were weakened.[51] (See Table 9 and Map 7.)

The Democrats could be cheered by their gains. The tobacco region was solidly theirs now. Granted, this was not a populous area, but the Democrats carried two of these counties by over 60 percent of the vote. They had gained on the Eastern Shore, and had even wrested Baltimore County from the Americans. They had a strong national party

[47] *Baltimore Sun*, November 2, 1857.
[48] *Ibid.*
[49] *Ibid.*, November 5, 1857.
[50] The most concise and accurate accounting of election outrages may be found in Schmeckebier, *op. cit.*
[51] In the House of Delegates, Americans led forty-five to twenty-seven. In the Senate, Americans outnumbered Democrats fifteen to seven.

with a platform which increasingly appealed to those Marylanders who thought of themselves as Southerners. Southern Maryland, the area of most extensive slaveholding in Maryland, gave the Democrats a greater percentage of its votes with each election.[52] On the Eastern Shore the Democrats registered a gain in 1857 over 1856 in four of the seven counties, and those were the four counties in that region with the greatest proportion of slaves in their population.[53] In the state as a whole, slaveowning areas tended to vote Democratic.[54] At the head of the ticket Groome ran well against Hicks. Outside of Baltimore, Groome carried eleven of twenty-one counties and beat Hick's popular total by 1,179 votes. (See Table 9 and Map 7.)

The downfall of the Democrats continued to be Baltimore. If the Democrats could have matched the Americans evenly in the city, the 1857 election would have been very close. An even split in the ten House of Delegates seats from Baltimore would have cut the Americans' margin in the lower chamber from eighteen votes to eight. The American state ticket would have been in serious trouble without the fraudulent votes from the city. Fillmore would likely have won in 1856 without chicanery in Baltimore; in 1857 Hicks would probably have lost. The Americans had to hold Baltimore, and they went to great lengths to do so.

IV

The real meaning of Baltimore, however, was not that it was badly used by politicians, but that it was so eminently usable, so openly available for such violent goings-on. Baltimore's shabby politics was only the most visible symptom of a much deeper sickness, as the fever merely represents the attacking virus. Baltimore was socially, as well

[52] The percentage of the vote captured by the Democrats in the six counties of Southern Maryland averaged 44.3 in 1852; 44.65 in 1853; 56.85 in 1855; 56.4 in 1856; and 59.1 in 1857. The decline in 1856 was probably accounted for by the popularity of Fillmore, who was also running as a Whig and who was well liked in Maryland for his support of the Compromise of 1850.

[53] The breakdown by county was as follows:

County	Percentage of Population Slave	Percentage of Vote Democratic	
		1856	1857
Talbot	29.9	54.9	55.7
Queen Anne	29.4	45.0	50.5
Somerset	24.9	45.4	49.9
Kent	23.1	39.8	47.2
Dorchester	22.7	43.1	42.1
Worchester	18.3	53.8	52.7
Caroline	8.3	53.8	48.4

[54] The coefficient of correlation between the extent of slaveholding in a county and the percentage of the vote obtained by Democrat Groome in 1857 is +0.558.

Table 9. Comparison of the Presidential Vote in 1856 with the Gubernatorial Vote in 1857, Showing the Declining Strength of the American Party

County	Percentage of the Vote American		
	President 1856	Governor 1857	Difference
Southern Maryland			
Anne Arundel	52.9	48.7	−4.2
Calvert	53.0	51.1	−1.9
Charles	37.8	35.8	−2.0
Montgomery	51.8	48.0	−3.8
Prince George's	47.3	40.4	−6.9
St. Mary's	19.0	21.3	+2.3
Eastern Shore			
Caroline	46.2	51.6	+5.4
Dorchester	56.9	57.9	+1.0
Kent	60.2	52.8	−7.4
Queen Anne's	55.0	49.5	−5.5
Somerset	54.6	53.1	−1.5
Talbot	45.1	44.3	−0.8
Worcester	46.2	47.3	+1.1
Western Maryland			
Allegany	46.3	43.6	−2.7
Baltimore	52.6	49.6	−3.0
Carroll	52.8	50.7	−2.1
Cecil	50.5	48.8	−1.7
Frederick	53.0	51.3	−1.7
Harford	59.6	56.9	−2.7
Howard	58.7	52.5	−6.2
Washington	50.4	50.2	−0.2
Baltimore City	63.1	68.5	+5.4
Average for Maryland	55.0	54.9	−0.1

Average American percentage of the vote in counties carried in 1857 (10), 52.8
Average American percentage of the vote in counties lost in 1857 (11), 43.4

as politically, a desperately unhealthy place. Maryland's metropolis was not alone in its difficulties, for other cities shared problems similar to Baltimore's, but this knowledge was cold comfort to Baltimoreans.

American cities have always been exploited and scorned; Baltimore was no exception. Thomas Jefferson's aversion—"The mobs of great cities add just so much to the support of pure government, as sores

Map 7. The Election of American Thomas H. Hicks to the Governorship of Maryland, 1857

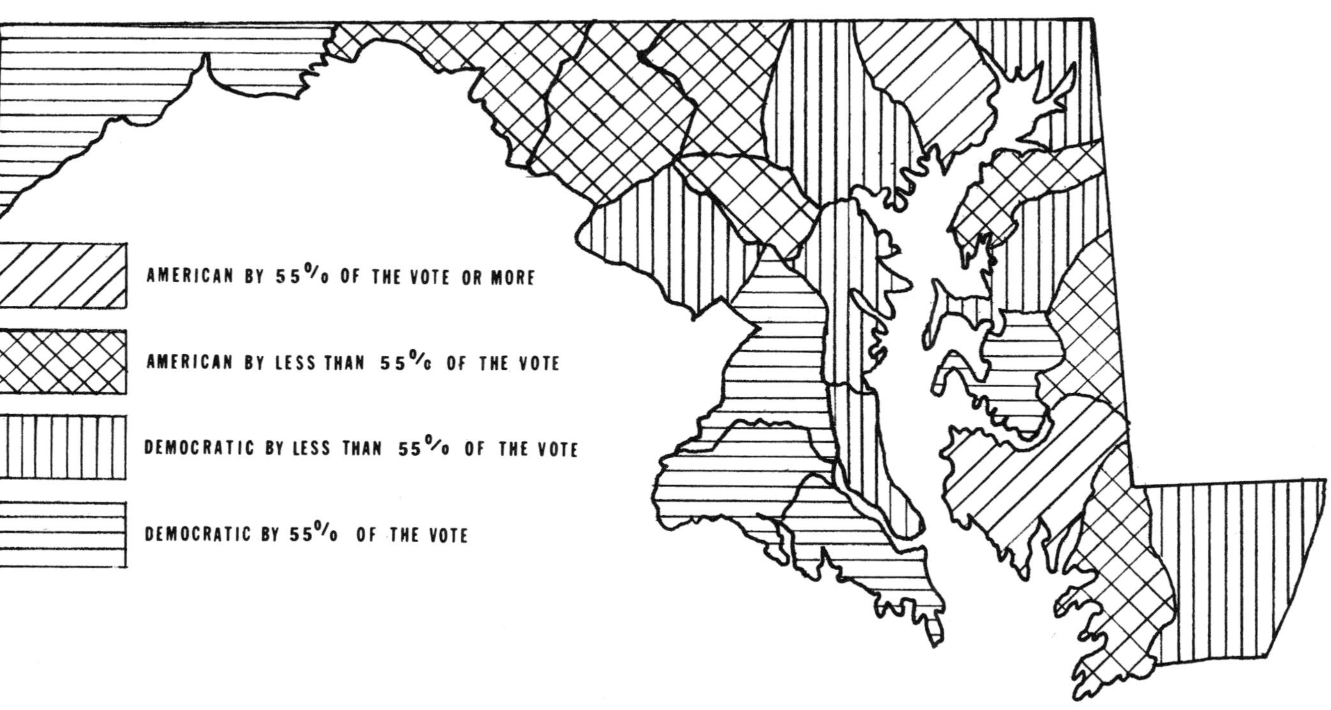

do to the strength of the human body"—has been a point of faith for Americans.[55] The pastoral ideal elevated country living and rural pursuits. "Commercial prosperity is ruinous to morals," warned the *Planters' Advocate*, and "commercial superiority [*is*] destructive of States."[56] The editor of the *Cambridge Democrat* showed to what extremes such sentiments can go. He praised extravagently the rural life in preference to the "hot bricks and dust of town;" yet the metropolis of which he complained was a sleepy river hamlet of 1,800 people.[57] People thought of cities as being intrinsically hopeless. Given this attitude, cities suffered from suspicion, fear, and gross neglect. As powerful as New York, Boston, Philadelphia, and Baltimore were, they remained unrespectable. They were centers of wealth, but they were also gaudy, noisy, and dangerous. One obvious effect of the mistrust of the city was its chronic underrepresentation in state legislatures. From the time Baltimore began to grow, late in the eighteenth century, for example, it was not represented in the General Assembly in a strength proportionate to its population. Repeatedly Baltimoreans had to fight, cajole, and threaten to get any increase in their allotted number of delegates. Even after the new constitution of 1851 readjusted Baltimore's representation, the city dwellers were the most underrepresented people in the state, by a wide margin.[58] The inevitable result of a negative approach to cities was that the prophecy was fulfilled. Left to grow and sprawl unattended, cities lived up to their detractors' worst predictions. On top of the emotional handicap, and perhaps as a result of it, came deficiencies in municipal government, lack of planning and services, an insufficient number of police, and inadequate political institutions. By the middle of the nineteenth century America already faced the problem of the cities.

Baltimore was part of this problem. It was the third largest city in the country; over a fifth of a million people lived there in 1860. It had more than tripled in size in forty years. Its port was jammed with trade. Manufacturers and wholesalers employed tens of thousands of people. The unique geography of the upper Bay made Baltimore an

[55] Adrienne Koch and William Peden, *The Life and Selected Writings of Thomas Jefferson* (New York: The Modern Library, 1944), p. 280. For full development of the antiurban theme, see Morton White and Lucia White, *The Intellectual versus the City* (Cambridge, Mass.: Harvard University Press, 1962).

[56] July 10, 1851.

[57] July 6, 1853.

[58] For example, in the west, Frederick County had one delegate for every 7,765 people (one for every 6,399 whites). In Prince George's County of Southern Maryland, each delegate represented 6,410 people (3,217 whites). On the Eastern Shore, in Dorchester, there was one representative for every 6,410 persons (one for every 3,885 whites). Baltimore, on the other hand, had one delegate per 21,242 persons, or, figuring on the basis of its white population, one for every 18,952.

upland city on the ocean; the Fall Line was but a few miles inland from the deep-water ship channels. Foreigners clogged the port; German was the most prominent of the foreign tongues heard in the city.[59] The city still possessed considerable charm amid the confusion; its seafood and terrapin were renowned, and almost every traveler seemed to comment on the beauty of Baltimore's women. In its activity, too, there was an impressive, crude strength. Nevertheless, Baltimore had grown too big, too fast. This cancerous expansion produced a social climate in which crime flourished.

News of violent crime packed the Baltimore press. At the far right of every front page, every day, Marylanders found stories of the latest assaults, arson, and rowdyism. Old crimes reappeared in the reports of court decisions. Whatever world and national events filled the columns of the *Sun, American, Clipper,* and *Patriot,* the crime bulletins were always there in small, dense type. When banker George William Brown addressed the Maryland Institute in March 1853, he chose as his subject the problem of crime in the streets. For his text he simply read from the *Baltimore American* the events of Thanksgiving 1852. On that solemn holiday the paper reported two cases of attempted robbery, one of arson, and two gang wars.[60] Violence in the streets and alleys of the city was depressingly common. The most distinctive feature of this constant violence was gang warfare.[61] A lively street corner society flourished in the city. Young men adrift, with little or nothing to do, banded together for companionship, protection, and a sense of belonging. Colorful names added to the cachet of toughness the clubs offered—names like the Rip Raps, Gladiators, Thunderbolts, Red Necks, Butt Enders, Rough Skins, Hard Times, Plug Uglies, and Blood Tubs.[62] Aside from the record of assaults and lawbreaking compiled by each individual member, the gangs would waylay unwary citizens or, more likely, one another.

Baltimore was famous for mayhem. Little ports all around the Bay dreaded the excursion parties from Baltimore, because along with their money they brought fights, drunkenness, and disorder.[63] Residents of the rural areas immediately around Baltimore were its most outspoken

[59] Baltimore's total foreign-born population in 1860 was 52,497. The census of 1860 did not give breakdowns by country of origin for each locality, but a safe estimate is that over half of Baltimore's immigrant population was German.

[60] Schmeckebier, *op. cit.*, pp. 41–42.

[61] Most northeastern cities had such gangs in the period before the Civil War. Richard Maxwell Brown, "Historical Patterns of Violence in America," in *Violence in America: Historical and Comparative Perspectives,* ed. Hugh Davis Graham and Ted Robert Gurr (New York: Bantam Books, 1969), p. 47.

[62] Schmeckebier, *op. cit.*, pp. 43–44.

[63] See, for example, *Cambridge Democrat,* June 29, 1853.

critics. "Outrage and rowdyism appear to be on the increase in Baltimore," clucked the *Baltimore County Advocate*. "Hardly a day passes but we hear of a respectable citizen being waylaid, robbed, insulted, or abused.[64] "The spirit of rowdyism still triumphs in Baltimore," the county paper said later. "Street fights with firearms, and highway robberies are of almost daily occurrence."[65] In a more sympathetic vein, but no less condescending, the *Advocate* pitied "The people of Baltimore [who] are drowning out their existence by breathing the impure air of the city."[66] An Annapolis editor expressed "shame and disgust" at the violence in Baltimore.[67] From as far away as Worcester County, on the seacoast, Marylanders expressed loud indignation about the situation in the metropolis.[68] Granted, some of the distaste for Baltimore was grounded in jealousy. "Beautiful Baltimore," sneered the *Worcester County Shield,* "has been petted and pampered and indulged . . . until some of her citizens begin to think that Baltimore is *all* Maryland."[69] Rural resentment against the merchants who handled farm products also hurt Baltimore. The *Planters' Advocate* of Upper Marlboro complained bitterly about the city tobacco warehousemen and merchants, "who have never failed to plunder us."[70]

Even Baltimoreans had little faith in their city as a place in which to live and work. John Pendleton Kennedy, for example, was easily one of the leading citizens of the city; he had had a law practice there, and by the 1850s was operating a large grain mill at Ellicott's Mills, west of the city. Kennedy participated actively in the social, cultural and political life of the town. He served as a director of the fledgling Maryland Historical Society. His elegant home on the southeast side of Mount Vernon Place was a social center for Baltimore, and from there Kennedy interrupted his writing and literary pursuits to participate in a myriad of civic activities. He was of Scotch-Irish extraction and, though the family home was in Martinsburg, Virginia,[71] in his mature years Kennedy was an urbane man and very much a part of Baltimore. Yet even he found the city wanting. His admiration for Baltimore was limited to a romantic conception of what the city was supposed to have been like in its early years—in effect, before it became truly a city; since that mythic time late in the previous

64 December 11, 1852.
65 *Ibid.*, January 1, 1853.
66 *Ibid.*, March 13, 1852.
67 *Maryland Republican*, November 8, 1856.
68 See, for example, the editorial "More Plug-Uglyism," *Worcester County Shield,* July 25, 1857.
69 *Ibid.*, February 8, 1853; see also *Upper Marlboro Gazette,* March 23, 1853.
70 October 25, 1851.
71 Martinsburg is now in West Virginia.

century Baltimore had "sadly . . . retrograded."[72] Indeed, in his many popular novels Kennedy raptly endorsed the pastoral ideal. In *Swallow Barn, or a Sojourn in the Old Dominion,* he wrote:

You will never know your friend so well, nor enjoy him so heartily in the city as you may in one of those large, bountiful mansions whose horizon is filled with green fields and woodland slopes and broad blue heavens. . . . There is a fascination in the quiet, irresponsible, and reckless nature of these country pursuits, that is apt to seize upon the imagination of a man who has felt the perplexities of business.[73]

Kennedy could have moved, of course; he did own a house in the pleasant, rolling country near his business in Baltimore County. Instead, he chose to spend most of his time in the city, complaining all the while. The city, it seemed, was a necessary location for business, writing, and social contact, but it was only to be used and not to be trusted or admired.

Newspaper editors are usually notorious for local chauvinism and booster enthusiasm, but Baltimore's editors were glum about city life. The *Clipper* predicted a flight to the suburbs. "The time will arrive," the paper warned, "when a considerable portion of the more wealthy citizens of Baltimore will locate themselves and families in the country. . . . The superior healthfulness of the country will be a strong inducement."[74] Even the *Sun,* largest of the Baltimore papers and firmly devoted to the city, entered a brief against the urban existence. In an 1850 editorial addressed to "our American youth," the editors of the *Sun* said:

Instead of putting their faces towards the city, those in the country had far better cast about them for the best means of establishing a personal [economic] interest. . . . It would be a hard task to convince any half dozen young men indiscriminately selected from the throng in our city streets of the truth of such a proposition as this, in the midst of the refinements, the luxuries, and the vices of city life.[75]

72 John P. Kennedy, "Baltimore Long Ago," manuscript essay or speech, Kennedy Papers, p. 21.

73 William R. Taylor, *Cavalier and Yankee: The South and American National Character* (Garden City, N.Y.: Doubleday & Co., 1961), p. 66.

74 Reprinted in *Baltimore County Advocate,* January 8, 1853. Baltimore's heat and humidity made it very unpleasant in the summer. Resorts like nearby Green Spring Valley, or Old Point Comfort, Virginia, advertised regularly in the Baltimore newspapers and evidently did a thriving business among those who could afford it. As one Baltimore merchant wrote to his wife, who was vacationing in Morgantown, Virginia (now West Virginia), "I would advise your longer breathing the fresh air and reposing in that retirement from our heat, and our hot and dry chorus—that sweet City Melody." Charles F. Mayer to Mrs. Mayer, undated typed copy, Brantz Mayer Papers, Maryland Historical Society, Baltimore.

75 August 26, 1850; see also *ibid.,* August 30, 1850.

The editors clearly did not trust the city—but they did see its siren charm for farm youths. This ambivalence was typical of American attitudes about the city in the nineteenth century. Obviously cities were valuable and offered many attractions; rapidly increasing numbers of people lived in them. As the *Sun's* editors realized, the young would not heed their warning, just as Kennedy ignored his own lyrical endorsement of the nonurban life. The city, it seemed, had the people but not their allegiance.

Baltimore's problems, like those of other major nineteenth-century U.S. cities, arose from a complex of social and physical factors. Baltimore's population was a volatile mixture of foreigners, the young, the large number of lower-class laborers peculiar to industrial areas, an extensive free black population, and itinerants of all types—seamen, railroad workers, commercial travelers, drifters.[76] All these people were jammed into narrow streets and long blocks of row houses. The stumpy, block-on-block design of the town demanded alleys that cut into the heart of each square to service the stores and shops, and that provided housing for many of the city's blacks, both slave and free. These alleys formed a maze of concealment and escape for criminals. The streets were scarcely better than the alleys; most were unpaved and very poorly lit. There were no municipal sewers, nor would there be any for many decades. Baltimore, in short, suffered from the same sorts of ills that plagued other cities, but it had reached this condition in half the time required elsewhere.

Managing a city like Baltimore would be difficult under the best conditions; under existing conditions it was nearly impossible. The police force, for example, was a study in arrested civic development. Until late 1858 the ridiculously small Baltimore force was not uniformed. The regular duty roster supplied one policeman per ward by day, and scarcely more night watchmen.[77] These men received no professional training, and the job offered nothing in the way of status or pay which would attract good men. Policemen were often recruited from the very elements they were expected to control. A bill to enlarge and professionalize the police force passed the city council in 1853, but it was eventually vetoed by the mayor after a long struggle.[78] Worst of all, policemen were political appointees. It was manifestly absurd to ask political placemen to supervise the

[76] The census of 1860 reported 23,947 white males between the ages of fifteen and thirty living in Baltimore. The same census reported 25,680 free blacks and 52,497 foreign-born in the city.

[77] Schmeckebier, *op. cit.*, p. 42. One old, pedestrian study of the Baltimore police force is marginally useful; See De Francias Folsom, *Our Police* (Baltimore: J. D. Ehlers & Co., 1888).

[78] *Baltimore Sun*, March 20 and June 14, 1853, and November 7, 1854.

elections on which their jobs might depend, but such was the practice. Even if the police could be persuaded to arrest someone, the American judge of the criminal court, the notoriously corrupt and alcoholic Henry Stump, was likely to let them go. Frequently Stump was said to be drunk on the bench. He was successfully impeached and convicted in 1860 for conduct unbecoming to his position.[79] After the 1858 elections the police force was somewhat enlarged by Mayor Swann, and new regulations were laid down. To judge from the elections of 1859, however, no real improvement resulted. Real police reform waited until 1860, which was anywhere from ten to thirty years behind the need for it.

Fire fighting was not a municipal service, and the private groups that were organized to carry it on were sometimes worse than useless.[80] These volunteer groups were usually manned by young men who did not have regular jobs; the notion of firefighting appealed to their sense of excitement. Fire company headquarters were often near—or in—a tavern. Most fire companies were street gangs entrusted with a civic function. They could do their job with vigor when they chose to; letters of thanks from grateful merchants or homeowners occasionally appeared in the papers. But it seems likely, too, that members of the informal street gangs also belonged to the fire companies. Certainly the fire-fighting outfits served as social clubs.[81] Each company had its own territory, but they were always invading one another's domain. Pitched battles between the companies, with fists, clubs, and firearms, became routine. Often members of one company would start a fire, wait for the other company's members to show up, then jump them.[82] The two most prominent offenders seem to have been the United Fire Company and the New Market Company. In 1850 the mayor drew sharp boundaries for the two, but to no avail.[83]

Politics in Baltimore was bedeviled by these violent elements—by the gangs, the fire companies, the inadequate and partisan police force, and social conditions that were conducive to crime and violence.

[79] See Chapter V.

[80] Fire companies were a problem in other cities, too, as in New York; see Stephen Ginsburg, "Above the Law: Volunteer Firemen in New York City, 1836–1837," *New York History*, 50 (1969): 165–86.

[81] See, for example, the report of the excursion of the Mechanical Fire Company to New York, *Baltimore Sun*, June 17, 1853.

[82] In 1858, 130 of Baltimore's 225 fires were set deliberately, although how many of this alarmingly high number of arson incidents can be laid to feuding fire companies is uncertain. Schmeckebier, *op. cit.*, p. 42.

[83] The United was to stay west of Sharp Street and south of Camden and Baltimore Streets. The New Market Company was to stay north of Fayette and west of Charles. *Baltimore Sun*, March 6, 1850.

Election violence was very familiar in Baltimore and other major cities by the 1850s. Foul play was taken for granted. In one edition of the *Sun*, for example, the paper commented both on the details of some election mayhem and also on the "courtesy and urbanity" of the election.[84] In 1847, when Maryland's elections were calmer, the *Sun* found occasion to congratulate the citizenry for voting "so amicably," yet in 1847 many election abuses were routine.[85] "Cooping" was the commonest and foulest method of "roughing" an election. Unsuspecting voters were kidnapped and held prisoner in some convenient house known as a "coop." Either they were prevented from voting or, if they could be threatened, coerced, or frightened into it, they were driven from poll to poll in wagons and voted numerous times.[86] Derelicts and bums were often led through the polls in this fashion. One victim testified to voting eighteen times in a single election. Edgar Allan Poe was found dead in a Baltimore gutter a few days after he had apparently been "cooped" in 1849.[87] By 1850 the local papers were referring casually to a "well known coop" and "a number of political coops."[88] Delegates to the constitutional convention of 1850 complained that street toughs were interfering with the polls in Baltimore.[89]

Street violence in general, and on election day in particular, began to reach intolerable levels in the 1850s under the reign of the Know-Nothings. In 1853, with the worst election atrocities yet to come, the *Sun* complained:

> Few who have not been induced to acquaint themselves upon the subject, have any adequate idea of the lawless, mischevious, malevolent, defiant spirit by which multitudes . . . of the city are activated. This spirit is diffusing itself, and increasing the ferocity of its tone, more and more every year.[90]

The bloody rioting of the elections of 1855 and 1856 startled even Baltimoreans who had grown used to such things. The street gangs and their more respectable cousins, the fire companies, became political clubs that acted as an extension of the party process. Fire-company engine houses were used as gathering places for ward

84 *Ibid.*, October 1, 1850.

85 *Ibid.*, October 6, 1847.

86 For numerous examples of specific acts of election violence, see Schmeckebier, *op. cit.*, Steiner, *op. cit.*; and Maryland, General Assembly, *House and Senate Documents*, 1860, "Baltimore City Contested Election."

87 Schmeckebier, *op. cit.*, p. 43, n. 1.

88 *Baltimore Sun*, October 1, 1850.

89 Steiner, *op. cit.*, p. 36.

90 March 20, 1853.

meetings; the Lafayette Engine House in the Seventh Ward and the Patapsco Engine House in the Eleventh were two such meeting places.[91] The American regime in Baltimore found the turbulent elements of the city very useful; they aimed the gangs at their political enemies and turned them loose. The police, inept and politically controlled, were both unable and unwilling to stand in the way of the mobs. The Democrats, too, had their vandals, notably the Bloody Eights from the Eighth Ward. Nonetheless, the Know-Nothings permitted, and probably even encouraged, the interference of Baltimore's turbulent elements with the free election process. By the mid-fifties, voting in the city was a very risky business, even by Baltimore standards.

The use the politicians had for the gangs was obvious; the gangs' interest in politics is less clear.[92] For one set of toughs, nativism had a plain attraction; it appealed to their prejudice against outsiders. The Democratic gangs, on the other hand, probably responded to ethnic and class ties, as well as to the threat of Know-Nothing attack. Politics in the mid-fifties played on the same allegiances that dictated gang structure—nationality, religion, and, as an extension of these, the neighborhood. Politics in this way came right down to the streets, where those so inclined used brick ballots. That the election-day warfare was a bit more than mere brainless violence was shown by the active appearance of the gangs in political rallies, at least in the American party. As the dignitaries were being introduced to a post-election American rally in Baltimore in 1856, for example, the *Sun* reported that "the Plug Ugly Club" came in with flags and posters, to a "thunderous shout" from the galleries.[93] It is conceivable, of course, but not provable, that the gangs were literally in the employ of the parties. Whether cash was involved or not, however, the gangs received a payoff in the form of unofficial sanction to pursue their favorite hobbies, fighting and terrorism.

The role of the gangs (and of the young generally), the police, and the court system in Baltimore's elections can be clarified by a close

[91] *Ibid.*, August 18, 1853.

[92] By its nature the relationship between political leaders and the street gangs would be hard to prove and define exactly. Police records were very sketchy, and, since the police looked the other way during election difficulties, arrest records and court records are unreliable. Henry Winter Davis, for example, was often referred to as the master of the Baltimore mob (as, for instance, by Henry Adams in his essay "The Great Secession Winter of 1860–61," in *The Great Secession Winter of 1860–61, and Other Essays,* ed. George Hochfield [New York: Sagamore Press, 1958]), but no one has ever proved his connection with the gangs, or shown any closer relationship than one would normally expect a candidate to have with his constituency.

[93] November 29, 1856.

examination of the 1856 outrage as it was culled from the columns of the newspapers. Most of the victims were young men, as were the few who were arrested. Innocent bystanders included a girl whose arm was severed by a three-ounce, two-inch-long shot apparently propelled by a small field piece; an old man who was knicked in the arm; and a shopkeeper on Aisquith Street who was mortally wounded in the head by a stray bullet. Aside from these, however, the number of teenagers involved in the bloody accounts was notable; some were in their early teens, a sort of junior auxiliary to the gangs. Twenty people were wounded when a rock fight between the "Junior Calithumpians" and the "Junior Mount Clare Association" grew into a riot between the senior gangs. The police suffered some casualties, even apart from the fatality in the Eighth Ward already noted. In the Fourth Ward a policeman was hit in the hip. In the Eighth Ward an acting policeman from the special force was shot in the calf, while one of the regulars suffered an arm wound and two others checked in with a gashed hand and a broken hip, respectively. In the Second Ward, two special policemen and another regular were shot. A man identified as a "city watchman" died on November 16 when his wounds led to lockjaw. Indeed, police casualties outnumbered arrests; scarcely half a dozen arrests were made in the midst of all the carnage, and in a few of these cases the charges were ultimately dismissed. The deep involvement of the gangs was pointed up after the election when the American Club, the Ashland Club, and other groups showed up en masse for the funeral of an American who had been shot in the Democratic Eighth Ward. The suspect in another election-day incident was arrested in the headquarters of the Empire Club.

Aside from the use of violence, unscrupulous politicians were abetted by the current methods for voting. Ballots were not supplied by the civil authorities but by the candidates or the parties themselves. Voters then went to the polls and deposited the ballots in full view of all. For one thing, this made ticket splitting very difficult. Even worse, however, with this system it was possible—though technically illegal—to print your party's ballot with distinctive markings or on colored paper so that no matter how the voter folded it, his choice was plainly visible. The Democrats may have invented the marked ticket device; at any rate, the Americans used it widely.[94] All who approached the polls without properly marked ballots were scared off or physically barred from voting. The sight of a battered voter staggering from the poll was usually enough to discourage any others. One of the American gangs would borrow tubs of blood from

[94] Schmeckebier, *op. cit.*, p. 87.

a nearby slaughterhouse—hence their name, the "Blood Tubs"—and throw this gore all over their victims. The effect was well calculated and frightening. Furthermore, the polling places themselves were often situated in rough neighborhoods, at political headquarters, or in saloons.[95] An election judge in the Fifth Ward complained that the American administration had put the polls in an out-of-the-way area called Loudenschlager's Hill, on Baltimore Street.[96] Second Ward voters found their polls across the street from a coop, which was, in turn, three doors down from the "Rough Skins" club.[97]

Social conditions, civic attitudes, and political practices all conspired to make a mockery of Baltimore elections. Each party was guilty of roughing the elections; the Americans' culpability was only a matter of degree. Driven as they were by greed for office, the politicians of both parties exploited the conditions they found in the metropolis.

95 *Ibid.*
96 "Baltimore City Contested Election," pp. 27–28.
97 *Ibid.*, p. 32.

V

PRELUDE TO CRISIS: REFORM AND JOHN BROWN

Because of the outlandish fraud practiced in the Baltimore polling of 1857, several Democrats contested the result. William Pinckney Whyte, loser in the Third Congressional District (Baltimore), took his case to the House of Representatives, where a committee recommended that American J. Morrison Harris should be ousted and the seat declared vacant. The House itself, however, rejected the recommendation and seated Harris.[1] Defeated Democrat Henry P. Brooks, from the Fourth District, also challenged the seating of winner Henry Winter Davis. The House refused to hear the case. The Democratic candidates to the House of Delegates from Baltimore contested their defeat, too, but their petition was caught in the crossfire of yet another skirmish between Ligon and the Americans.

The Two Hundred Fifty-second session of the General Assembly met on January 6, 1858. The Americans dominated both houses. The striking feature of this session was the inexperience of the members; the turmoil of Maryland politics was producing a large turnover. Only two American delegates in the 1858 legislature had served in the 1856 session, and the Democrats also showed many new faces. Like its predecessor, the 1858 American assembly ignored

[1] Laurence Frederick Schmeckebier, *History of the Know Nothing Party in Maryland*, The Johns Hopkins University Studies in Historical and Political Science, ser. 17 (Baltimore: The Johns Hopkins Press, 1899), p. 89. Schmeckebier asserted that the Democrats in the House acquiesced in Harris's seating because certain American congressmen convinced them that an antislavery man would be sent if Harris were rejected. The idea of Baltimore electing an antislavery congressman was patently absurd, and it is not logical that Harris was kept for that reason. Why the committee's recommendation was rejected by the House is not clear.

nativism and concentrated instead on a clash with the Democratic governor.

Ligon was leaving office and, as his parting shot, he attacked the Americans again for their shady tactics in Baltimore:[2]

> I record my deliberate opinion that the election was fraduently conducted; that in the exclusion of thousands of people from the polls there has been no expression of the popular will; and that the whole of the returns from this city are vicious, without a decent claim to official recognition anywhere, and in all their character a gross insult to our institutions and laws, and a most offensive mockery of the great principles of political independence and popular suffrage.[3]

As an added insult, Ligon released his message to the press before he sent it to the General Assembly. The House responded by tabling the message—an unprecedented move—by a strict party vote.[4] The message was then read at the next meeting, where only one hundred copies were ordered printed, also an unprecedented slur.[5]

Then the Americans mounted a counterattack; they drafted a sharp condemnation both of Ligon's message and of his conduct during the elections. They called the message "a libel upon the people of that great commercial metropolis in our state."[6] The resolutions also blamed Ligon for the very disruption he decried, because of his abortive attempt to intervene with militia. The House also censured Ligon for spending $1,712.44 to get muskets from Virginia. Fist fights nearly erupted several times during the debate over these resolutions. Arguments continued past midnight. On one occasion only fast and firm action by the Speaker of the House, J. Summerfield Berry, prevented outright violence on the floor of the chamber.[7] The condemnatory resolutions were adopted by strict party vote in both houses.[8] When the ten unsuccessful Democrats from Baltimore arrived to contest their defeat, the House of Delegates refused to print their protest, and the Committee on Elections threw out their claim, blaming all the trouble on the governor. In one stroke they dismissed the claimants and scored another hit against Ligon.

Redoubtable nativist Andrew B. Cross came back with yet another

[2] Maryland, Governor's Message, *House and Senate Documents,* 1858.

[3] *Ibid.*, p. 28.

[4] The vote was 41 to 28; all yes votes were cast by Americans; 27 of the no votes were cast by Democrats, and the other was registered by a dissenting American.

[5] Eventually 5,000 copies were printed, along with the complete correspondence between Ligon and Swann from the previous fall.

[6] Maryland, House of Delegates, *Journal,* 1858; pp. 101, 396-99.

[7] *Ibid.*, p. 131; and Maryland, Senate, *Journal,* 1858, p. 152.

[8] Maryland, House of Delegates, *Journal,* 1858, pp. 101, 396–99.

petition for the suppression of convents.[9] Once the House of Delegates Judiciary Committee received the proposal, it simply vanished. A nativist attempt to prohibit state courts from granting any more naturalization certificates failed after the second reading of the bill.

The only proposal which aroused much interest among the American majority in the General Assembly was a plan to revise the constitution. The proposed alterations in the constitution centered on an increase in the appointive powers of the governor and on the institution of a strict population basis for representation in the General Assembly. To many Marylanders the proposed changes seemed to be a power grab by the Know-Nothings.[10] The Americans proposed the constitutional revision, and they backed it heartily. Finally, the General Assembly ordered a referendum on the question of calling a constitutional convention. The vote on calling a referendum split almost perfectly on party lines, Americans for and Democrats against, although a few Americans from rural regions voted against the plan.[11]

The constitutional convention proposal was not popular anywhere except Baltimore. In the June referendum the voter turnout was light, and the counties rallied to overcome a 5,000-vote majority for the convention in the city. The defeat had been expected.[12]

The 1858 General Assembly compiled a mediocre record. Even the Know-Nothing *Baltimore Clipper* saluted adjournment with "thanks . . . that we have just passed from an epoch shrouded in pestilential vapors."[13] The *Clipper's* pique was partly inspired by disappointment over a state printing contract.[14] That the legislators in Annapolis would offend such a powerful party organ is one more testmony to their ineptness.

Once the Assembly adjourned, 1858 became a dull year in Maryland. Marylanders devoted much of their energy to recovering from the recession which had begun in 1857. The only important elections in Maryland in 1858 were the Baltimore municipal contests in October.

9 *Ibid.*, p. 281.

10 Since the constitution of 1851 was due to be reviewed regularly after each census, and next in 1861, the desire of the Know-Nothings to do it in 1958 was not logically explicable in any terms other than political survival. Increasing the governor's spoils would enhance the longevity of the party; the Americans had a lease on the chief executive's chair for the next four years. Cut off as they were from national parties, any increased patronage would be very valuable to them. Also, if apportionment were assigned strictly on the basis of population, Baltimore would gain enormously in the state legislature, and by 1858 Baltimore was the chief support of the American party.

11 Maryland, House of Delegates, *Journal,* 1858, p. 806; Maryland, Senate, *Journal,* 1858, p. 354.

12 *Baltimore Sun,* June 9, 1858.

13 Schmeckebier, *op. cit.*, p. 96.

14 *Ibid.*

American Mayor Thomas Swann was induced to run again after first bowing out.[15] The Democrats were nowhere in sight; their spirit and machinery had been devastated by the defeats of the past three years. At last a group of independents rallied just before the election. In a vain but defiant gesture they nominated Colonel A. P. Shutt to stand against Swann.[16] Intimidation replaced open riot in the election, but fraud still ruled. The result was no contest. Shutt withdrew about noon on election day, partly to protest against the fraud and partly to keep any more people from being hurt.[17] Swann won with 19,144 votes to 4,859 for Shutt; 3,428 of Shutt's votes came from the consistently Democratic Eighth Ward. All but one member in each branch of the new city council were Know-Nothings.[18]

The 1858 Baltimore elections were important because the election riots which accompanied them finally galvanized voters to change the system. Independent citizens moved to fill the gap left by the demoralized Democratic opposition. The independents had opposed the American candidates both in 1857 and in 1858 as incipient reformers. They showed a spirit of defiance that was impressive in a hopeless situation. Furthermore, critics now fully recognized just how crucial Baltimore was to the entire American apparatus in Maryland. One paper said of the 1858 election that the Baltimore Americans were "driven by desperation and bound to win."[19] Then, on November 1, a movement for reform of the city elections began to take shape. A "City Reform Association" held its first meeting on November 2, 1858.

The rise of the reform movement and the final collapse of the American regime in Maryland began in 1859, quietly at first, but definitely. In March the Democrats won handily at the Frederick municipal elections.[20] Frederick had been loyal American country. Then the Baltimore Americans began to fight among themselves. Without the rallying point of a strong opposition, they turned on one another at the primary elections for delegates to the city and state conventions. Various factions set their gangs on the others; Americans were kept from the polls by fellow Americans.[21] The disorder was so striking that the *London Illustrated News* ran a feature on it.[22]

Still, election reform, not dissension, was the biggest threat to the

15 *Baltimore Sun,* September 9 and 22, 1858.
16 *Ibid.,* October 13, 1858.
17 Schmeckebier, *op. cit.,* p. 97; *Baltimore Sun,* October 14, 1858.
18 *Baltimore Sun,* October 14, 1858.
19 Schmeckebier, *op. cit.,* p. 97.
20 *Frederick Herald,* March 8, 1859.
21 *Baltimore Sun,* August 17, 1859.
22 Schmeckebier, *op. cit.,* p. 100.

Americans. Loss of Baltimore would mean the loss of everything. Marylanders from both parties realized that. When the Democrats met at their state convention in Frederick in late July, they made a clear issue of American corruption in Baltimore; "the staple talk of the convention was vituperation of Baltimore City," complained the American *Frederick Herald*.[23] American politicians from rural districts faced the awkward job of defending their invaluable Baltimore machine and its reprehensible methods. Already some county representatives had defected from the party because of the constitutional issue in the General Assembly; the suggestion of increased representation for Baltimore was too much for them. It was doubtful that the Americans could hold back the indignation which was rising across the state. To oppose the reform of Baltimore elections was political suicide in some areas, but to allow it would be equally destructive of the party's fortunes. Some American editors tried manfully to defend Baltimore against Democratic criticism, but with little success.[24] Ironically, the mounting outrage of the rural regions made control of Baltimore all the more important to the Americans. They were trapped without a national affiliation, dependent on a downward spiral of violence and disorder.

The elections of 1859 gave reform its first real test. As usual, the Baltimore municipal elections preceded the state contests by one month, and, as usual, Marylanders watched them closely. Reform gathered momentum in August when both the *Baltimore Sun* and the *Baltimore American* came out in favor of a change in city administration.

The *American* called for a town meeting to act on reform of the city's politics.[25] Held on September 8, this central meeting established ward committees with the power to make nominations for city council. The meeting, like other reform gatherings at this time, was composed of a prominent group of business- and professional men; representatives of the skilled and clerical trades also participated.[26] Many businessmen were there because Baltimore's growing and well-deserved reputation for gory elections was actually frightening away business.[27] One leading reformer, for example, was George William

[23] *Frederick Herald*, August 2, 1859.

[24] See, for example, *ibid.*

[25] *Baltimore American*, August 2, 1859.

[26] Of the 172 members of the City Reform Association listed in the *Baltimore Sun*, November 3, 1858, I have been able to identify the occupation of 141 from the city directory: proprietors, 65; professional, 40; clerical, 6; skilled, 29; unskilled, 1. Most of the proprietor group were retail or commission merchants.

[27] *Baltimore American*, September 9, 1859.

Brown, a prominent banker whose concern for civic order had been publicly expressed many times.[28]

These zealous but unpracticed reformers were the only opposition the Americans faced. The enfeebled Democrats had retired for the time being, though they cheered the reform effort. Despite the Democrats' support, however, the reformers were an independent group which began outside formal party organizations. Some individual reformers were clearly identifiable as Democrats,[29] but Henry Winter Davis's charge that the reformers were nothing but "Locofocos and a few carping timid merchants"[30] was not true. If the Democratic party had been strong enough to mount a reform campaign on its own, without sharing the issue with the City Reform Association, it would have done so. Davis took pains to discredit the movement because he seemed genuinely concerned about its growing influence. He personally took the stump to condemn reform. With typical audacity he accused the reformers of promoting violence themselves with their "vigilante tactics."[31]

The 1859 municipal elections were rough; the gangs were out in force. The newest addition to the arsenal of electoral intimidation was the shoemaker's awl, which evidently made its first appearance during this election. A sharp, short instrument, like a stumpy icepick with a curved tip, the awl was easily concealed, handy, could be justified as a tool and not a weapon, and left a vicious puncture wound if brandished with enough force. For all the customary carnage, however, the reformers made solid gains. They captured six of the thirty city council seats.[32] The Americans paid them the tribute of taking unprecedented measures in the November elections to beat off this alarming new resistance. Between the municipal and state elections, however, Marylanders had to confront a new challenge, an event which confused their politics and gave them a fright from which they never fully recovered

I

In July 1859 a man calling himself "Isaac Smith" rented a piece of ground called the Kennedy farm several miles southwest of Fred-

[28] See p. 109.

[29] Among the 168 members of the City Reform Association at its founding were some identifiable Democrats—notably, S. Teackle Wallis, John H. Thomas, and Charles Howard. Jean H. Baker (*The Politics of Continuity: Maryland Politics from 1858 to 1870* [Baltimore: The Johns Hopkins University Press, 1973]) also found the reformers to be heavily Democratic.

[30] Henry Winter Davis to Samuel F. DuPont, October 25, 1859, Samuel F. DuPont Papers, Eleutherian Mills Historical Library, Greenville, Del.

[31] *Baltimore Sun*, September 2, 1859.

[32] *Ibid.*, October 14, 1859.

erick. "Smith" stood just under six feet tall; he was slender, stooped, and wiry, and he sported a full beard, mostly white. In truth, "Smith" was John Brown, who was already notorious in Kansas; he had killed several persons and had a price on his head:[33] His sons were with him in Maryland, bound by filial ties and solemn oaths to support the antislavery cause that consumed their father's life. Brown came to Maryland with a daring plan to seize the federal arsenal at nearby Harpers Ferry, Virginia, and to start a slave insurrection which would strike down the institution of black bondage in America.[34] The mountain chain that runs to the heart of the South was to be his fortress. The hills of Maryland were his starting place.

Brown's operations were remarkably well guarded. No Marylanders knew of or even suspected what was being prepared out in western Maryland. Brown had with him a force of twenty-one men, five of them black, and two women besides. He brought with him dozens of Sharp's carbines and—a curiously romantic and archaic touch—950 pikes. Maryland authorities later found a cache of hand-printed constitutions for the state Brown hoped to establish with his insurgents.

The night of Sunday, October 16, was rainy and foggy when Brown moved out from the Kennedy farm about 8:30 P.M. Eighteen of the men went with him while the rest stood guard. As they came down from the heights around the Potomac River, each carried a rifle, two pistols, and a knife. Sometime between 10:30 and 11:00 P.M. they crossed the railroad bridge over the Potomac rapids and attacked both the town and the federal armory at Harpers Ferry. Their surprise was perfect. By Monday morning they had secured both objectives. It was not until midday that news of what had happened at Harpers Ferry leaked to the rest of the nation.

Brown's announced plan never had a chance of success. Slaves did not flock to his banner; indeed, few slaves lived in the Harpers Ferry region. His tactical position was pitiful. He carried the arsenal and town but let himself be imprisoned by the steep mountains and the river. Public reaction was swift and violent. Militia from Virginia and Maryland quickly surrounded the area. Some came from as far away as Baltimore. Brown was forced to retreat to the railroad engine house, where he made a stand with his followers, a few slaves forcibly brought in from the nearby countryside, and several white hostages. On Tuesday, October 18, a group of U.S. Marines under

[33] All of the details of the Harpers Ferry raid used here are found in several accounts. See especially the standard biography of Brown, Oswald G. Villard, *John Brown, 1800–1859* (Boston and New York: Houghton Mifflin, 1910); and the more recent one by Stephen B. Oates, *To Purge This Land with Blood: A Biography of John Brown* (New York: Harper & Row, 1970).

[34] Harpers Ferry, of course, is now in West Virginia.

Colonel Robert E. Lee stormed the engine house, forced the door, and captured Brown. Brown was wounded in the fight. Ten of Brown's company were killed or mortally wounded, including two of his own sons. Some escaped; most survivors were apprehended and tried. The entire affair, from Kennedy farm to capture, lasted less than forty-eight hours. Brown was charged with, and convicted of, treason against the state of Virginia, conspiring with slaves to rebel, and eight counts of murder. Forty-five days after his capture, on December 2, 1859, the Virginia authorities hanged John Brown.

Brown's raid was never a practical threat to Virginia, Maryland, or the South, or the institution of slavery—but that did not matter. John Brown may have failed miserably at his avowed purpose, but he struck terror into the slaveholding states. He triumphed in frightening the South, and, if he thought panic would speed emancipation, he was wrong. What Brown's raid really accomplished was to tap a deep vein of fear in slaveholding society, fear of servile insurrection. He raised visions of another Southampton or Santo Domingo.[35] Also unsettling was the effect Harpers Ferry had on sectional relations. Brown had received financial backing from several Northern antislavery leaders, and after his death some abolitionists hailed him as a martyr to the cause of freedom, a man not repudiated but mourned and honored. So it struck many Southerners that the North had launched and condoned a murderous assault on Southern institutions, honor, and lives.

Maryland shared in the shock of Harpers Ferry. When the news broke on Monday, October 17, all was confusion. The Tuesday morning *Baltimore Sun* mirrored the alarm and the lack of knowledge which affected everyone away from the scene.[36] A huge headline screamed,

SLAVE INSURRECTION
AT HARPERS FERRY
HEADED BY 250 ABOLITIONISTS
U.S. ARSENAL SEIZED

First reports were wild: "250 whites with a gang of negroes," read one report; the leader was said to be "a middle aged man with gray

[35] In 1831 Nat Turner led a slave revolt in Southampton County, Virginia, in which fifty-seven whites are killed. In 1791 the mullatoes and black slaves of Santo Domingo, inspired by the French Revolution, rose up and attempted to take over the island; during the reign of terror which followed, thousands of whites fled the island and many who did not make it were slain. Perhaps as many as ten thousand émigrés from Santo Domingo settled in the Southern United States. Both incidents were prominent in the consciousness of Southerners at the time of Harpers Ferry.

[36] October 18, 1859.

hair, beard, and moustache," named "Andress" or "Anderson;" one overwrought correspondent claimed that 500–700 "insurgents" were in arms. Later dispatches were a bit more rational. One correspondent noted that the few local slaves grouped with Brown behaved more like prisoners than frenzied revolutionaries. Then, the latest report in the Tuesday edition identified Brown himself—"of Kansas notoriety." From October 18, Brown was on the front page of the Baltimore dailies every day for two weeks. His entire trial was reported copiously. Late into the next spring, news of Brown, of one of his men, or of the Harpers Ferry incident was scarcely ever absent from Maryland's newspapers or Marylanders' minds. After Brown, fear was never again very far from the surface.

After the jolt of the event itself came the lingering alarm over what it all meant. Analysts appeared everywhere, most of them crying doom. The more judicious citizens at least realized that the raid itself was a fiasco. "The whole affair dwindles into insignificance as the literal facts are brought out from the uncertainty peculiar to the first demonstration," admitted the *Sun.*[37] But the symbolic meaning of the act brought a more somber response from the same paper:

> Intelligent men, however, will learn in time that there can be no compromise with a thing, in itself, hostile to the spirit of our national compact. It may take subtle and more insidious forms than that in which the insurgents of Harpers Ferry have exhibited it, but it is the same thing, however, its hideous deformity may be disguised to serve and end of political ambition, and its fruits must be repulsive sectionalism and internecine strife. The lesson is timely.[38]

Marylanders concluded that Brown's raid was ample evidence of a venomous ill will held by too many Northerners. The *Sun,* for example, researched and reprinted opinion from Northern newspapers in great detail, and came away amazed at the support Brown received from press and pulpit.[39] Such support was attributed to antislavery fanatics in general and to the Republican party in particular; repudiation of Brown by William Seward, Abraham Lincoln, and other Republican leaders did nothing to alter this impression. Brown, said the *Sun,* was "a pupil of the [Joshua] Giddings school—he has been taught to believe that the killing of a slaveholder was an act which God would approve."[40] The whole affair illuminated "the . . . fanaticism

[37] *Ibid.,* October 19, 1859.
[38] *Ibid.*
[39] See, for example, *ibid.,* October 21 and 25, 1859.
[40] *Ibid.,* November 5, 1859. Joshua Reed Giddings (1795–1864) was a pioneer in political antislavery. Originally a Whig, then a Free-Soiler and a Republican, Giddings represented a district in the Western Reserve of Ohio in Congress and earned the reputation of a vigorous, unrelenting foe of slavery.

which, unhappily, exists in a certain portion of the Union."[41] One Washingtonian said "that a heavy responsibility falls upon persons in the North as abettors of Murder and Treason."[42] More precisely, the Republicans were blamed. "Brown's act," said the judicious *Sun*, even allowing that Brown might be insane, "is one of the legitimate fruits, one of the natural consequences, the inevitable results of the Republican doctrines."[43] One Marylander wrote that the Republicans were merely a branch of the abolitionist clique which sponsored Brown.[44] An editorial from the *Washington Constitution* asked—"pertinently," said the *Sun*—what the result would have been if a Republican like Seward had been President.[45] The best hope left for Marylanders was that the North would come to its senses or, in the words of the *Frederick Herald*, that "the consequences upon the Southern mind of this desperate experiment of abolition . . . will be recognized in the North as pregnant with danger to the Union."[46] Meanwhile, the Maryland militiamen who went to Harpers Ferry came home to parades and congratulations, and were honored as heroic defenders against Northern fanaticism.[47]

Marylanders also took some concrete steps to guard against any more Browns. They were visibly upset that he had operated undetected in Maryland for so long. After October 18, strangers were expected to give good account of themselves. Governor Hicks empowered the sheriffs in western Maryland to add extra deputies and to "arrest and detain" any suspicious persons.[48] People in Hagerstown were frightened to learn of reference in Brown's personal correspondence to a black clergyman in their town. The minister, one Thomas Henry, had been suspected of abolitionist ties in the past, but by the time he was exposed through Brown's papers he had sold all his goods and left.[49]

The concrete effects of the Harpers Ferry incident on Maryland politics are difficult to gauge exactly. Certainly the tension of the sectional quarrel was increased. A calm had fallen over the argument between North and South in 1859, but Brown shattered that. Since 1860 was a presidential election year, the issue of slavery was bound to come to the fore again. Nonetheless, Brown's raid, and the interpretation of it as a logical consequence of Republican doctrine, surely heightened the sense of crucial importance that hung on Republican

41 *Ibid.*
42 "Ion," *ibid.*, October 21, 1859.
43 *Ibid.*, November 7, 1859.
44 *Ibid.*, October 22, 1859.
45 *Ibid.*, October 21, 1859.
46 *Frederick Herald*, October 19, 1859.
47 *Baltimore Sun*, October 20, 1859.
48 *Herald and Torch Light* (Hagerstown, Md.), November 1, 1859.
49 *Baltimore Sun*, November 16, 1859.

victory or defeat. In Maryland, at least, evidence of increased military activity and intensified excitement began in the winter of 1859, well before the 1860 campaign began.[50] Thanks to Brown, Marylanders entered the crucial year with nerves already on edge.

The Democrats probably benefited most from Harpers Ferry. Their star was already rising in Maryland and, as the champion of Southern rights, they stood to gain most by an affront to those rights. By late October Maryland Democrats claimed that Harpers Ferry would never have happened but for the Know-Nothings' feeble allegiance to the South, and they cited particularly the pro-Republican tendencies of Henry Winter Davis.[51] The Americans counterattacked by accusing the Democrats of raising a cry over "Harpers Ferry" and "the niggers" solely to confuse and distract the voters in the coming state elections.[52] Henry Winter Davis privately blamed the Harpers Ferry panic for Democratic gains at the November polls.[53]

II

The biggest statewide office at stake in November 1859 was comptroller, where American incumbent William Purnell faced Democrat A. Lingan Jarrett. Half the state Senate and all of the House of Delegates seats were to be filled, and U.S. Congressmen were to be chosen. Baltimore was once again the key to the state offices, and the election turmoil there was the worst since 1856. One week before the election the Americans held a rally in Baltimore's Monument Square.[54] Congressman Davis addressed the meeting while standing under a large replica of a shoemaker's awl. A portable blacksmith forge was set up to supply awls to the party faithful. The transparencies which decorated the scene—cloth posters illuminated by lanterns—were openly gruesome. They depicted Americans sticking awls into fleeing reformers. One showed a clenched fist and the motto, "With this we'll do the work." "The head of a Reformer" on another transparency was bleeding profusely. The Americans even lapsed into profanity, if not quite into rhyme; one design said, "Reform movement, Reform man, if you can vote, I'll be d——d." Worst of all, the threats were carried out. Election day was a blood bath. Cooping was epidemic. Innocent voters were beaten, stabbed, and on occasion shot; several died. Among other outrages, the unsuccessful candidate for

[50] See Chapter VI.

[51] *Planters' Advocate*, October 26, 1859.

[52] *Frederick Herald*, November 8, 1859.

[53] Henry Winter Davis to Samuel F. DuPont, November 11, 1859, DuPont Papers.

[54] See *Baltimore Sun*, October 28, 1859; and Schmeckebier, *op. cit.*, pp. 101–2.

Congress in the Third District, William Preston, was seriously beaten.

When the ballots were counted, only Baltimore saved the Know-Nothings from total disaster. The Democrats carried three of six congressional seats: they might have carried five, but American victories in the Third and Fourth districts were secured by Baltimore votes. Officially, Purnell won the comptroller's race, but only an outrageous 12,783-vote majority in Baltimore achieved that. Jarrett carried the rest of the state by 2,492 votes. Purnell carried only seven counties, and two of those by exactly one vote each. (See Table 10 and Map 8.) Most damaging to the Americans in the long run were the Democratic gains in the legislature. The House of Delegates went overwhelmingly Democratic, forty-five to twenty-nine, almost exactly reversing the ratio of the previous session. The new Senate was also Democratic, twelve members to ten. It was not even clear that the Americans could hold onto what little the debacle had left them. Defeated Democrats in the Third and Fourth districts, the ten Democratic Delegate losers from Baltimore, and Jarrett all moved to contest their defeat on the grounds of fraud in Baltimore.

The violence of November 1859 marked the climax of American rule in Maryland. The party had been forced to the ultimate absurdity. So dependent were the Americans on their control of the city streets that they finally went too far. In order to win one more time they made it impossible to win that way again. Corruption finally overreached itself. The real victor of November's carnage was the reform impulse, the determination never to allow another crooked election.

III

The impact of the Democratic victories showed up immediately when the General Assembly met in January 1860. This Two Hundred Fifty-third session of the state legislature was a turbulent one; many important issues had to be met in an emotional atmosphere. With their nerves already on edge from the Harpers Ferry raid and the political upheavals of two months past, the legislators faced a crushing load of business—reform of the police and election systems of Baltimore, the impeachment of a politically powerful judge, contests for the ten delegate seats from Baltimore, and a savage fight over the chartering of a street railway company. The capital was alive with lobbyists, including a committee of slaveholders seeking a drastic alteration in the state laws governing free Negroes.[55]

[55] *Baltimore Sun,* October 28, 1859. For the General Assembly's reaction to other issues, including the slaveholders' attempt to place severe restrictions on free Negroes, see Chapter VI.

TABLE 10. THE AMERICAN PARTY DEBACLE OF 1859: COMPARISON OF THE AMERICAN VOTE IN THE GUBERNATORIAL RACE OF 1857 WITH THE AMERICAN VOTE IN THE COMPTROLLERSHIP RACE OF 1859

	Percentage of the Vote American		
County	Governor 1857	Comptroller 1958	Difference
Southern Maryland			
Anne Arundel	48.7	49.5	+0.8
Calvert	51.1	44.9	−6.2
Charles	35.8	47.5	+11.7
Montgomery	48.0	47.1	−0.9
Prince George's	40.4	42.7	+2.3
St. Mary's	21.3	23.0	+1.7
Eastern Shore			
Caroline	51.6	50.1	−1.5
Dorchester	57.9	50.0[a]	−7.9
Kent	52.8	52.5	−0.3
Queen Anne's	49.5	48.8	−0.7
Somerset	53.1	53.9	+0.8
Talbot	44.3	42.7	−1.6
Worcester	47.3	46.4	−0.9
Western Maryland			
Allegany	43.6	47.1	+3.5
Baltimore	49.6	48.1	−1.5
Carroll	50.7	51.0	+0.3
Cecil	48.8	50.0[a]	+1.2
Frederick	51.3	50.3	−1.0
Harford	56.9	47.7	−9.2
Howard	52.5	46.3	−6.2
Washington	50.2	49.7	−0.5
Baltimore City	68.5	77.3	+8.8
Average for Maryland	54.9	55.9	+1.0

Average American percentage of the vote in counties carried in 1859 (7), 51.1
Average American percentage of the vote in counties lost in 1859 (14), 45.1

[a]American by one vote.

Baltimore was the focal point of the session. The violence of the 1859 Baltimore elections became the first topic of business when the defeated Democratic candidates to the House contested the seating of the Americans. During the debates and investigations of this challenge, all the sordid details of the city's fraud and riot became common knowledge and were enshrined forever in the public records

Map 8. An American Party Debacle: Defeat of the American Candidate for Comptroller of Maryland, 1859

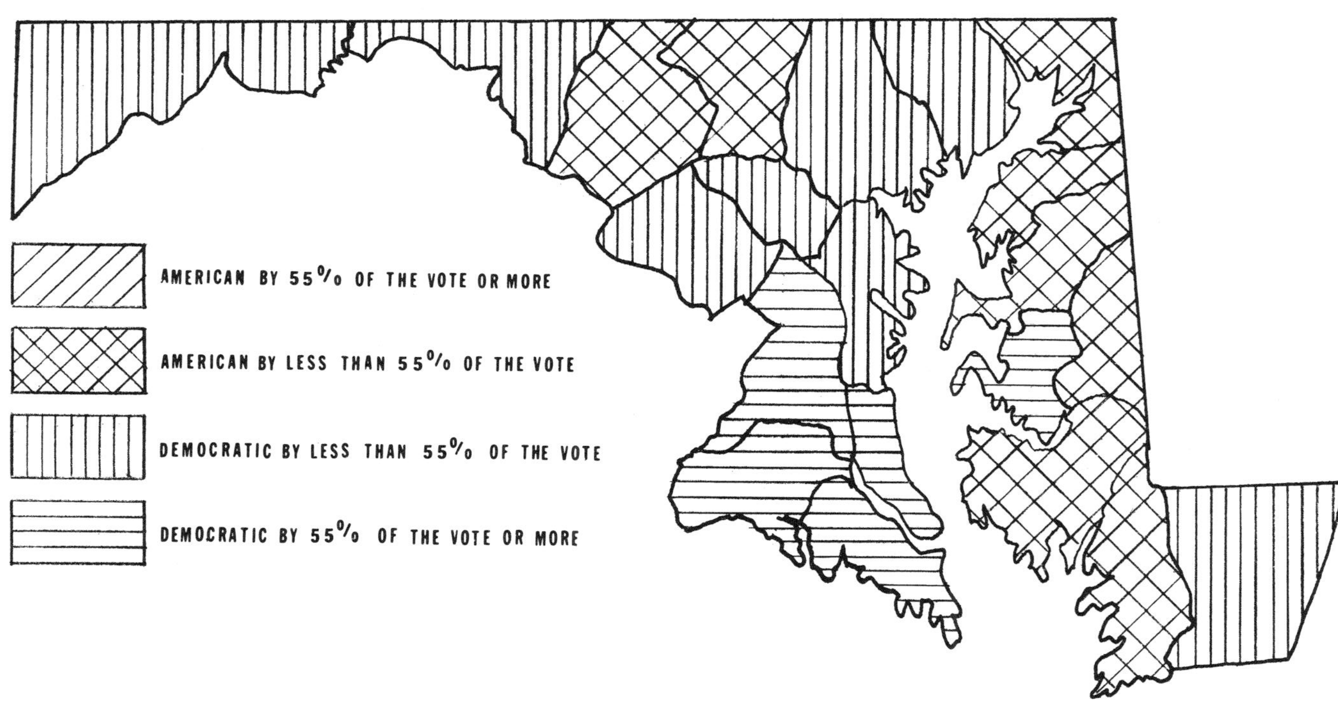

of the House. Ten thousand Baltimoreans signed memorials to the General Assembly praying for relief from corruption.[56] Any remaining doubts about the prevailing climate of crime in Baltimore vanished on January 18, when someone fired a shot at two delegates who were investigating the situation.[57]

The General Assembly first moved to deny the Americans any office obtained by fraud. The legislature declared vacant the office of clerk of the circuit court for Baltimore on the grounds that no legal election had taken place in the city. For the same reason it declared Democrat Jarrett the winner in the comptroller's race, since he had carried the election outside Baltimore.[58] The House did not eject the Baltimore American delegates, however, until the last day of the session. The Democrats held such a majority that they did not need to expel those ten, only nine of whom were present and voting anyway.[59] In addition, if the House declared the seats vacant before the end of the session, a special election would have to be called, and until reform was accomplished no one wanted another election in Baltimore.

The City Reform Association drafted and sent to the General Assembly three interlocking bills for the purification of the city elections. Keystone of the reform arch was the Metropolitan Police Act, which took control of the Baltimore force away from the corrupt city administration and put it in the hands of a state-appointed board of police commissioners. A new Election Law then put election judges under police control. A third enactment corrected abuses in the selection of juries in the city. The Democrats adopted all three measures as party positions after they caucused with a reform delegation early in January.[60] The combined set of laws passed both houses, after a bitter fight, on February 2.[61]

The American members faced a very difficult problem. So blatant were the abuses of the Baltimore elections that reform was awkward to oppose. Americans from the counties were under popular pressure

[56] *Ibid.*, January 19, 1860.

[57] *Ibid.*

[58] In fact, Jarrett never took office. Governor Thomas H. Hicks refused to swear him in. A long, complicated dispute ensued, in which incumbent Purnell simply continued to occupy the office and to function as comptroller until he resigned, whereupon Hicks appointed American Dennis Claude to succeed him.

[59] The reluctant American who never showed up to claim his seat was William A. Wisong, formerly a Democrat and in 1860 an official of a Baltimore bank.

[60] *Baltimore Sun*, January 13, 1860.

[61] *Ibid.*, February 3, 1860. The violent fifties still affect Maryland. The power to appoint the Baltimore police chief remained with the state when the present Maryland constitution was drafted in 1867. As a consequence, Baltimore is powerless to chose its own chief law enforcement officer even today.

to support the clean-government bills which would destroy the party by snatching away those precious, fraudulent Baltimore majorities. Speaking generally, the Americans fought the reform bills with all the votes and parliamentary obstructions they could muster. Just days short of the final vote on reform, the American House caucus of January 31 decided to allow each individual to vote as he would, while the group entered into the *Journal* a protest against the partisan spirit of the reforms.[62]

The combined reforms of 1860 ended the era of condoned violence in Baltimore elections. A new five-man state-appointed police board quickly took charge of the municipal force. At the head of the board was wealthy Democrat Charles Howard, descendant of an old Maryland family and a founding member of the City Reform Association. Dishonest officers were removed outright, and the remainder were put on a civil service basis. The force was enlarged, and, though the same sorts of persons were recruited for the force as before, a new spirit of pride and professionalism animated the police.[63] Furthermore, the courts no longer undid the work of the police; jury selection became more equitable, and the alcoholic Judge Stump lost his seat on the bench. The astonishing peace and order of the 1860 elections in Baltimore stood as a tribute to the effectiveness of the reforms.

Reform was only part of the agony endured by the General Assembly, however. Much, much more confronted them and the people they represented. Reform was the culmination of a long chain of domestic grievances in Maryland, but it only prepared the way for the crucial test of allegiances to come.

62 *Ibid.*, February 1, 1860.

63 A breakdown of the new police force by previous occupations showed that, of 348 patrolmen, 34 were shoemakers, 66 were carpenters, 19 were blacksmiths, and 16 each came from the occupations of tobacconist, caulker, and painter. Also included were 10 machinists and 36 laborers, while the balance represented semi-skilled trades.

VI

1860: THE DEFERRED DECISION

For Marylanders, the crisis of allegiances began in earnest in 1860 and lasted at least until the middle of 1861. This was an anxious time. In the eighteen months after New Year's Day, 1860, Marylanders had to decide who they were, where they were going, and where their loyalties and values lay. As difficult as clear-cut decisions on these questions were, furthermore, the overlapping of local and national issues confused the choices even more. What Marylanders ardently desired was clear, but what they would do was still very much in doubt. The desire was for fanatics and sectional extremists to be silenced, for the Union to be preserved, and for the whole problem to go away. "The sound sentiment" for Maryland, editorialized the *Baltimore Sun*, was very simple—"let us alone."[1]

I

As 1860 opened, Maryland was rapidly becoming an armed camp. With Harpers Ferry clearly on their minds, Marylanders organized militia companies in the winter and spring of 1860-1861 faster than the state could supply them with arms. A single issue of the *Baltimore Sun*, for example, noted the formation of rifle companies in Frederick, Brook Hill (Frederick County), Leonardtown, and Port Tobacco.[2] Two companies appeared in Harford County, one was formed in St. Mary's County, and Frederick added a cavalry unit.[3] By May 1860 the "late revival of the military spirit" was a well-remarked phenom-

[1] January 2, 1860.
[2] *Ibid.*, December 24, 1859, and April 3, 5, and 14, 1860.
[3] *Ibid.*, January 9, 27, and February 1, 1860.

enon.[4] The connection between this ferment and Brown's raid was clearly spelled out by a group in Montgomery County, which simultaneously formed a rifle company and adopted resolutions damning Northern sympathy for Brown.[5]

So serious was the flight to arms that even before the end of 1859 the state adjutant general reported that the arsenal was out of rifles for the use of volunteer companies, and that the entire 1860 allotment was already more than spoken for.[6] Even a larger-than-usual $70,000 appropriation for munitions by the General Assembly of 1860 was not sufficient. Governor Hicks had to appeal for caution to prevent the complete denuding of the state arsenal. Significantly, the governor's concern over the depletion of the central arms supply was phrased in terms of "events lately transpiring upon our own borders."[7]

With the Harpers Ferry excitement still very much in mind, the Two Hundred Fifty-third session of the Maryland General Assembly convened on January 4, 1860. It was overloaded with important issues. Foremost on the agenda was the reform of Baltimore's elections, and that issue alone would have made the session memorable (see Chapter V). But, in addition, the legislators had to grapple with the question of Maryland's proper relations with the rest of the Union. They were asked to respond to initiatives from both North and South.

From the Vermont legislature came copies of resolutions denouncing slavery and opposing its extension into the territories. These resolutions received no consideration in the Maryland General Assembly; they were quickly tabled. True to their border-state cautiousness, however, the members declined to take any stronger action.

More serious was a feeler from South Carolina; that state, as usual, led the extreme Southern response to John Brown's raid. Under the prod of Governor William H. Gist, the Palmetto State called for a convention of Southern states to take "concerted action" and invited Maryland to participate. Gist's invitation did not appeal to Marylanders. Attempting to ease border-state fears of radical action, Gist subsequently explained in a letter to Hicks that "concerted action" did not mean secession. Hicks replied, in effect, that he was glad of this moderate purpose, but saw no reason for meeting at all; inaction was the most moderate course. The legislature formally upheld Hicks in his inert response to the South Carolina proposals.[8] Offered a

[4] *Ibid.*, May 5, 1860.
[5] *Ibid.*, January 4, 1860.
[6] Letter to Oscar Miles, reprinted in *ibid.*, December 24, 1859.
[7] From the Governor's Annual Message, text in *ibid.*, January 7, 1860.
[8] *Ibid.*, March 9, 1860.

chance to identify themselves with the extreme Southern sectionalists, Marylanders declined.

Internal affairs, however, unavoidably raised the question of Maryland's proper sectional identity. By 1860 nearly half of all black Marylanders were free. The cause of this shift was essentially economic; as tobacco culture lost its old monopoly on Maryland's agriculture, it became economically unfeasible to keep slaves on many farms. Instead of caring for slaves in infancy, old age, and sickness, Maryland farmers occasionally found it more convenient to sell them south or to let them go free, hiring them back as day labor at planting and harvest time. The process had been going on steadily for decades by 1860.[9]

In that already troubled year, a growing unrest among slaveholders over the "free Negro problem" matured into action. A slaveholders' committee appeared among the several lobbying groups in Annapolis in 1860. In addition to that committee, petitions from several Southern and Eastern Shore counties increased the pressure on the General Assembly to do something to reduce the number of free Negroes presently living in Maryland and to make manumission difficult.[10] Maryland slaveowners were agitated over the erosion of slavery as an institution and the pernicious effect which free Negroes allegedly had on slaves.[11] The legislature responded by passing the Jacobs Bill.

The Jacobs Bill exposed the decay of slavery as a vital interest to many Marylanders. Named after Curtis W. Jacobs, the Eastern Shore delegate who chaired the House Committee on the Colored Population, the bill would have forbidden manumission and forced free Negroes to hire themselves out on an automatically renewable basis on terms virtually identical to slavery. Those who did not hire themselves out voluntarily would be assigned masters by local commissioners. The bill was, in effect, quite similar to the post-Civil War Southern "black codes" that so infuriated Northern opinion. However,

[9] For elaboration of this point, see Jeffrey R. Brackett, *The Negro in Maryland* (Baltimore: N. Murray, 1889); and James M. Wright, *The Free Negro in Maryland, 1639–1860*, Columbia University Series in History, Economics, and Public Law, vol. 97, no. 3 (New York: Longmans, Green & Co., 1921). Maryland slaveowners sometimes accomplished manumission by encouraging slaves to run away or by simply refusing to pursue them when they absconded on their own. See Elwood L. Bridner, Jr., "The Fugitive Slaves of Maryland," *Maryland Historical Magazine*, 66 (1971): 34–35. Further study of the slavery situation before the Civil War is in progress, notably in a Ph.D. dissertation, "Slavery in Maryland, 1850–1860," by Lawrence McDonald, University of Maryland, College Park.

[10] Petitions from Anne Arundel, Cecil, Somerset, and St. Mary's counties were sent to the House Committee on the Colored Population.

[11] See Maryland, House of Delegates, *Documents*, 1860, document "L," the report of the Committee on the Colored Population.

two provisions in the Jacobs Bill spoke truly of the decrepit state of slavery in Maryland. First, the bill was to be limited in its coverage to certain Eastern Shore and Southern counties only. Second, it was to be submitted to a popular referendum in those areas.[12]

In the fall referendum the Jacobs Bill was crushed. Maryland's slaveholders refused to be bound to a policy of no emancipation and reinforced slavery. In anticipation of possible passage of the ban on manumissions, however, Maryland slaveowners freed a large number of Negroes during the summer of 1860.

The Jacobs Bill, as its author asserted, forced the legislators to ponder "whether Maryland shall be a Southern state, or whether she shall go into the arms of the abolitionists."[13] The behavior of Congressman Henry Winter Davis in Washington posed the same question in a different light. In the protracted contest over the election of a Speaker of the House, Davis broke a close canvass by supporting former Whig William Pennington of New Jersey. Pennington was a compromise candidate, technically a member of a "People's party" in his home state. But he was distinctly a northern candidate, and he received Republican party support after the regular Republican candidate, John Sherman, repeatedly failed to attract enough votes to end the deadlock.

Davis's vote was one more step in his own private journey towards the Republican party. Motivated as always by a nearly irrational hatred for the Democratic party and for indecisiveness and timidity in politics, Davis feared another long, drawn-out contest for the speakership. The tumultuous and time-consuming election of Nathaniel P. Banks to the speakership in Davis's first term (1855-1857) had soured him on such proceedings.[14] "Oh," he complained to Samuel F. DuPont in late 1859, "the folly of timidity in the face of the Demo-

[12] Unfortunately, no evidence exists for the workings of the committee which drafted the bill. Scarcely more information is available on its course through the General Assembly. Delegate Jacobs himself wanted sterner measures than the final bill—"House Bill #44"—provided. Maryland, House of Delegates, *Journal*, 1860, pp. 364, 468. No record of the votes on the Jacobs Bill is available, except for the roll call on final passage. The bill succeeded by a 38 to 14 count in the House:

	By Party		By Section		
	American	Democrat	Eastern Shore	Southern Maryland	Western Maryland
For (38)	9	29	14	10	14
Against (14)	13	1	1	0	13

[13] *Baltimore Sun*, March 7, 1860.

[14] Henry Winter Davis to Samuel F. DuPont, January 4 and 13, 1856, Samuel F. DuPont Papers, Eleutherian Mills Historical Library, Greenville, Del.

crats–[who are] sure to beat us . . . if we remain divided."[15] Davis's frustration mounted after the session commenced and he saw his fellow Know-Nothings "truckling" to the Southern Democrats.[16] "On the Democratic side audacity, on the Republican side, obstinacy, among my friends, weakness, vacillation," he complained to DuPont.[17] Fearing a deal between the border-state Americans and the Southern Democrats, he cast his vote for Pennington.

Only a fool–and Davis was certainly not that–could not have predicted the abuse that was hurled at Davis from all quarters of Maryland because of that vote. With only one dissenting vote and three abstentions, the General Assembly voted a ringing censure of Davis's gross misrepresentation of Maryland's interests and feelings. In doing so, they accurately reflected their constituents' opinion. The *Baltimore Sun* reported that somewhere in Cumberland a group of citizens supported Davis's vote; if true, this was the only recorded pro-Davis opinion in the entire state.[18] From that same town, 600 persons signed a memorial condemning Davis in strong language.[19] He was burned in effigy in Maryland and throughout the South. In the eyes of many Marylanders, moreover, Davis seemed to have been paid his thirty pieces of silver. One of his trusted lieutenants, S. Owings Hoffman, was made House sergeant at arms, and Davis himself moved to second place in the powerful Ways and Means Committee.[20]

Pressured from within and without the state to adopt some position on slavery and sectional tension, the Two Hundred Fifty-third session finally passed a set of resolutions in March 1860. The resolutions were guarded, equivocal, and etched in fear:

> We deem it inexpedient to call a Southern convention in the present excited condition of the country, relying upon the belief that the recent outrages against the South have already awakened the patriotism and justice of the majority of our Northern brethren.

Had they stopped there, the legislators would have been on record with an overly optimistic but unambiguous statement of belief. But

[15] Davis to DuPont, November 28, 1859, *ibid.* Who the "us" is in Davis's reference is not clear. He probably meant the entire opposition to the Democrats. Indeed, one of his cherished dreams was a fusion of all the Democrats' opponents. See Gerald S. Henig, "Henry Winter Davis and the Speakership Contest of 1859–1860," *Maryland Historical Magazine,* 68 (1973): 1–19.

[16] Davis to DuPont, December 27, 1859, DuPont Papers.

[17] Davis to DuPont, January 9, 1860, *ibid.*

[18] February 20, 1860.

[19] *Ibid.*

[20] *Ibid.,* March 4, 1860.

1860 was not a year in which Marylanders could express themselves with assurance, so the resolutions continued.

But should this fond hope result in shameless failure, our earnest protest be totally disregarded, and the disruption of these states rendered inevitable, . . . Maryland will then be prepared to meet her sisters of the South in a Southern convention for the protection of Southern rights.[21]

This giving with one hand and taking with the other was typical of Marylanders' attitudes in early 1860. First came the timid expression of good will and confidence. Then the conditions—"shameless failure," "totally disregarded," and "inevitable" disruption—suggested action but actually promised little. Rhetoric was as far as Marylanders could bring themselves to go; the call to action was hesitant and hedged. Within the legislature, sentiment on the resolutions was roughly divided between Americans who wanted to ignore the issue entirely, and Democrats who wanted as least some action to be taken. Also, the Western Maryland representatives were naturally less inclined to speak out on the slavery issue than their Southern and Eastern counterparts.[22]

Most Marylanders in early 1860 agreed that their state was allied with the South. In practice, this alliance was ringed by caution and qualification. A Southern Maryland meeting, for example, followed the legislature's hesitant lead by drafting a set of thoroughly proslavery, pro-Southern resolutions, then finished them off with a paean to the Union and expressions of their own unshakable determination to uphold it.[23] Marylanders were yet unready to admit that those two allegiances might be incompatible.

The legislative session, meanwhile, moved to a climax of confusion. Sleepy Annapolis and the local politicians who populated the General Assembly were evidently not made to stand much excitement. When the prearranged adjournment date arrived in mid-March, the legis-

[21] *Ibid.*, March 6, 1860; see also Maryland, House of Delegates, *Documents*, document "LL."

[22] Although no final vote on the resolutions was recorded, one key vote did appear in the House of Delegates *Journal*. Maryland's resolutions were the eventual result of a special joint committee which studied the South Carolina invitation. When that invitation first arrived in the General Assembly, American Delegate Claude Dennis, of Somerset County, moved to table it and not to consider the issue at all. The motion lost on a roll-call vote as follows:

	By Party		By Section		
	American	Democrat	Eastern Shore	Southern Maryland	Western Maryland
For (28)	23	5	6	2	20
Against (35)	4	31	12	8	15

[23] *Baltimore Sun*, March 24, 1860.

lators were edgy from two months of frenetic decisionmaking. On the very last day of the session a legislator and a lobbyist for a group which was seeking unsuccessfully to obtain a street railway charter for Baltimore exchanged shots in the rotunda of the historic State House. The lobbyist fell with a ball in his hip.[24] Speaker of the House E. G. Kilbourne, of Anne Arundel County, hastily adjourned the session, even though several important bills were awaiting final action. Fearful of the Speaker's safety, the sergeant at arms escorted Kilbourne home.[25]

Almost immediately, requests to call a special session of the General Assembly began to arrive at Governor Hicks's office.[26] But Hicks had apparently seen enough of the disrupting effects of the Assembly meeting. He choes to let matters rest as they were.

II

During these tense days leading public figures often felt called upon to appeal to Marylanders for calm. The governor did so in his annual message. A typical 1860 plea for peace was the February speech of Baltimore merchant Brantz Mayer.[27] "This is a year not of absolute disorder or of real danger, but of annoyance and discontent," Mayer tried to reassure his listeners; it was the customary plea for calm. Tensions arose, he asserted, from the machinations of "trading politicians" who kept up a "passionate tumult . . . in the *political* world."[28] No "revisionist" historian of the twentieth century ever argued more insistently than Mayer that sectional conflict was the product of inept leadership fabricating tensions in the public mind. Mayer wound up

24 Accounts of the affair are confused, but apparently the fracas was over the failure of the street railway scheme. A Philadelphia group petitioned the legislature for a charter to operate horse-drawn street cars in Baltimore. A complicated struggle resulted, with charges and countercharges of corruption, influence peddling, misrepresentation, and fraud. Mass meetings in Baltimore for and against the plan argued the questions of fares, monopoly, outsiders controlling the line, and so on. Though the controversy has not earned space in this narrative, it was quite bitter and received considerable attention in the press. In the affair in the State House, the lobbyist, Thomas H. Gardiner, accosted Delegate Richard B. McCoy of Harford and knocked him down. McCoy, who was armed for some reason, shot Gardiner in the hip. McCoy was then beaten up by friends of Gardiner and kicked in the face; the sheriff found him unconscious behind the stairs. The issue at stake is not the point of the story. What is significant about the fracas is that it demonstrated the taut nerves and overheated emotions of the session. It would be interesting to know for certain why McCoy was carrying a gun, and how many other firearms were in the hall.

25 *Baltimore Sun,* March 12, 1860

26 *Ibid.*

27 A manuscript draft of the speech is in the Brantz Mayer Papers, Maryland Historical Society, Baltimore.

28 Italics in the original.

his address with a hymn to the past. His whole speech was titled "True Americanism Considered in the Lives of Calhoun, Webster, and Clay." George Washington received as much attention in the speech as did the three stars of the title, and Mayer lamented the lack of a contemporary hero of like magnitude to rally the nation.

Mayer packaged fear, political mistrust, hope in the basic soundness of people, and a reverent appeal to the past in one oration. For all their internal divisions, most Marylanders could have applauded that speech as enthusiastically as did the audience at the Maryland Institute. Yet the stories about John Brown appeared regularly in the newspapers, and the arming of the state went on.

III

It was in this frame of mind that Marylanders had to confront the most important presidential election in living memory. They worried about it. "We live in a state between the Disunionists of the South and the Black Republicans of the North," wrote one concerned citizen as he looked ahead, "and the ascendency of either will be alike subversive of our happiness and prosperity."[29] Indeed, the presidential campaign of 1860 became one of the longest, most heated contests in the history of that office, seething with excitement and even violence right up to election day itself. The ultimate irony was that after the ballots were counted it became obvious that the contest in Maryland had been decisively affected by local passions which had little to do with the national questions that were supposedly up for solution.

In Maryland the presidential contest of 1860 was a two-way race. Even though four names were on the ballot, only Southern Democrat John C. Breckinridge and Constitutional Unionist John Bell had any chance of winning Maryland's electoral votes.

A "Black Republican" from Illinois, even a relatively inoffensive figure like Abraham Lincoln, was out of the question as a presidential choice for all but a handful of Marylanders. Republicans, in fact, were so unpopular in the state that they were in physical danger. Montgomery Blair, Republican leader from Silver Spring, was menaced by a mob in Baltimore.[30] A Charles County Republican—who optimistically predicted fifteen or twenty Lincoln votes there—announced that he would stand by his preference, "although it may cost me my life."[31]

[29] *Port Tobacco Times*, February 3, 1860.

[30] William Marshall to Montgomery Blair, May 5, 1860, Montgomery Blair Papers, Library of Congress, Washington, D.C. Marshall was a judge in Baltimore. Silver Spring is only a few miles north of Washington.

[31] N. Burnham to Montgomery Blair, October 10, 1860, *ibid.*

When a few hundred Baltimore Republicans attempted to hold a rally, their parade route was nearly the scene of a monumental riot. "Wonderful to relate," said the *Baltimore American*, with apparent pride in the temperate behavior of the populace, "there was no one killed and no one badly beaten."[32] The crowd contented itself with pelting the marchers with stones, eggs, and garbage. From Clarksburg, in Howard County, one Lincoln supporter lamented that he had intended to announce his choice, but that "everyone declared if I did they would not patronize me any more and I have to live by my trade."[33]

When they did speak out, Republicans in Maryland stressed their moderation, especially in contrast to the secessionist tendencies of Breckinridge. In a speech delivered in October, Montgomery Blair asserted that, if Breckinridge were not a disunionist himself, his "controlling partisans" were. Douglas and Bell would both admit slavery into the territories. Blair ridiculed the Constitutional Unionists' position that there was "nothing at stake" in the slavery question. He ended his appeal by disowning abolitionism and by claiming that "the Republicans stand where the fathers of the constitution and where Clay and Benton stood"—for free territory.[34]

The most conspicuous of the few Lincoln voters were the radical Germans. The leading Republican newspaper in the state, both in 1856 and in 1860, was Baltimore's *Die Wecker*, edited by immigrant forty-eighter Wilhelm Schnauffer.[35] The Germans in Maryland were sharply divided between the old stock, who arrived in the eighteenth century, and the new wave of political immigrants, who came in the late 1840s and early 1850s. The latter were abolitionist to a man.[36] These forty-eighters were concentrated in Baltimore, where Lincoln received half of his Maryland votes. Germans were prominent in the ill-fated Republican rally in Baltimore.[37]

The tiny network of Maryland Republicans in 1860 found their awkward position made worse by the party's failure to nominate a better-known or more conservative candidate, like Montgomery Blair's favorite, Judge Edward Bates of Missouri.[38] Blair and German-born

32 November 1, 1860.

33 William L. Donenbury (?) to Montgomery Blair, November 6, 1860, Blair Papers.

34 Manuscript speech, *ibid.*

35 Karl Heinrich Schnauffer, founder of the paper and mentioned in Chapter III, was dead by 1860. Wilhelm Schnauffer was his nephew.

36 Dieter Cunz, *The Maryland Germans* (Princeton: Princeton University Press, 1948), p. 281; and Louis P. Henninghausen, *History of the German Society of Maryland* (Baltimore: n.p., 1909), p. 351.

37 *Baltimore American*, November 1, 1860.

38 E. Stabler to Montgomery Blair, June 21, 1860, Blair Papers.

George Wiss went to the Republican national convention in Chicago with instructions to vote for Bates.[39] Still, as the election approached, small Lincoln clubs appeared in Carroll, Frederick, and Allegany counties, at least.[40]

In truth, Lincoln had somewhat more strength in Maryland than open voting exposed. A tenuous bond of sympathy existed between some Bell supporters and Lincoln. This sympathy was certainly limited, and because of its clandestine nature, is now hard to trace.

The most outspoken advocate of cooperation between the Constitutional Unionists and the Republicans was Henry Winter Davis. Davis's speakership vote for Pennington was no shock to insiders. At least as early as 1859 he was calling privately for the fusion of Americans and Republicans behind a safe conservative in 1860.[41] He was friendly with several Republicans, including Justin S. Morrill of Vermont, who shared his desire for protective tariffs. David Davis, Lincoln's campaign manager, was Henry Winter Davis's cousin, and although the two Davises were never on close terms, this connection was influential in drawing Lincoln's attention to the maverick Marylander.[42]

Davis also had his eye on the political future. Like most Marylanders, he expected the Democratic rupture to give the election to Lincoln.[43] He artfully maneuvered to stay on good terms with the Republicans while ostensibly campaigning as a Bell man. He offered to campaign for Lincoln outside Maryland.[44] After the election Lincoln and his advisers, including Thurlow Weed, seriously considered Davis for a cabinet post.[45]

The underground Maryland Republicans had two problems, whether to field Lincoln electors in Maryland, and whether to expose themselves personally as Republicans. Davis sought to avoid a Lincoln-Bell confrontation at all costs, both in Maryland and elsewhere in the Middle Atlantic states. He felt that the two candidates would divide anti-Democratic strength.[46] His impractical solution was a combined ticket of Bell-Lincoln electors.[47] This prompted a Marylander to call one of Davis's speeches "A Lincoln pronunciamento in Bell clothing,

39 Reinhard C. Luthin, *The First Lincoln Campaign* (Cambridge, Mass.: Harvard University Press, 1944), p. 60.

40 See correspondence in Blair Papers.

41 Luthin, *op. cit.*, p. 153; and Henry Winter Davis to Justin Morrill, August 20, 1859, Justin Morrill Papers, Library of Congress, Washington, D. C.

42 See Williard L. King, *Lincoln's Manager, David Davis* (Cambridge, Mass.: Harvard University Press, 1960).

43 Henry Winter Davis to Samuel F. DuPont, July 1860, DuPont Papers.

44 King, *op. cit.*, pp. 147–48.

45 *Ibid.*, pp. 168–69, 173–74.

46 Henry Winter Davis to Samuel F. DuPont, July 1860, DuPont Papers.

47 William Marshall to Montgomery Blair, May 27, 1860, Blair Papers.

or rather an eccentric Republican sheep with a Union Bell on its neck."[48] Montgomery Blair, head of the Republican party in Maryland, disagreed with Davis. Blair and the avowed Republicans held the Baltimore congressman in contempt for his "cowering." They also felt the need to give their organization visibility and respectability by choosing electors.[49] A slate of Republican electors was duly put forth, with Blair heading the ticket.

Aside from calculating politicians, some rank-and-file Bell voters seemed sympathetic to Lincoln, but they were intimidated. "A public demonstration would crush us down as things now stand," said one cautious Maryland Republican.[50] His reluctance to support Lincoln openly was probably shared by others. "I know quite a number that will vote for Bell," declared a plucky Republican from Charles County, "and yet they are willing Lincoln should be elected, and some say they hope he will be."[51]

The candidacy of Stephen A. Douglas fared scarcely better than Lincoln's. The state's Democrats never liked Douglas's doctrine of popular sovereignty. When state Democratic organizations had to choose between the Breckinridge and Douglas wings, Maryland's Southern leanings steered them unerringly to Breckinridge.[52] The only prominent Douglas spokesman in Maryland was the half-blind former Whig Reverdy Johnson.[53] The Breckinridge spokesmen placed heavy emphasis on their claim that they, and not the Douglasites, were the regular party organization in Maryland.[54] The already exhausted Douglas made one brief, desultory tour through Maryland in September.

Lacking an effective organization and a strong appeal, Douglas ran a poor third in Maryland in 1860. Marylanders clearly joined Douglas and Lincoln together as unacceptably anti-Southern.[55] Douglas's only sizable bloc of votes outside Baltimore came from mountainous Allegany County, where a heavy proportion of Catholics gave the

48 Ollinger Crenshaw, *The Slave States in the Presidential Election of 1860* (Baltimore: The Johns Hopkins Press, 1943), p. 118.

49 William Marshall to Montgomery Blair, May 27, 1860, Blair Papers.

50 George M. Palmer to Montgomery Blair, October 1860, *ibid.*

51 N. Burnham to Montgomery Blair, October 29, 1860, *ibid.*

52 *Baltimore Sun,* March 21, 1860; *Frederick Herald,* March 21, 1860.

53 Correspondence between Stephen A. Douglas and Reverdy Johnson is found in the Reverdy Johnson Papers, Maryland Historical Society, Baltimore. This communication is very scant, but clearly indicates a personal friendship between the two men. See also a letter from Douglas to Johnson in the *Annapolis Gazette,* September 2, 1858.

54 *Baltimore Sun,* September 6, 1860; see also Crenshaw, *op. cit.,* pp. 72, 82.

55 Crenshaw, *op. cit.,* p. 74. The coefficient of correlation between the vote received by Lincoln in the countries of Maryland in 1860 and the vote received there by Douglas in the same election is +0.685.

area a Democratic inclination, but where Breckinridge's slavery appeal was not so effective.

Only one clear-cut difference—the emphasis of their appeals—separated the two leading contenders for Maryland's electoral vote, Breckinridge and Bell. Although both men were from border states, only Bell and the Constitutional Unionists adopted an anti-sectional appeal. Breckinridge, the Southern Democrat, bluntly called on Marylanders to tie their allegiances to the South.

Breckinridge's campaign foreshadowed his success with Maryland's old society, in the areas of heavy slaveholding. In contrast to the Union-above-everything approach of the Bell spokesmen,[56] the Breckinridge men put first emphasis on the need for a friendly federal attitude toward slavery, especially in the territories. They dismissed Douglas's popular sovereignty as unconstitutional and dangerous. They attacked Bell as being unsafe on the key issue. A Montgomery County Breckinridge newspaper expressed "abhorrence of the silence and noncommitalism of the convention which has recommended Mr. Bell upon this most vital and all-important question of slavery in the territories."[57] Baltimore Democrats distributed 5,000 copies of a Breckinridge speech in which he criticized the Constitutional Unionist platform:

> Gentlemen, they tell us that they are advocating the principles of "the Constitution, the Union, and the enforcement of the laws." I presume that there is scarcely a man in this assembly—perhaps no one North or South—who will admit that he is against the constitution, the Union, and the enforcement of the laws.[58]

At a large rally in Monument Square, Baltimore, the Breckinridge people hung a huge sign which read "Maryland Must and Will Be True to the South."[59] The *Baltimore Sun* frequently reported speeches by Southern Democrats who regarded the question of slavery protection in the territories as the paramount issue in the election.[60]

Breckinridge's appeal, therefore, was pitched at the slaveholders and other Southern sympathizers in Maryland. The results showed a clear connection between the Breckinridge vote and the strength

[56] See pp. 146–47.

[57] *Montgomery County Sentinel* (Rockville, Md.), June 20, 1860.

[58] *Baltimore Sun*, September 7, 1860.

[59] *Ibid.*, October 23, 1860.

[60] For example, on September 29, 1860 the *Sun* reported a speech by former Governor Wise of Virginia in which he declared he would "regard Lincoln's election as an open declaration of war against the Southern States." William L. Yancey was recorded in the same paper as saying that, "if the Union is to be sustained by trampling upon the Constitution and oppressing my section because it is the weaker . . . then I am a traitor and you can make the most of it." *Ibid.*, November 5, 1860. See also Crenshaw, *op. cit.*, p. 112.

of slaveholding in a locality.[61] All five counties carried by the Southern Democrat were areas of entrenched slavery and a high percentage of Negro population.[62] In St. Mary's and Charles counties, where Democrats were strengthened by a substantial proportion of Catholics as well as slaveowners, Breckinridge polled over 60 percent of the vote. In six other Eastern and Southern counties Breckinridge ran close behind Bell.

John Bell, who carried sixteen of Maryland's twenty-one counties, campaigned under the banner of the new Constitutional Union party. The party was formed to fill the ideological gap between Douglas and Breckinridge, and was based, in the words of its platform, on "the Constitution, the Union, and enforcement of the laws."

It was only fitting that a party based on antisectional attitudes be launched in Baltimore. Marylanders took a leading part in its formation.[63] On May 9, in the First Presbyterian Church of Baltimore, a group of former Whigs and Americans renewed old contacts and met in convention. With a minimum of dissension and uproar the convention chose bland John Bell of Tennessee to head the ticket.[64] Edward Everett of Massachusetts was chosen for the second spot. "Youth," according to one commentator, "was conspicuous by its absence."[65] The Constitutional Union appeal was based on the one viable contribution of the American party—a deprecation of sectionalism. John P. Kennedy spoke for the party when he fumed, "The whole of the present slavery agitation is a trick."[66] Brantz Mayer, also a leader of the Maryland Constitutional Unionists, impatiently dismissed the accusations of both North and South as "false issues . . . political bugaboos, that are as harmless and hollow as ghosts manufactured out of sheets and pumpkins."[67] Henry Winter Davis agreed: "The way to settle the slavery question is to be silent on it."[68] Ceaselessly, the

[61] The coefficient of correlation between the percentage of the vote for Breckinridge in the Maryland counties and the percentage of whites who owned slaves in the Maryland counties, on a county-by-county basis, is a significant +0.672. The coefficient between Breckenridge's percentage of the vote and the percentage of a county's population which was Negro is +0.691.

[62] All Maryland counties carried by Breckinridge had a Negro population of at least 35 percent; they were Charles County (Negro population, 64.9 percent), Prince George's County, (58.7 percent), St. Mary's County (66.5 percent), Talbot County (48.7 percent), and Worcester County (35.2 percent).

[63] See *Baltimore Sun*, March 9, 1860.

[64] Joseph H. Parks, *John Bell of Tennessee*, Southern Biography Series (Baton Rouge: Louisiana State University Press, 1950).

[65] Paul R. Frothingham, *Edward Everett* (Boston and New York: Houghton Mifflin, 1925), p. 408.

[66] John P. Kennedy to Sir Richard Pakenham, February 19, 1860, copy, John Pendleton Kennedy Papers, Peabody Institute Library, Baltimore.

[67] Manuscript speech, Mayer Papers.

[68] Henry Winter Davis, *Speeches and Addresses* (New York: Harper & Brothers, 1867), p. 158.

Constitutional Union spokesmen in Maryland pressed the importance of preserving the Union against the pointless agitation of the territorial slavery question—a question they considered already settled by geography and climate.

The Constitutional Unionists accordingly rebuked their major opponent, Breckinridge, for being too extreme on the question of slavery. The *Baltimore American* said, "It is impossible to accept Mr. Breckinridge's personal worth or individual fealty to the constitution as a compensation for the rampant and controlling spirit of disunion which is a distinguishing feature of his supporters."[69] The *Frederick Herald* referred to Breckinridge men as "the seceders."[70] The *Frederick Examiner*, meanwhile, bluntly asserted: "The irretrievable choice is . . . between 'Bell and the Union' or 'Breckinridge and Disunion!' There is no evading this issue."[71]

In their pursuit of calm the Constitutional Unionists minimized the danger Lincoln presented to the institution of slavery and denied that his election would be a justification for secession. "Let us not fall into the fatal error of thinking that the great interests of the Union are irrefutably lost by the election of an administration we do not like," Kennedy warned.[72] All the "eternal howl" by Southerners on the slavery question was simply a Democratic trick to frighten the voters, said Henry Winter Davis.[73] A Bell newspaper called on its readers "to fight together against Democracy and sectionalism."[74]

The Bell campaigners followed the Know-Nothings in advocating Unionism, and the Bell voters had clear antecedents in the American party. Eighty percent of the county election districts that went for Bell in 1860 had voted Know-Nothing in both of the two previous statewide elections. Across the state, Bell's votes in 1860 came from the same areas as Fillmore's had in 1856.[75] It was this nativist connection which proved to be Bell's undoing in Baltimore.

69 September 7, 1860.

70 July 21, 1860.

71 October 31, 1860.

72 John P. Kennedy, *The Great Drama: An Appeal to Maryland* (Baltimore: J. D. Toy, 1861), p. 6.

73 Davis, *op. cit.*, p. 152.

74 *Harford Times* (Havre de Grace, Md.), March 17, 1860.

75 A strong statistical correlation exists between the vote received by Bell in 1860 and the vote received by the American candidates for statewide office in 1855, 1857, and 1859. The coefficient of correlation between the percentage of the vote received by Bell in 1860 and the percentage of the vote received by the American candidate for comptroller in 1855, county by county in Maryland, is +0.916. Between the Bell percentage and the American gubernatorial percentage in 1857 the coefficient is +0.914. Between Bell's percentage and that of the American comptroller candidate in 1859 the coefficient is +0.822. The coefficients of correlation between Breckinridge's county-by-county vote in 1860 and previous Democratic candidates' percentages also are strongly positive.

This is not to say that the Constitutional Union party was simply the Know-Nothing organization under a new name. The new party totally discarded nativism. Also, it was animated by a resurgence of old Whiggery. Many of the leading Constitutional Unionists were former Whigs who had been repelled by nativist excesses and had been politically underground for almost a decade. The national figures of the party were conspicuous former Whigs, men like John J. Crittenden, Bell, and Everett. The *Baltimore Sun's* Washington correspondent, scanning the delegates heading for the Baltimore convention, remarked many a "veteran politician of the Clay school."[76]

In Maryland, John Pendleton Kennedy was such a Whig; he had not been happy since Henry Clay died.[77] Sometimes called a Know-Nothing, he firmly denied it. "I may vote their ticket—in part, perhaps," he admitted, but only because "I can certainly never vote for the Democratic nominee." In the Constitutional Union party he found a home again, coming out of semiretirement to be a leader of the Bell movement in Maryland. He was very enthusiastic about the party's convention in Baltimore, calling it "a most worthy and striking assemblage of representatives of the old Whig party."[78]

The combination of old Whigs and Americans proved an uneasy alliance at best. Despite the prominence of respected old Whigs like Kennedy and Brantz Mayer, and despite the omission of any nativism in the party platform, the taint of Know-Nothingism still clung to the Constitutional Unionists. Kennedy, for one, was visibly upset that the new party was not able to avoid the nativist stigma; he gloomily foresaw disaster. "The distinctive tone of Americanism," he complained in his diary, "cannot but offend."[79]

The fundamental split between the truly moderate old Whigs and the Americans was evident from the beginning of the new party. Seating fights disrupted the state Constitutional Union convention in Baltimore on April 19. Two sets of delegates appeared from Baltimore, one which had been chosen at a Constitutional Union mass meeting and the other which was sponsored by the city convention of the American party itself. After a rancorous debate, a compromise was reached which seated a split delegation headed by American mayor Thomas Swann.[80] It was this situation which so distressed Kennedy. Swann further perpetuated the basic differences within the party by emphasizing that the American organization still existed on the

[76] May 5, 1860.
[77] See Chapter II.
[78] John P. Kennedy, Journal, May 9, 1860, Kennedy Papers.
[79] *Ibid.*, April 19, 1860.
[80] *Baltimore Sun*, April 20, 1860.

local level, and that their association with the Constitutional Unionists was simply a loose affiliation aimed at the presidential election.[81]

As a result of the Know-Nothing stain, droves of Catholic voters avoided Bell.[82] In St. Mary's County (both Southern and Catholic) Bell drew only 19 percent of the vote. In the mountainous west slavery was not an issue, but Bell ran poorly in Allegany County, where the Catholic population was second only to that in St. Mary's. In Frederick County, German-language pamphlets promoted Bell's chief competitor, Breckinridge, as the enemy of Know-Nothingism.

Without an understanding of Bell's entanglement with Know-Nothingism, the results of the 1860 election are inexplicable (see Table 11). Breckinridge defeated Bell in Maryland by 522 votes. Bell expressed what must logically be regarded as the majority sentiment in Maryland; the entire course of Marylanders from 1850 to 1860, from their advocacy of the Compromise through the election of 1860, evidenced their overwhelming conservatism. Bell was the candidate of a party born in Baltimore and led by several Marylanders. He carried sixteen of twenty-one counties, and compiled a 1,830-vote advantage over his principal opponent in those counties. But he lost the state because he lost badly in Baltimore.

That Baltimore should vote in tandem with its old enemy, the most conservative and Southern section of the old society, was the result of the reform issue. Reformers still were very active in Baltimore. They won essential help from the General Assembly early in the year when the legislature passed the election and police reform laws, but the consummation was not until fall, when the Know-Nothings were ousted for good. Reform swept everything before it, including Bell.

The Baltimore Democrats made a strategic alliance with reform in 1860. Most reform organizers were themselves Democrats. Adam Denmead, for example, was both a prominent reform leader and one of the Democrats who were contesting the results of the Baltimore House of Delegates election of 1859.[83] Also, the Baltimore Democrats as a party did not nominate any candidates for local office in 1860; they supported the reform slate. Many prominent Democratic leaders worked actively for the deform ticket.[84] Davis fumed that the entire reform movement was a disguised Democratic plot.[85] But, despite

[81] *Ibid.*

[82] The coefficient of correlation between Bell's percentage of the vote in Maryland counties and the percentage of the Catholic population of those counties is −0.843.

[83] *Baltimore Sun,* February 7, 1860.

[84] *Ibid.,* October 18, 1860.

[85] Henry Winter Davis to Samuel F. DuPont, August 1859, DuPont Papers; Davis to Justin Morrill, September 14, 1859, Morrill Papers.

TABLE 11. THE PRESIDENTIAL ELECTION OF 1860 IN MARYLAND

	Votes Cast for Each Candidate, with Percentage			
County	Breckinridge	Bell	Douglas	Lincoln
Allegany	979 (23.2)	1,521 (36.0)	1,203 (28.5)	522 (12.3)
Anne Arundel	1,107 (47.1)	1,041 (48.4)	98 (4.5)	3 (0.0)
Baltimore	3,305 (46.0)	3,388 (47.2)	449 (6.3)	37 (0.5)
Calvert	386 (46.6)	399 (48.1)	43 (5.3)	1 (0.0)
Caroline	616 (42.8)	712 (49.4)	100 (6.9)	12 (0.9)
Carroll	1,791 (39.9)	2,295 (51.2)	339 (7.6)	59 (1.3)
Cecil	1,506 (39.1)	1,792 (46.6)	393 (10.2)	158 (4.1)
Charles	723 (60.4)	430 (35.9)	38 (3.2)	6 (0.5)
Dorchester	1,176 (46.9)	1,265 (50.5)	31 (1.2)	35 (1.4)
Frederick	3,167 (43.2)	3,616 (49.3)	445 (6.1)	103 (1.4)
Harford	1,527 (43.0)	1,862 (52.4)	82 (2.3)	81 (2.3)
Howard	530 (34.2)	830 (53.5)	189 (12.3)	1 (0.0)
Kent	694 (41.8)	852 (51.3)	74 (4.5)	42 (2.4)
Montgomery	1,125 (46.3)	1,155 (47.6)	99 (4.1)	50 (2.0)
Prince George's	1,048 (53.0)	885 (44.8)	43 (2.2)	1 (0.0)
Queen Anne's	879 (46.9)	908 (48.5)	87 (4.6)	0 (0.0)
St. Mary's	920 (67.1)	261 (19.0)	190 (13.9)	1 (0.0)
Somerset	1,339 (45.2)	1,536 (51.8)	89 (3.0)	2 (0.0)
Talbot	898 (50.1)	793 (44.3)	98 (5.6)	2 (0.0)
Washington	2,475 (45.7)	2,567 (47.4)	283 (5.2)	95 (0.7)
Worcester	1,425 (55.6)	1,048 (40.9)	90 (3.5)	0 (0.0)
	27,326 (44.0)	29,156 (46.9)	4,463 (7.2)	1,211 (1.9)
Baltimore City	14,956 (49.1)	12,604 (41.5)	1,503 (5.0)	1,083 (4.5)
Maryland	42,282 (45.8)	41,760 (45.2)	5,966 (6.5)	2,294 (2.5)

the close working relationship and the overlapping personnel between the reform association and the Democrats, the groups were not the same. The people who had bestirred themselves and organized the reform effort were not just Democratic leaders; the Democratic organization in Baltimore was standing by disspiritedly when independent reformers first took the field. Furthermore, neither the reformers nor the Democrats sought outright fusion. The reformers were a private clean-government group which enjoyed strong cooperation from one of the established parties.

When all these forces came together in the elections of 1860, the Democrats tied themselves to a popular local issue while the Constitutional Unionists supported the discredited and unrespectable

Know-Nothings; inevitably, Breckinridge benefited. Democratic advertisements specifically damned Bell as "the sympathizer and supporter of Know-Nothingism.[86] The charges were made plausible by Bell's one-time association with the American party. The charges were given additional weight when a handful of drunken Know-Nothings attacked a Breckinridge parade on election eve.[87] Kennedy's pessimistic prediction about what "the distinctive tone of nativism" would do to the Constitutional Union campaign was quite correct. Breckinridge carried Baltimore, and Maryland with it.

Statistics also demonstrate the connection between support of reform and Breckinridge strength. In the municipal elections of October 10, 1860, the reform candidate for mayor carried all of Baltimore's twenty wards in an uncommonly quiet and well-policed election. The *Sun* accurately diagnosed the intensity of local feeling about reform: "Not a single candidate—not a man, whatsoever his character and standing heretofore, who had the hardihood to stand before the people as an antagonist of Reform, has been spared. The blow has fallen upon all indiscriminately."[88] The blow even fell on Bell a month later. The areas of reform strength in October and the areas of Breckinridge strength in November were identical (see Table 12). The ward-by-ward pattern of the two elections shows that, while the reform mayor, George William Brown, ran ahead of Breckinridge, the patern of his support and that for Breckinridge coincided.

In this way were Maryland's eight electoral votes awarded. On the surface it was an illogical result; the counties which had increasingly been going Democratic reverted to the heir-apparent of the Know-Nothings, Constitutional Unionist Bell. Baltimore, which had been the birthplace of the first American victories, and which had sustained the party in recent years, chose Breckinridge. That Southern Maryland, the personification of the old society, should vote in tandem with Baltimore, pinnacle of the new, strained rational calculation. Small wonder, then, that Henry Winter Davis could only shake his head over "this insane canvas."[89]

What is clear is that Breckinridge's victory could not safely be interpreted as an endorsement of his campaign pledges, nor could Bell's defeat be seen as a rejection of his moderate approach. Bell seemed the logical majority choice in Maryland; the history of the

[86] *Baltimore Sun,* November 5, 1860.
[87] *Ibid.,* November 6, 1860.
[88] *Ibid.,* October 11, 1860.
[89] Henry Winter Davis to Samuel F. DuPont, November 7, 1860, DuPont Papers.

TABLE 12. REFORM AND BRECKINRIDGE IN 1860: BALTIMORE

Ward	Votes for Mayor: Reform Candidate[a]		Votes for Breckinridge	
	No.	%	No.	%
1	776	(65.2)	721	(59.6)
2	1,176	(78.8)	1,153	(76.1)
3	963	(62.1)	788	(50.9)
4	726	(61.9)	646	(52.2)
5	970	(61.3)	834	(54.2)
6	779	(55.2)	677	(46.7)
7	969	(61.3)	945	(57.9)
8	1,007	(79.5)	776	(69.7)
9	1,106	(76.2)	860	(59.6)
10	1,161	(72.9)	902	(56.0)
11	932	(73.5)	641	(51.1)
12	577	(60.9)	425	(43.2)
13	783	(61.1)	634	(48.8)
14	908	(56.4)	656	(42.4)
15	1,032	(64.1)	839	(51.9)
16	925	(60.3)	800	(50.5)
17	836	(66.0)	806	(64.4)
18	807	(55.4)	721	(48.0)
19	631	(60.1)	471	(42.8)
20	715	(63.7)	655	(57.6)

NOTE: The coefficient of correlation between Brown's percentage of the vote, ward by ward, and Breckinridge's percentage of the vote in the same wards is +0.844.

[a] The reform candidate for mayor was George William Brown. The election was held October 10, 1860.

state for the past decade had been a continuous testament to sectional moderation and refusal to take sides. Bell swept the most populous counties, leaving Breckinridge to pick up the pieces in the enclaves of the old society. And logic suggests that a candidate of Bell's Unionist persuasion would have carried commercial Baltimore. The business and civic leaders of Baltimore were later uniformly conservative and cautious in the secession crisis and supported the Unionist stand of American Governor Thomas H. Hicks. The answer to this puzzle, and to Breckinridge's victory in Maryland, was the reform issue, which swept away the former American Bell on a wave of indignation. The same business leaders who later proved their Unionism were leading elements of the reform movement, men like George William

Brown, the banker, men whom Davis tried to laugh off as "the mercantile gentry." But in the fall of 1860 they were not thinking about Unionism as much as about reform, and the zeal which buoyed up the local Democrats spilled over onto Breckinridge in November. In sum, the election had affected no choice at all between the "South first" emphasis of one candidate and the "Union above all" approach of the other. Maryland's crisis of allegiance was still to be faced.

VII

THE CRISIS OF ALLEGIANCE

MARYLANDERS WATCHED with gloomy resignation as the election results came in from around the country. Most Marylanders were like John P. Kennedy, who marked election day in his diary with restraint; this public-spirited man, who had concerned himself with politics most of his life and who had helped to found the Constitutional Union party, was distracted by business. A curious calm had fallen on Kennedy and on Maryland.[1] When the inevitable results of Lincoln's election were clear, the *Sun* tersely observed, "As we cannot offer . . . readers . . . one word of congratulation on so inauspicious a result, we are disposed to do no more than announce the fact this morning, and await the developments that may ensue."[2]

In the developments of the secession winter Maryland occupied a critical position. Lincoln's aim was to hold the upper South, especially Virginia and Maryland, loyal to the Union. Recalling these tense months, Lincoln's secretaries later labeled Maryland itself "of more immediate and vital importance than . . . any [other] border slave state."[3] Maryland surrounded the national capital on three sides, and her secession would have separated Washington from the remainder of the Union.

For Marylanders the dilemma of the state's position was acute. If the nation should tear apart, Maryland would be right on the seam;

[1] Only one instance of violence was reported in Baltimore on election day. A spitoon was hurled from Bell headquarters and struck a policeman, who unwisely pulled a revolver. The gun discharged accidentally, wounding another policeman. *Baltimore Sun*, November 7, 1860.

[2] Like most people, Marylanders expected Lincoln's election, which was, in the words of the *Frederick Examiner* (October 17, 1860), "a gloomy probability."

[3] John G. Nicolay and John Hay, *Abraham Lincoln: A History*, 10 vols. (New York: Century, 1917), 4: 93.

indeed, the state itself might be bisected. Maryland had a heterogeneous population, no natural line of defense to the North, no clear voice in national councils, and no immediately obvious course of action. Both sections watched Maryland with mixed hope and fear, while Marylanders themselves knew only that they faced grave danger. "May God in his mercy avert the dangers . . . which so threateningly . . . impend," said the *Frederick Herald*.[4]

Marylanders earnestly hoped that the Union would hold together. "We all wish that the Union shall be preserved intact," said the *Baltimore Sun*.[5] The Presbyterian churches of Baltimore called a mass "Union prayer meeting" shortly after the election.[6] Pleading for conciliation, Senator James A. Pearce said, "The Union has given us, for seventy years . . . a blessing of inestimable value."[7] Maryland's course throughout the1850s spoke of its citizens' devotion to the Union both by sentiment and by self-interest. But wishing would not make the crisis of allegiance go away.

The first reaction in Maryland to Lincoln's election was pro-Southern; Marylanders were at least partially inclined toward secession. The *Sun* erroneously labeled Breckinridge's Maryland victory "an appropriate demonstration in defense of Southern rights and institutions."[8] The North, the editors argued, had committed "practical disunion" by reneging on the fugitive slave law under the influence of "an intolerant minority," and they listed numerous Northern violations of Southern rights.[9] The columns of Maryland papers bristled with exciting, bellicose reports of the progress of secession in South Carolina and elsewhere. On November 12 the *Frederick Herald* urged a serious, deliberate consideration of secession for Maryland.[10] The *Centreville Advocate* and the *Patapsco Enterprise* decidedly leaned toward secession.[11] Thanksgiving Day, 1860, was celebrated in an atmosphere of unhappy excitement about the subject, reported John P. Kennedy.[12]

By the end of November, however, a calmer, more balanced approach seemed dominant. There was less talk of dissolving the

[4] November 12, 1860.
[5] November 16, 1860.
[6] *Ibid.*, November 19, 1860.
[7] Reprinted from the *Kent Conservator* in *ibid.*, November 27, 1860.
[8] *Ibid.*, November 7, 1860.
[9] *Ibid.*, November 8, 21, and 22, 1860.
[10] November 12, 1860.
[11] George L. P. Radcliffe, *Governor Thomas H. Hicks of Maryland and the Civil War*, The Johns Hopkins University Studies in Historical and Political Science, ser. 19 (Baltimore: The Johns Hopkins Press, 1901), p. 19.
[12] John P. Kennedy, Journal, November 29, 1860, John Pendleton Kennedy Papers, Peabody Institute Library, Baltimore, Md.

Union and more about saving it. Kennedy was correct when he said it was "scarcely possible that this wicked frenzy can last much longer."[13] Within a week after counseling possible secession. the *Frederick Herald* bemoaned the way newspapers kept the public agitated on that question when calm was needed. Wait for patriotism to reassert itself, the editor advised.[14] One week later that same journal advocated strict "neutrality."[15] The *Kent Conservator* recommended "prudence, calmness, deliberation."[16] On November 27 the *Sun* itself called for "calm, deliberate counsel," whereas two weeks earlier it had chided Mayor George W. Brown for giving the very same advice.[17]

Advice was plentiful, too plentiful, in fact. A babble of voices offered suggestions on what to do. The mayor of Balimore, on the one hand said that there was "no doubt about the course" Maryland should pursue—"adhere to the Union"—but then he added, "so long as she can do so with honor and safety."[18] On the other hand, a farmer from Carroll County took it for granted that "our sympathies are, of course, wholly with the South."[19] Demand our rights, suggested N in the *Sun,* then proceed to economic reprisals against the North, and, if that failed, secede.[20] "The *Frederick Herald* advocated "armed neutrality."[21] C sent his plan to the *Sun,* setting forth a very explicit set of steps to follow, from a first convention of fifteen Southern states, through suggested constitutional changes, and on to possible secession.[22] Yet another correspondent proposed strengthening the enforcement of the fugitive slave law in the North, and offered both a justification and a plan for secession.[23] Many Breckinridge organizers continued to meet weekly after the election as a kind of forum for arguing about the direction of events.[24] Yet this surfeit of discussion, advice, and plans added up to nothing.

The confusion and conflicting advice were maddening. A letter from Baltimore to the *New Orleans Picayune* described Baltimore as "almost paralyzed by the extreme excitement."[25] On November 11,

13 *Ibid.*, November 30, 1860.
14 November 20, 1860.
15 *Ibid.*, November 27, 1860.
16 Reprinted in the *Baltimore Sun,* November 27, 1860.
17 *Ibid.*, November 12 and 27, 1860.
18 *Ibid.*, November 12, 1860.
19 *Ibid.*, November 28, 1860.
20 *Ibid.*
21 November 27, 1860.
22 December 3, 1860.
23 *Ibid.*, December 9, 1860.
24 *Ibid.*, November 16, 1860.
25 Carl M. Freasure, "Union Sentiment in Maryland, 1856–1860," *Maryland Historical Magazine,* 24 (1929): 214.

the *Sun* ran as tortured and emotional an editorial as had ever appeared in that staid journal:

We talk of the value of the Union . . . but who can appraise it? . . . We are utterly at a loss for a single suggestion towards the result we all desire. We all wish that the Union shall be preserved intact, yet to propose so desirable a result, what can we say to the South? . . . "We think," says one; "We believe," says another; "Wait," says a third; "The Union," says a fourth; but not one feasible, rational, consistent, practical sentiment is to be found. In the meantime, the work of secession goes on [in the lower South], prepares for a demonstration, and hastens to a conclusion. And its people have us all at a disadvantage, because we can oppose no reasonable, convincing, constitutional argument against it.[26]

In the traditional New Year's Day editorial the *Sun* editors continued the note of pessimism. "All is uncertain, and conjecture is totally at fault in any attempt to outline, even the possible consequences of the sad and strange and unnatural rupture of our political Union."[27]

Erratic action supplemented the confusion of words. A group of "Southern Volunteers" materialized in Baltimore.[28] In nearby Reisterstown the pro-Southern element adopted the blue cockade as their emblem and called themselves "Minute Men."[29] The raising of Palmetto flags became for a time "all the rage" in Baltimore and its vicinity.[30] A militia regiment in Harford County petitioned the governor to muster it into active service so that it might defend Maryland from the "Black Republican hordes of the North."[31]

Pro-Union gatherings did not become widespread until December and January, but they did finally appear—in Frederick on January 5, in Baltimore on December 6 and January 10, in Cumberland on January 17, and then in many more places.[32] The resolutions of the Baltimore meeting of December 6 were typical: "If worse comes to worse . . . we will defend the State of Maryland in and not out of the Union."[33]

I

By the start of 1861 the trend in Maryland was towards Unionism. Two state leaders stood out as champions of the efforts to save the Union, and both endured a great deal of abuse for their efforts. Henry

26 November 16, 1860.
27 *Ibid.*, January 1, 1861.
28 *Ibid.*, November 24, 1860.
29 *Ibid.*
30 *Ibid.*, November 27 and December 1, 1860.
31 *Frederick Herald*, January 29, 1861.
32 *Baltimore Sun*, December 7, 1860.
33 *Ibid.*, December 7, 1860.

Winter Davis labored hard in Washington to fashion a compromise that would ease the crisis. In Annapolis, meanwhile, Governor Thomas Hicks became the center of the controversy over whether to call the General Assembly into special session.

In Washington, Henry Winter Davis was the most prominent Maryland spokesman. Discredited and unpopular at home, Davis nonetheless towered over the nonentities who made up the rest of the Maryland delegation.[34] Even though he was still technically a "South American"—a leftover Know-Nothing without a new affiliation—Davis had great influence in Republican councils. Overlooked now was his fight for preferment with Montgomery Blair, who also was a Marylander and a far more outspoken Republican party member. Davis was seriously considered for a cabinet post and, because of his long involvement in Maryland politics and his position in Congress, he was easily Maryland's noteworthy voice in Washington.[35]

Davis was a bright, educated, and energetic man. He originally came from Southern Maryland, but his home was Baltimore, where he had made an outstanding legal and political career. His speech was vigorous and direct, although his style—like his personal manner—tended too much toward sarcasm. His actions were usually pragmatic, whereas his justifications were dogmatic. Even to a shrewd and confident judge of statesmen like Henry Adams, Davis remained a puzzle.[36] He worked zealously through the secession winter to save the Union, yet his private correspondence revealed a tired and pessimistic man. As one of the few border-state congressmen with good connections to the incoming administration, he was under constant seige by office seekers. To his close friend DuPont he complained:

> If I wind up this letter with the formula of recommendation for an office don't suppose I am crazy . . . but merely that habit has overcome reason in this particular case. I fear I feel sure that as Napoleon died muttering *tété d'armee*, I should depart eulogizing the eminent fitness of some nobody for some place where nothing is to be done.[37]

[34] The Maryland congressional delegation consisted of Democrats James Stewart, Jacob Kunkel, and George W. Hughes, and Americans Davis, Edwin Webster, and J. M. Harris.

[35] Davis denied any cabinet ambitions or any claim to Lincoln's favor. He even disowned the efforts of his friends to secure him a cabinet post. Davis to Samuel F. DuPont, March 12, 1861, Samuel F. DuPont Papers, Eleutherian Mills Historical Library, Greenville, Del.

[36] See Henry Adams, "The Great Secession Winter of 1860–61," in his *The Great Secession Winter of 1860–61, and Other Essays*, ed. George Hochfield (New York: Sagamore Press, 1958).

[37] Davis to Samuel F. DuPont, March 12, 1861, DuPont Papers.

He had little confidence in the future. Buchanan's ambiguous message to Congress in December left him fuming.[38] Always decisive and vigorous, he chafed under the endless debate, the indecision, and his own powerlessness. He found the "South Americans" "utterly demoralized," and his fellow "conservatives" seemed "fools, fools."[39] "From now to the Fourth of March," he fretted, "is haymaking time for those who wish to make a safe revolution."[40]

Typical of Davis was his performance as Maryland's representative on the House Committee of Thirty-Three to study ways of compromising the secession crisis. Davis was a key man on the committee; he voted for its creation and participated actively in its work. Yet he professed to see no hope for the group's labors. "The Committee of Thirty-Three is a humbug . . . but as it will amuse men's minds it *may* do no harm. I voted for it—but why I don't know except that everybody seemed to be for it."[41] "I am getting utterly disgusted," he concluded.[42]

Davis's first active role in the Committee came shortly after it asembled. On December 13 he submitted a resolution urging Northern states to repeal all laws which acted to thwart the fugitive slave law—the so-called personal liberty laws; in doing this Davis squarely attacked one of the sorest points in the sectional quarrel and represented Maryland's interest well. The committee adopted these resolutions without difficulty.

Davis consistently sided with the Republicans on the committee. Because there were sixteen Republicans, Davis's vote could give them a majority even if all thirty-three men voted. For instance, on December 17, Thomas A. R. Nelson, of Tennessee, introduced a proposal to divide the Union once more along the Missouri Compromise Line. All Democrats and Southern Americans on the committee went for that idea—except Davis, who gave the Republicans a seventeenth negative vote to ensure defeat of the plan.[43] In this action Davis did not represent Maryland's sentiment accurately, since hostility to Republicans ran high in the state and since support for the Crittenden-Nelson plan was overwhelming there, among all parties.

Davis's next set of resolutions may have saved the Committee of Thirty-Three from breaking up completely. By December 20 the

[38] Davis to DuPont, undated, *ibid.*
[39] Davis to DuPont, January 1, 1861, *ibid.*
[40] Davis to DuPont, undated, *ibid.*
[41] *Ibid.*
[42] Davis to DuPont, January 1, 1861, *ibid.*
[43] David M. Potter, *Lincoln and His Party in the Secession Crisis* (New Haven and London: Yale University Press, 1942), p. 291.

committee was at an impasse. On December 14 Southern members had issued a manifesto declaring that "argument is exhausted" and that the situation was hopeless. For the next strained week these Southerners insisted that the Crittenden Compromise—which extended the old Missouri Compromise Line of 36° 30″ to the Pacific—was their absolute demand. The Northern members refused to accede, and dissolution of the committee seemed imminent. Blunt and unpredictable as usual, Davis on December 20 introduced resolutions for the admission of New Mexico and Kansas as states, slave and free respectively.[44] His proposals also required that any additional territory could be annexed to the United States only by a two-thirds vote of Congress and that in any such territory the status of slavery would be that which prevailed on that soil at the time of acquisition.

Coming from one who had been acting closely with the Republicans, these startling proposals caught the Southerners off guard, stalled their drive to break up the committee over the 36° 30″ line, and forced a week's adjournment for study. During that week tempers cooled, and the prospect of alternative compromises was intriguing enough to hold the committee together. Henry Adams, whose father, Charles Francis Adams, was on the committee, later asserted that Davis's bold stroke prevented permanent disruption of the debates and drove a wedge between the Border and the Gulf states.[45] The Republicans adopted Davis's resolutions in slightly revised form, and prestigious Charles F. Adams sponsored them. These measures were the first positive proposals advanced by the Republicans after their rejection of the Crittenden plan.

Davis's efforts came to nothing. At the turn of the year he predicted war within six months, and he saw it come to pass.[46] He would certainly be turned out of office himself in the next election. Thus he did his best to hide a genuine zeal to preserve the Union behind cynicism and wry humor. The one ray of cheer for Davis was the stubborn Unionism of his fellow American, Governor Thomas Holliday Hicks.[47]

[44] Charles Francis Adams, describing Davis's resolutions and their impact, said, "discussion was carried on rather heavily until Mr. Winter Davis first broke in with a cannon shot clear through the line." Charles Francis Adams, Diary, December 20, 1860, Charles Francis Adams Papers (microfilm), The Johns Hopkins University Library, Baltimore, Md.

[45] Henry Adams, *op. cit.*, pp. 18–21; see also Potter, *op. cit.*, pp. 290–91, 295. Davis explained to Charles Francis Adams that his purpose was "breaking the combinations they [the representatives of the seceding states] are trying to form." Charles Francis Adams, Diary, December 21, 1860, Adams Papers.

[46] Davis to Samuel F. DuPont, December 28, 1860, DuPont Papers.

[47] In Davis's correspondence and recorded remarks of this period there are many instances of praise for Hicks and his policy.

Hicks was an ordinary man, a farmer and state politician from the Eastern Shore who had moved up the ladder from county to state office. Once a Democrat, then a Whig, he served Dorchester County for two terms in the General Assembly. In 1857 it was the Eastern Shore's turn to provide Maryland's governor. As one of the more prominent and faithful of the new American party, Hicks won the Know-Nothing nomination and the election; he was fifty-nine years old.[48] Three years later he confronted a greater responsibility than any other Maryland governor has ever been asked to bear. A rather commonplace politician, at the end of his term, without a functioning party behind him, Hicks unavoidably encountered a situation of utmost peril. Nothing in his experience had prepared him for such a crisis.

Marylanders in 1860 thought in terms of a state response to the secession of the Deep South states and the inauguration of a "black Republican" president. As the secession crisis took shape they immediately began to ask, "What shall Maryland do?" The only existing agency which could plan a unified course of action was the state government. Since the legislature was not in session and was not scheduled to be so until 1862, Governor Hicks became the target for all demands that Maryland do something.

Specifically, a vocal segment of Marylanders asked Hicks to call the legislature into special session. Yet convening the General Assembly had definite hazards. For one thing, the older sections of the state, more involved with slavery and hence more inclined to be pro-Southern, were overrepresented in the legislature.[49] Furthermore, the General Assembly of 1860 had resolved "that should the hour ever arrive when the Union must be dissolved, Maryland will cast her lot with her sister states of the South and abide their fortune to the fullest extent." This was merely rhetoric when it was passed, but it was alarming rhetoric now that dissolution was in progress. Moreover, a legislative session would provide for a sharp, focused, intense debate, where rash action might be taken. The 1860 session of the General Assembly was certainly a discouraging precedent, having begun in bitterness, continued in confusion, and climaxed with chaos and pistol shots. "Public property and even private is in danger, and personal safety is at a discount should the legislature of this state be brought together," claimed one of Hicks's friends.[50] Hicks agreed.

[48] Hicks was a compromise candidate who had been chosen on the seventh ballot.

[49] The Eastern Shore and Southern Maryland had only 25.3 percent of the state's white population but controlled nearly half of the combined seats of the two houses of the General Assembly—forty-six of ninety-six places.

[50] Louis Schley to Thomas Hicks, Thomas Hicks Papers, Maryland Historical Society, Baltimore.

For a long time Hicks resisted the pressure to call the legislature. Contemporaries and historians alike have blamed him for cowardice and vacillation in this matter,[51] but, had he been a weakling, Hicks would have run from the sole responsibility for Maryland's course and turned the matter over to the General Assembly. He resisted, however, because he desired to keep Maryland in the Union and because he feared the consequences of secession for his border state.

Hicks's devotion to the Union was firm. He intended "to uphold the Union . . . until every honorable and constitutional and legal effort is exhausted."[52] He held that Lincoln's election was no cause for secession. Indeed, he even insisted that the president-elect might turn out satisfactorily if given opportunity and support.[53] He wrote to Mississippi Governor A. H. Handy that the proper description of Maryland was "conservative, and above all things devoted to the Union."[54] When he received word of Mississippi's secession he scribbled on the envelope, "Mississippi has seceded and gone to the devil."[55] "Disunion is no remedy for southern wrongs," Hicks was quoted as saying in the *National Intelligencer,* "and Maryland should not seem to give countenance to it by convening her legislature at the bidding of South Carolina."[56]

Hicks offered his cautious support to the incoming Lincoln administration. In March he wrote to Secretary of State William Seward "to beg that the appointments for Maryland be deferred for a time. . . . Everything depends upon proper appointments to leading places in border states." He then continued: "I am not a Republican, but a Union man and supporter of your Administration as far as it may be wise and proper, and, thus far I have no fault with it. You gentlemen do not understand as I do the condition of things here and in the border states." He said that he wrote "not as a member of your party, but [as] one ready to aid you by faithful advice, and to hold up your hands as far as I can."[57]

The governor claimed to have definite information, from private sources, that, if convened, the legislature would at once declare in

[51] See, for example, the sketch of Hicks in Henrich E. Buchholz, *Governors of Maryland* (Baltimore: Williams & Wilkins, 1908).

[52] Frank Moore, ed., *The Rebellion Record,* 9 vols. (New York: G. P. Putnam's Sons, 1861–1868), 1: 109.

[53] Open letter from Hicks to Thomas G. Pratt *et al., Baltimore Sun,* November 29, 1860.

[54] Moore, *op. cit.,* 1: 109.

[55] Radcliffe, *op. cit.,* p. 35.

[56] Freasure, *op. cit.,* p. 215.

[57] Thomas H. Hicks to William H. Seward, March 28, 1861, Abraham Lincoln Papers, Library of Congress, Washington, D.C., and The Johns Hopkins University Library (microfilm), Baltimore, Md.

favor of the seceding states and authorize emissaries to deal with them in Maryland's name.[58] The federal capital would then be separated from the North, and civil war would result. On December 1, 1860, a writer for the *National Intelligencer* warned Hicks of a plot by seceders in the District of Columbia to organize their friends in Maryland.[59] While addressing a delegation from Talbot County in January, Hicks spoke of the plan to seize Washington as a reality, even noting that a force of 8,000 men was at that moment organized for the purpose. This frightening information, he said, was from "sources not accessible to the people of the state."[60] On February 19, however, the governor told a congressional investigating committee that he understood that the plot, though once quite active, had been abandoned as hopeless.[61] Hicks was not alone in believing in the existence of such a conspiracy.[62]

Certainly the appeals to call the legislature had a pro-Southern, even secessionist, tone about them. The resolutions of two separate Talbot County meetings connected the calling of the legislature with a declaration that Maryland was a Southern state.[63] Some Harford County citizens wanted the General Assembly convened so that it could call a convention specifically empowered to "entertain" the idea of seceding.[64] Prolegislature, anti-Hicks resolves were paired at a gathering of Southern sympathizers in Frederick.[65] In the course of a very pro-Southern speech the captain of a Carroll County militia group damned Hick's inactivity on the legislature question.[66]

Unionists, on the other hand, supported Hicks. Henry Winter Davis saw the beleaguered governor as the only hope for saving the District of Columbia from the disunionists.[67] Unionists in Baltimore County condemned secession and endorsed Hicks's course in separate resolutions; so did a meeting in Annapolis.[68] Unionist meetings in Perryville, Cosgrove's Mills, and other places in Cecil County supported Hicks's inactivity.[69] The Boonsboro (Washington County) *Odd Fellow* approvingly dubbed Hicks "Old Gibraltar."[70] At a Worcester County

58 *Cecil Whig* (Elkton, Md.), January 19, 1861; and *Baltimore Sun*, January 21, 1861.
59 Unknown correspondent to Governor Hicks, December 1, 1860, Hicks Papers.
60 *Cecil Whig*, January 19, 1861. The words are the reporter's, not Hicks's.
61 *Baltimore Sun*, February 14, 1861.
62 See *ibid.*, January 16 and 22, 1861; and *Cecil Whig*, March 2, 1861.
63 *Baltimore Sun*, January 19 and February 3, 1861.
64 *Ibid.*, January 10, 1861.
65 *Ibid.*, January 15, 1861.
66 *Ibid.*
67 Davis to Samuel F. DuPont, January 13 and 26, 1861, DuPont Papers.
68 *Baltimore Sun*, January 11, 12, and 24, 1861.
69 *Cecil Whig*, January 19, 26, and February 2, 1861.
70 *Ibid.*, January 19.

gathering the introduction of anti-Hicks resolutions made several Unionists leave the hall.[71] Future Maryland Governor Augustus W. Bradford, a firm Unionist, supported Hicks.[72] Senator James A. Pearce was the only visible Unionist who said early in 1861 that a special session should be called, and he took this position only because he believed that Unionist sentiment would prevail there.[73]

As the winter passed, the pressures on Hicks increased from all sides. From friends of Lincoln's he received encouragement, entreaties never to "waver from [your] high and noble stand," and "authorized" promises from the president-elect to ask Hicks about Maryland patronage.[74] From a Union mass meeting in Philadelphia came a letter of effulgent praise which was designed to keep Hicks firm in his course.[75] Mississippi, Alabama, and Georgia, on the other hand, all sent representatives to see the Maryland governor.[76] Papers which had previously endorsed Hicks were calling him a "despot" by January.[77] An anonymous Southron threatened to shoot Hicks, "if it takes twenty years," because the governor was "a damned black Republican."[78] Teagle Townsend, state senator from Worcester County, openly announced his intention of going to Annapolis to "offer . . . personal violence" to Hicks, and he received an ovation from his audience.[79]

Through all the pressure, Hicks believed he represented the best interests of Maryland and the majority sentiment as well.[80] "I think I know the sentiment of . . . [Maryland's] citizens in this matter," he told the governor of Mississippi.[81] In pursuit of his stout conservatism Hicks limited himself to one positive official act. The state of Virginia issued a call for a "Peace Conference" to bring together representatives from each state to seek a remedy for the national crisis. Hicks appointed seven commissioners to act in Maryland's name when the conference convened in Washington on February 4, 1861. The Maryland delegation was headed up by venerable Reverdy Johnson, but consisted of such a cluster of colorless individuals that it excited

71 *Baltimore Sun,* February 8, 1861.

72 *Cecil Whig,* January 26, 1861.

73 *Baltimore Sun,* January 14, 1861.

74 J. M. Lucas to Governor Hicks, January 11, 1861, Hicks Papers. The Lincoln administration did ask Hicks about patronage.

75 G. H. Mindel to Governor Hicks, March 14, 1861, *ibid.*

76 George Beall, "The Persuasion of Maryland to Join the Federal Union" (typescript), Maryland Historical Society, Baltimore, p. 15.

77 See, for example, *Frederick Herald,* January 22, 1861.

78 "Southern Rights" to Governor Hicks, April 23, 1861, Hicks Papers.

79 B. Everett Smith to Governor Hicks, April 24, 1861, *ibid.* The letter was hand-carried to Annapolis because the public mails were deemed unsafe.

80 Open letter to Thomas G. Pratt *et al.*, *Baltimore Sun,* November 29, 1860.

81 Moore, *op. cit.,* 1: 109.

considerable complaint.[82] The conference met for two weeks and recommended an amendment to the Constitution along the same lines as the Crittenden compromise. Congress took no action on the recommendation.

Though Hicks was ultimately forced to convene the legislature, he bought time for Unionism. The anti-Hicks movement was very strong around New Year's Day. Then a note of caution began to enter the endless arguments in the press and in the public meetings. As time went by, the conservative Unionist element began to reassert itself, led by commercial interests and rallied by Hicks's stubborness. Eventually the "activists"—as I shall call those who were pushing for a special legislative session or a convention or both—found themselves unable to plan and execute a program.[83]

When the governor remained firm against calling the General Assembly, frustrated activists sought to take matters into their own hands. Early in January, for example, a meeting in Prince George's County resolved that, should Hicks remain unmoved by the tenth of the month, the Speaker of the House of Delegates and the president of the Senate would be justified in calling a session.[84] Most activists, however, saw the unconstitutionality of such a move, and preferred instead to move directly toward the object for which the General Assembly was to be convened—a state convention.[85]

[82] Maryland sent seven men to the "peace conference": Reverdy Johnson, A. W. Bradford, William Goldsborough, John Crisfield, J. Dixon Roman, Benjamin C. Howard, and John F. Dent. Dent almost always voted with the Virginia delegation, dissenting from Maryland's vote whenever that was ranged against Virginia. With the exception of Dent, the Maryland delegation acted as a broker between the demands of the Northern and Southern delegations. The convention was reported briefly in Crafts J. Wright, *Official Journal of the Conference Convention Held at Washington City, February, 1861* (Washington: M'Gill & Witherow, 1861), and more completely, though unofficially, in Lucius E. Chittenden, *Debates and Proceedings of the Conference Convention, 1861* (New York: D. Appleton & Co., 1864).

[83] The choice of terms here is delicate. "Secessionist" would definitely be too strong a sobriquet for these people. "Southern sympathizers" also is misleading, as well as a bit awkward. I have chosen the term "activists" because it sums up the common denominator shared by all shades of opinion within the convention movement—they all sought to move Maryland into some positive, active response to the crisis, in contrast to the policy of inertia favored by the governor.

[84] *Baltimore Sun*, January 4, 1861.

[85] For the legislature to assemble itself was clearly unconstitutional; only the governor could call an extra session. A popular convention was certainly extra-constitutional; the basic law made no mention of it. The movement for a popular convention had the advantage of being at least not directly forbidden, since it was not intended to propose amendments to the state constitution. In addition, the threat of an unofficial popular convention had brought about desired changes in the state constitution in 1836 and 1850.

The movement for a popular convention was afoot by January 1861. It began in a plethora of local meetings. There was no clarion call, but rather a spontaneous combustion of frustration. All counties and Baltimore were represented at an activist meeting in Baltimore on January 10 and 11. Some localities had so little time to organize a delegation that citizens from that area who happened to be in Baltimore on the tenth were, in effect, drafted for the meeting.

This Baltimore convention had no clear mandate or direction; on the contrary, the first day was spent in fierce bickering which revealed considerable pro-Hicks sentiment from the Northern counties. On January 11 the meeting managed to report a set of milk-and-water compromise resolutions which paid tribute to the "Union," gave a strong vote of confidence to the Crittenden proposals then before Congress, and made a feeble request that Hicks call not a convention but merely a referendum on whether or not to have a convention.[86] The activists who organized the meetings must have been dismayed by the meekness of the resolutions. This first effort in Baltimore foreshadowed the curious impotence of the convention movement.

On February 2 a local meeting was held in Baltimore. The dais was overloaded with Breckinridge Democrats who praised the constitution, damned Hicks, and vowed to go with the South if a real split should come. From this group came a call for a state meeting in the metropolis on February 18, to consider specifically the calling of a convention.

Delegates to the state meeting of February 18 to consider a popular convention talked tougher, but acted no more vigorously, than their predecessors of January 11. Six county delegations missed the start of the session. Again the meeting required two days to agree on a set of resolutions. Instead of calling for a convention, the resolutions simply said that one was desired. The meeting then adjourned until March 12, both to give Hicks time to act and also to confront him with a deadline.[87] Significantly, this meant that Maryland would do nothing until well after Lincoln's inauguration on March 4. Furthermore, by appealing once more to the obstinate Hicks, the delegates exposed their own deep reservations about the drastic, even illegal, nature of an unofficial convention.

The activists spent enormous amounts of effort on nothing; the proposed call for a convention never materialized. The March 12 meeting limited itself to appointing six observers to the Virginia

[86] *Baltimore Sun,* January 11 and 12, 1861.
[87] *Ibid.,* February 18 and 20, 1861.

convention, which was in session.[88] By this time, cautious Unionism was ascendent in Maryland.

The activists and avowed secessionists almost always proved to be former Breckinridge supporters. Though by no means all Breckinridge voters were pushing Maryland toward the Southern Confederacy, the pre-eminence of Breckinridge Democrats in the pro-Southern meetings and in the convention movement was overwhelming. For example, Oden Bowie, Breckinridge man from Prince George's County, asked the legislative officers to call a special session on their own, without the governor.[89] In charge of the Baltimore activist meeting of February 2 were Joshua Vasant, A. C. Robinson, S. Teackle Wallis, Charles Wethered, T. Parkin Scott, Benjamin Presstman, C. J. M. Gwinn, and E. M. Kilgour–Breckinridge Democrats to a man. They issued the call for the state convention, which met on February 18 and passed resolutions condemning Hicks and Davis in strong language.[90] In this meeting the lead was taken by such Breckinridge men as J. C. Groome, former Governor Lowe, John Contee, and Augustus R. Sollers.[91] Lowe and Kilgour presided over a Frederick meeting which passed, in the words of the *Baltimore Sun,* "strong Southern resolutions." The *Cecil Whig* exaggerated only slightly when it belittled the activists as a "portion of the late Breckinridge party."[92]

The Unionists were in an awkward position; they could take little positive action except to hold on and hope for the best. Defense of the status quo always makes a weaker rallying point than some dramatic change. Alarmed at the uproar created by the convention movement, the *Frederick Examiner* pleaded with the Unionists to organize, lest the "minority of disunionists . . . overcome the conservatism of the Union men and drag Maryland into the revolution."[93] On the other hand, Unionists were aided by the inertia of the situation; Maryland was, after all, in the Union and it would take a terrific wrench to move it out. Although the Unionists managed to hold only one statewide meeting before April 19–in Baltimore on January 10–the unanimity and enthusiasm of that meeting were impressive. Contrast the evasive resolutions of the proconvention meetings with the unequivocal stand of the Unionists, who declared that they held the Union sacred and pledged: "we will discountenance whatever may

88 The delegates as to the Virginia convention urged that meeting to regard Hicks as totally unrepresentative of Maryland.

89 *Baltimore Sun,* January 4, 1861.

90 *Ibid.,* February 2, 1861.

91 *Ibid.,* February 19, 1861.

92 *Cecil Whig,* January 17, 1861.

93 Reprinted in *ibid.,* March 2, 1861.

suggest even a suspicion that it [the Union] can in any event be abandoned."[94]

Bell, Douglas, and Lincoln supporters worked together in efforts to support the Union. Bell-Everett politicians from 1860 showed up prominently in Unionist meetings in 1861. John P. Kennedy was one. Baltimore merchant Brantz Mayer was another. Comptroller Purnell and Governor Hicks himself were both Americans and Unionists, as were Senator James A. Pearce and future Governor Augustus W. Bradford. Most Bell-Everett newspapers were later Unionist in their editorial policy. Douglas Democrats like Henry F. May—Davis's long-time foe—were conspicuous Unionists who said flatly that Maryland could defend her honor better in the Union than out of it.[95] Reverdy Johnson, the leading Douglas Democrat in Maryland, worked tirelessly to preserve the Union and served on the Maryland delegation to the peace convention. Charles F. Mayer, cousin of Brantz Mayer, stood solidly for Douglas in 1860 and for the Union in 1861. Douglas Democrat Samuel S. Maffitt later ran for comptroller on the Union ticket headed by Bradford.

In the counties of Maryland the Bell, Lincoln, and Douglas voters were doubtless as Unionist as their leaders. The entire Constitutional Union campaign in Maryland was aimed at saving the Union, downplaying sectionalism, and reasserting the spirit of compromise exemplified by Clay and the other great departed Whig statesmen. Kennedy represented such a spirit of compromise. So did Henry Winter Davis, for all his consorting with Republicans. A majority of the Douglas voters of November also could be counted as Unionists during the succeeding months. The handful of Lincoln voters were most likely to be Unionists.

Unionism, then, was the majority sentiment in the counties of Maryland early in 1861. If a majority of the Bell, Douglas, and Lincoln voters were antisecessionist, the 1860 vote gives a rough indication of Unionist strength. In the counties of Maryland, Bell, Douglas, and Lincoln totaled 54 percent of the vote to Breckinridge's 46 percent. Though some of these non-Breckinridge voters may later have favored a league with the seceding states, that portion must have been small, and it was probably balanced by Breckinridge voters who later could not face the actuality of secession for Maryland.

Baltimore, as usual, was something of an anomaly. Although the city went for Breckinridge, the majority there was probably Unionist, too. The Breckinridge vote was not a true indication of Baltimoreans' identification with the Southern rights position. Commercial interests

[94] *Baltimore Sun*, January 11, 1861.
[95] *Ibid.*, February 18 and 20, 1861.

led the city cautiously to support the national government and Hicks's conservative position.

In 1861 Baltimore was a manufacturing and commercial center of the first magnitude. The key to the town's success was trade. This trade moved on two major arteries, the Chesapeake Bay and the Baltimore and Ohio Railroad; the Chesapeake and Ohio Canal and the rail lines to central Pennsylvania and Philadelphia did a brisk business, too. Much of the Bay trade was to or from South America. From that area Baltimore imported principally guano, coffee, and copper ore; out through the Bay went flour, grain, coal, and miscellaneous provisions like boots, textiles, clothing, and hardware.[96] The Bay also allowed a thriving coastal trade to and from the Northeast, a trade which was supplemented by rail connections to Harrisburg and Philadelphia. This trade sent out agricultural and mining products, as well as some finished goods, in exchange for manufactured items that were to be sold by Baltimore's commission merchants. Baltimore's interior trade via the Baltimore and Ohio Railroad and the Chesapeake and Ohio Canal brought in lumber, grain, livestock, coal, and even some cotton. Out to the interior went a vast assortment of finished goods and South American imports. Summarizing Baltimore's trade in 1860, one authority estimated that for Baltimore merchants the western connections were at least as important as the Southern markets and had greater potential for growth, while trade with the Northeast was the most lucrative of all.[97] The romance of Southern rights and Maryland's aristocratic colonial heritage paled before the cold facts of commerce in 1861.

Ideally for business, of course, the Union would remain intact. Secession of the lower South meant loss of markets, loss of cotton supply (not as crucial in Maryland as elsewhere), and probable loss of outstanding debts. Manufacturers also feared that a tariff-free South would flood the American continent with cheaper European goods. But, should the Union finally, tragically divide, Maryland's commercial interests dictated that the state should stay with the North. If Maryland joined the South the cherished Baltimore and Ohio would very likely be cut off at the Alleghenies, certainly at the Ohio, Since the South would have no navy, Chesapeake Bay trade would be at the mercy of the federal fleet, and would probably be shut off altogether. The indefensibility of Maryland's border with Pennsylvania was not lost on Maryland's merchants either.

Some Marylanders did put forth commercial arguments for a

[96] William B. Catton, "The Baltimore Business Community and the Secession Crisis, 1860–1861" (Master's thesis, University of Maryland, 1952), *passim*.
[97] *Ibid.*, pp. 78–85.

Southern connection, maintaining that Maryland would be the New York of the South, leaping instantly from third place in American commerce to economic dominance of Dixie.[98] Persons who argued so were not often in commerce themselves,[99] and such blandishments were largely lost on Maryland businessmen. Even if Baltimore survived the terrors of losing the western and Bay trade, the city would unquestionably lose the geographic advantage of being centrally located; as a Southern port, Baltimore would be far out on the periphery.

The businessmen of Baltimore could feel the threat of a divided Union already in the winter of 1860/1861; the mere prospect of a national schism was sufficient to depress trade. One observer noted of Baltimore:

> Stocks have gone down to almost nothing and many dealers therein are ruined. The banks have great difficulty in accommodating their customers. Money is abundant but capitalists will not let it out. . . . The leading hotel was reported to have closed more than half of its house and discharged two thirds of its servants. Other public houses in Baltimore were said to have suffered in proportion.[100]

The mayor's message to the city council complained, "The political troubles which now convulse the country have diminished the value of all descriptions of property and seriously interfered with business of every kind."[101] Compared with trade in December 1859, traffic on the Baltimore and Ohio Railroad in December 1860 was down by some $19,000, or 5.5 percent. The *Baltimore Sun* added morosely, "The onset of winter promises not fun and games, but the present gloomy aspect of business affairs, the dearth of employment in most of the mechanical branches, and the high cost of . . . the necessaries of life betoken a greater degree of suffering [than usual]."[102]

Faced with disaster, most of Baltimore's businessmen saw secession as its cause and consequently favored maintenance of the Union as its cure. Far more businessmen approved Hicks's inactive policy than condemned it. Two petitions from Baltimore which upheld the governor were dominated by businessmen's signatures—one with 1,300 signatures in December and a larger, 5,000-signature petition in Janu-

[98] See, for example, "Baltimore and the Southern Trade," *Baltimore Sun,* March 20, 1861.

[99] For example, Coleman Yellott made such a case in the columns of the *Sun* on January 26, 1861; Yellott was a lawyer.

[100] Freasure, *op. cit.,* p. 214. The hotel referred to was probably Barnum's, generally considered the best in Baltimore in 1860.

[101] *Baltimore Sun,* January 8, 1861. Remember that Brown was himself a businessman, a banker, and one of the wealthiest men of the city.

[102] *Ibid.,* November 21, 1860. See also *ibid.,* February 2, 1861.

ary. [103] Numerous Baltimore businessmen were active in Union meetings. At one point a large group of them chartered a Bay steamer to attend a Union rally in Easton.[104]

The commercial giant of Baltimore, the Baltimore and Ohio Railroad, led the way to Unionism. Under the direction of John W. Garrett the line offered its services to the national government immediately after the firing on Fort Sumter. Alexander Stephens later remarked, "the real crisis was passed in those early months, after the fall of Fort Sumter, when the South was waiting for Maryland to act, and Lincoln prevented the state from seceding—largely because of the fact that the overwhelming influence exerted by the Baltimore and Ohio was exerted in favor of the Washington government."[105] Lincoln called Garrett "the right arm of the Government in the aid he rendered the authorities in preventing the Confederates from seizing Washington."[106] Ironically, John Garrett's older brother, Henry, was a Southern sympathizer. The split between the Garretts was symbolic. Henry was still associated with the traditional family commercial and banking business. John was one of the new breed, younger, involved with the growing national economy and its prime mover, the railroad; he rejected the traditions and chose the Union.

"Workingmen" followed employers in their loyalty.[107] The three workingmen's meetings which are on record all strongly condemned secession, in Baltimore on January 9, in neighboring Towson on January 17, and in Annapolis on March 2.[108] Resolves of the Baltimore meeting declared that Maryland's industrial pursuits would be ruined by dissolution of the Union. "We are made to suffer by the present condition of the country," continued the resolutions, "and our situation may become more embarrassed if things continue as they are."[109] The miners of the western counties, especially Allegany, also were solidly Unionist.[110]

[103] Catton, *op. cit.*, p. 61. Freasure (*op. cit.*, p. 215) said that "nine-tenths of the business class of the city" signed the January petition. Hicks was also hailed by a meeting of merchants in Philadelphia. *Baltimore Sun,* March 14, 1861.

[104] Catton, *op. cit.*, p. 45.

[105] Harold A. Williams, *Robert Garrett and Sons* (Baltimore: Schneidereith & Sons, 1965), p. 42.

[106] *Ibid.*

[107] "Workingmen" is another of those troublesome, vague designations. As used at the meetings described here, it seems to denote skilled workers, but not necessarily self-employed workers. Unskilled laborers apparently were not "workingmen," but all conclusions about the group must be tentative and cautious for lack of precise evidence.

[108] *Baltimore Sun,* January 10, 19, and March 3, 1861.

[109] *Ibid.*, January 10, 1861.

[110] Katherine A. Harvey, *The Best-Dressed Miners: Life and Labor in the Maryland Coal Region* (Ithaca: Cornell University Press, 1969), pp. 146–49.

The Unionism that was numerically dominant in Maryland by spring 1861 was, it must be admitted, fragile. Most Marylanders, even those who denounced secession as illegal and unjustified, saw the North as the aggressor in the sectional conflict. Marylanders were especially sensitive to Northern disregard of the fugitive slave laws. Unionists also shared with the activists a high regard for the Crittenden Compromise proposals. Approval of the plan was automatic at every one of the numerous meetings held that winter, by all parties. Also, although the Unionists had the numbers, the activists had the more emotional case. In this situation Maryland could be severed from the Union by an explosion of feeling which overrode interest, blotted out reason, and substituted rage. Two incidents in the spring of 1861 threatened the control of the Unionists over the state.

II

President-elect Abraham Lincoln was scheduled to pass through Baltimore on Saturday, February 23, at the end of the speaking tour which wound up in Washington just ten days before his inauguration. Maryland newspapers reported Lincoln's progress through the North and East and carried synopses or even texts of the speeches he made on the way. His coming was anticipated with curiosity, excitement, and considerable alarm. A group of Baltimore Republicans petitioned Marshall of Police George P. Kane for protection and permission to accompany the president-elect in Baltimore and to hold a brief rally in his honor. Kane refused them, saying that it was a dangerous idea and that he could not promise protection. The *American,* which reported Kane's reaction, approved of it and called Lincoln "particularly obnoxious to the people and public sentiment of Baltimore.[111] The failure of the city authorities to plan a welcome for the president-elect or even to allow his followers to do so, was an ominous sign of ill-will. Dominant Unionism notwithstanding, Lincoln's passage through the state would be dangerous.

Baltimore was the riskiest stop on the president-elect's entire itinerary, not only because of the hostile sentiment there, but because of the physical arrangements that were required for his trip. Four passenger depots were scattered in various parts of Baltimore; all passengers from the North had to change trains in the city, and had to go from one depot to another through city streets. Lincoln was scheduled to arrive from Harrisburg, Pennsylvania, at the Calvert Street station around midday on Saturday, February 23, and to cross Baltimore by carriage to the Baltimore and Ohio tracks, stopping on

[111] February 26, 1861.

the way to greet well-wishers at the Eutaw House Hotel. The journey through the city streets would be well over a mile long.

As February 23 neared, Lincoln's friends began to hear alarming reports of trouble to come in Baltimore. Chicago detective Allan Pinkerton, originally hired by the Philadelphia, Wilmington, and Baltimore Railroad to protect their tracks and Bay ferries from secessionist sabotage, was working undercover in Baltimore when he discovered a group of Southern sympathizers plotting to assassinate Lincoln on his way through the city. Pinkerton was quite sure that the conspirators were in earnest; he later revealed details of the plot and named one of the leaders, a barber named Cypriano Ferrandini.[112] According to Pinkerton, a small band, chosen by lot from a larger group of conspirators, would create a row at the Calvert Street station, divert the police, and strike down the president-elect. A Bay steamer would be waiting to take the assassins to Virginia. On February 21, the alarmed Pinkerton rushed to Philadelphia, where Lincoln and his party were stopped at the Continental Hotel. Through fellow Chicagoan Norman B. Judd, the dectective met Lincoln privately and warned him to go to Washington without delay and without a ceremonial stop in Baltimore.

The weary Lincoln was skeptical, and, besides, he was scheduled to go to Harrisburg to meet the legislature and make a speech on Friday, the twenty-second; from there he would leave for Baltimore. He resolved to stick to his itinerary. But immediately after he left Pinkerton, Lincoln received a second and completely independent confirmation of the plot's existence. Frederick Seward, son of William H. Seward, was waiting in Lincoln's room, and told him that a group of New York city police detectives engaged by his father and himself had also found out about the would-be assassins.[113] Neither set of detectives knew about the other, and Lincoln was then convinced that the danger was real enough to warrant a change in schedule.

Lincoln went to Harrisburg on February 22 as arranged, but he did not wait for the Northern Central train to Baltimore on the morning of the twenty-third. Instead, he disguised himself with a soft wool cap pulled low, and left secretly that evening for Philadelphia

[112] The basic account of Lincoln's passage through Baltimore is taken from the judicious study by Norma Cuthbert, ed., *Lincoln and the Baltimore Plot, 1861* (San Marino, Calif.: Huntington Library, 1949). Cypriano Ferrandini was listed in the *Baltimore City Directory* in 1860, and for many years afterward, as a hairdresser and barber. Despite Pinkerton's positive assertion of Ferrandini's deep involvement with an assassination conspiracy, no legal action was ever taken against him.

[113] Whether the assassins uncovered by the New York detectives and those scouted by Pinkerton were the same is not known. It is conceivable that at least two separate plots on Lincoln's life existed.

by a special Pennsylvania Railroad train. Someone cut the telegraph lines to keep the president-elect's movements unknown. From Philadelphia he went to Baltimore by a special Philadelphia, Wilmington, and Baltimore train on the night of February 22/23. The rail line from Philadelphia terminated on the eastern edge of the harbor at the President Street station. Before dawn Lincoln passed through the city; because the cars could be drawn by horse from the President Street station to the Baltimore and Ohio tracks, Lincoln did not have to expose himself, as he would have if he had taken the train from Harrisburg. The secrecy was perfect, and the trip went off without incident. Lincoln and his party arrived in Washington around 6:00 A.M., February 23, roughly the time he was originally scheduled to leave Harrisburg.

In Baltimore on the twenty-third a large crowd gathered to see Lincoln. Perhaps ten to fifteen thousand people assembled near the Calvert Street station. Some were merely curious, others were outright hostile. The rumor circulated that Lincoln was already in Washington, but no one believed it. Finally the train arrived, carrying only Mrs. Lincoln and the children. Shouts and threats greeted the train; several persons called derisively for "the damned black Republican."[114] The crowd was stunned and angry to learn that the rumor was true and that Lincoln was already in the capital. Mrs. Lincoln and her party made their way nervously through the crowd and got out of town pushed and shaken and occasionally insulted, but unharmed.

Whether or not a plot to assassinate Lincoln existed and was actually going to be carried through[115]—it is fairly certain that at least some plans of this sort had been made—the emotional effect of Lincoln's midnight trip through Maryland was dismal. Unionists were embarrassed

[114] Cuthbert, *op. cit.*, p. 134. The description of Mrs. Lincoln's experience in Baltimore is essentially that given by a *New York Times* reporter. In their remembered biography of Lincoln his two secretaries, Nicolay and Hay, recalled the scene differently and said that the party had no difficulty. *Ibid.* Clearly, the contemporaneous account by the reporter squares with the facts of the Baltimore mob and its mood.

[115] Considerable controversy exists over the seriousness of the danger to Lincoln in Baltimore, and the various conflicting accounts by contemporaries are not much help. I agree with Pinkerton's view that a plot existed; it is highly improbable that he invented all the evidence and agents reports which Miss Cuthbert unearthed and reprinted in the volume cited above. But even Pinkerton was uncertain that the conspirators really had the nerve to go through with murder. If they had, the crowd scene at the station would have been perfect for their purposes. One Maryland Republican was definitely of the opinion that Lincoln's midnight trip was necessary. William Louis Schley was in Baltimore on the morning of the twenty-third, probably as a friendly greeter for the president-elect. He later wrote Lincoln that the conspiracy was "*meditated* and *determined.* By your course you have saved *bloodshed and a mob.*" Schley to Abraham Lincoln, February 23, 1861, Lincoln Papers; italics in the original.

and infuriated because confidence in the incoming administration was nearly wiped out by the Baltimore escapade, and that made their position more difficult. The *Sun* summarized the overwhelming disgust of most Marylanders: "Had we any respect for Mr. Lincoln . . . [this] would have utterly destroyed it."[116] Lincoln seemed cowardly because of the precaution, or, if not cowardly, ridiculous. The spectacle of the chief executive smuggling himself into the capital in disguise was completely disheartening. Some Marylanders were offended to think that Lincoln held them in so little regard as to shun them entirely; that they had snubbed him first made no difference. Mayor Brown later complained that the people of Baltimore were not only slighted but slandered.

> If Mr. Lincoln had arrived in Baltimore at the time expected, and had spoken a few words to the people who had gathered to hear him, expressing the kind feelings which were in his heart with the simple eloquence of which he was so great a master, he could not have failed to make a very different impression from that which was produced not only by the want of confidence and respect manifested towards the city of Baltimore by the plan pursued, but still more by the manner in which it was carried out. . . . Fearful accounts of the conspiracy flew all over the country, creating a hostile feeling against the city, from which it soon afterwards suffered.[117]

Lincoln himself recognized the damage the trip had done. "You . . . know," he told Ward Lamon, who had been with him on the trip, "that the way we skulked into this city [Washington] has been a source of shame and regret to me, for it did look so cowardly!"[118] Presidential prestige, already perilously low in Maryland, virtually disappeared on February 23.

The Unionist cause weathered that setback, however, and regained its strength through March 1861. Lincoln was inaugurated without incident on the fourth. The last feeble convention of the activists adjourned on March 13. Except for the alarming situation of the federal troops under seige in Charleston Harbor, excitement waned for a time. Marylanders waited. Then, on April 12, firing on Fort Sumter began, and civil war with it.

III

Marylanders were stunned, if not totally surprised, by the firing on Fort Sumter. John P. Kennedy noted ironically that war had broken

116 February 25, 1861.

117 George William Brown, *Baltimore and the Nineteenth of April, 1861* (Baltimore: N. Murray, 1887), p. 12.

118 Cuthbert, *op. cit.*, p. xv.

out on Henry Clay's birthday.[119] Lincoln responded with a call for 75,000 troops to put down the armed rebellion against the United States. Of this number, Maryland was asked to supply four regiments (3,120 men) to aid in subduing what many Marylanders were accustomed to calling "our sister States of the South." Federal forces prepared to pass over Maryland soil to protect the threatened national capital. Everyone knew that Maryland's role was crucial, but no one knew for sure what to do. On April 16 and 17 crowds milled through the streets of Baltimore gathering especially near the offices of the *Sun* and *American* on Baltimore Street. Fistfights between persons of different views were common; agitation was universal.

The opening of hostilities and the call for troops put Hicks on the spot. Resisting the call for a special session was one thing, but denying the president's demand for troops was quite another. Evasion was no longer possible. The governor must, it seemed, either uphold the Republican administration or defy it. Hicks, however, found one more compromise to try, although the middle ground was shrinking under him. He hurried to Washington on April 15 and saw Lincoln, General Winfield Scott, and Secretary of War Cameron. Able to impress upon them the dangers of asking Marylanders to participate in "coercion" of the South, he secured a promise from the administration that no troops raised in Maryland would be asked to leave the state except to guard the District of Columbia from attack. The next day, April 16, Hicks told John P. Kennedy of the arrangement, and two telegrams sent by Secretary Cameron on the seventeenth confirmed in writing what Hicks had been assured of earlier.[120] For the time being, Hicks made no move to summon any troops.

With this problem at least temporarily solved, the next crisis came over the transport of troops to Washington from the North. Troops had to cross Maryland to reach the capital. Given the temper of Marylanders, their divided sympathies, and clear opposition to the use of force against the South, violence could be avoided only by the most adroit handling of the situation. There being neither time nor wisdom enough for adroitness, Maryland nearly erupted into open rebellion. Baltimore was the pivot of the problem. South-bound troops had to make the same kind of exposed transfer between trains that had endangered Lincoln, and no other rail routes from the North existed except those which passed through Baltimore. The city was in an uproar by April 17, in anticipation of the coming troops. Southern

119 John P. Kennedy, Journal, April 13, 1861, Kennedy Papers.

120 *Ibid.*, April 16, 1861; and Maryland General Assembly, *House and Senate Documents*, 1861, document "A."

recruiters were active in Baltimore.[121] Palmetto flags appeared several places around town. In this atmosphere the passage of large numbers of armed Northern troops, visible symbols of perceived Northern coercion, was almost certain to cause trouble. Their passage was a raw confrontation between Maryland's lingering Southern sympathies and the federal government's resolve to maintain the Union by force. Sensing trouble, Mayor Brown issued on the seventeenth a proclamation urging calm and avoidance of rash and provocative acts. As he himself admitted, "I cannot flatter myself that this appeal produced much effect. The excitement was too great for any words to allay it."[122]

Order began to break down on April 18. Word came from Harrisburg that two companies of U.S. artillery, under Major George Pemberton, and four companies of unidentified militia would arrive at the small Northern Central Railroad station on Bolton Street, at the north end of town: they were due at 2:00 P.M. While many citizens prepared to confront the troops, Mayor Brown went to Bolton Street, as he put it, "to receive them." But before the troops arrived he was called away to consult with the governor. When the soldiers passed through the streets the crowd prudently avoided the regular U. S. artillery, but they harrassed the un-uniformed and unarmed militia mercilessly. The crowd grew quite large as the soldiers neared their destination at the Camden Street depot on the west side of the harbor. But for this day, at least, the Baltimoreans hurled nothing more than verbal abuse, and sang "Dixie."

That night a meeting was held in Taylor's Building, on Fayette Street near Calvert, by a group calling itself the "Southern Rights Convention." T. Parkin Scott led a large group of speakers; he told the audience that only lack of organization had made Southern men powerless that day, and he ominously urged them to prepare resistance for any other Northern troops that would follow. Bellicose resolutions in favor of the South, just short of being treasonable in their tone, also were approved.[123] News of Virginia's secession on April 17 measurably heightened the excitement in Baltimore on the 18th. Many Marylanders had long maintained that their state should follow Virginia if that state left the Union. Tension grew with every hour. The mayor issued another proclamation asking citizens to avoid rash

[121] *Baltimore Sun,* April 17, 1861.

[122] Brown, *op. cit.,* p. 36. Throughout this narrative of the events of April 19 I will rely heavily on Brown; with a few exceptions his book is by far the best source for the incident. Unless otherwise noted, material about the riot is from this work, and was checked against newspaper accounts and other documents.

[123] *Baltimore Sun,* April 19, 1861; see also John P. Kennedy, Journal, April 18, 1861, Kennedy Papers.

acts, and the governor, who had come to the city that afternoon, did the same. If Brown's proclamation of the seventeenth was ineffective, these on the eighteenth were small voices lost in the storm. Unable to control the city, the two officials sent urgent pleas to the president. "The excitement is fearful. Send no troops here," pleaded Hicks.[124] Added Brown, "it is not possible for more soldiers to pass through Baltimore unless they fight their way at every step."[125]

More Northern troops were rumored to be due on the nineteenth, but no one in Baltimore knew for sure when, how many, or from where. The only certainty was that the people of the city were extremely excitable and that an undetermined number of them had vowed to resist the passage of any more soldiers. Mayor Brown always maintained afterwards that, if he had been notified on April 19 of the exact details of the military's movements, he, with the police, could have kept order and prevented bloodshed.[126] Certainly the commanders of the troops arriving on the nineteenth expected trouble, but evidently they and the director of the Philadelphia, Wilmington, and Baltimore Railroad did not trust the city officials of Baltimore and so kept them in the dark. Consequently, Mayor Brown was at his office on the morning of the nineteenth when word came that an unknown number of troops were due to arrive momentarily. At the urging of Police Marshall George P. Kane, Brown rushed to the Camden Street station, where he found Kane supervising a rapidly growing force of city police. Why Kane was at the station where the troops would likely depart the city, and not at the depot of arrival, is a puzzle. Perhaps he did not know where the troops would arrive; if so, his move to Camden Street was the only logical one left to him. There he, the mayor, and several other city officials waited.

The troops arrived from Philadelphia at the President Street station at approximately 11:00 A.M. They were fully uniformed and armed, and, worst of all, they were from Massachusetts—an "abolitionist"

124 Thomas H. Hicks to Abraham Lincoln, April 18, 1861, Lincoln Papers.

125 George William Brown to Abraham Lincoln, April 18, 1861, *ibid.* Brown recalled this telegram, and Hicks's, too, as being sent on the nineteenth, and he reported them as such (*op. cit.*, p. 57). But the originals in the Lincoln papers both carry the date April 18, and it seems unlikely that the date was incorrectly entered on both, and then not corrected by the recipient when they were filed. The clash of citizens and troops referred to, then, must be the incident on April 18 and not the bloody affray with the Sixth Massachusetts Regiment. Most subsequent authorites, including Radcliffe (*op. cit.*), follow Brown's claim that the often-quoted telegrams were sent April 19. It would appear, however, that writing twenty-five years after the fact Brown was off by one day on the date of these telegrams.

126 The government of Massachusetts later sent its sincere thanks to Brown and the other city officials for their efforts toward preserving peace and order, however, futile. Brown, *op. cit.*, pp. 53–55.

state in the eyes of Marylanders; this made them doubly offensive to the agitated Baltimoreans. With the Sixth Massachusetts Regiment was an unarmed regiment of Pennsylvania militia; the total aggregation was nearly 1,700 men. Both regiments faced a journey of a mile and a half across the waterfront area down Pratt Street, one of the busiest thoroughfares in the city. The only people who might protect them were at the other end of the line—waiting, confused, and powerless to help. The troops moved out into certain disaster.

From the outset the movement of the troops through Baltimore on April 19 was a botched job. Despite the hazards of a long journey through the waterfront, the officers in charge did not keep their troops in a mass, but began sending them to Camden Street as soon as the units were formed. Seven companies made the trip safely by going at top speed in horse-drawn trollies, but this only aroused the crowd on the street. The last of these cars suffered heavy damage from rocks and paving stones and arrived at the west side of the harbor with its windows shattered. When the people on the street realized what was in progress, they began to obstruct the tracks with cobblestones, bricks, sand, and a stray anchor or two from the wharves. The rest of the Massachusetts troops—about 200 men—were then forced to march the entire route through a mob which was beginning to sense its power.

The next hour was chaos. Mayor Brown was waiting at the Camden Street station when the first seven companies of the Sixth Massachusetts Regiment arrived. The damaged last car and the absence of the expected remainder of the regiment was ominous. Then a messenger told him of the mob on Pratt Street. Brown left immediately for the scene while a messenger ran to fetch Kane, who had returned to the police station. As the Mayor rushed down Pratt Street, he saw the last four companies of the Sixth Massachusetts hurrying at double time while a shouting crowd milled around them. Bricks and cobblestones were flying everywhere, and, occasionally, bullets were fired as the mob pressed its attack; harassed and tormented, the troops fired back. Brown ran to the head of the column and began to march with it, doing his best to lend an air of calm authority. He persuaded the officer in command, Major Follansbee, to stop marching at the double-quick, in hopes that this, too, would restore a sense of order. "We have been attacked without provocation," Brown remembered the officer said to him, and he also recalled that he told the major, "You must defend yourself." For the moment Brown's show of firmness stalled the riot. But before the troops had gone another block the accumulated fury and frustration of the crowd spilled over again. First the stones began to sail out of the crowd. Then rioters rushed the soldiers and grabbed at their muskets. One soldier shot his assailant in the hip and soon the whole line began firing at will. No order to fire was given. No discipline or direction controlled the riflemen. Brown rushed down the column waving his furled umbrella and screaming "For God's sake, don't shoot!" People fell in bunches. He ran out from the column to try to quell the citizens, but in vain. Just then Marshall Kane ran onto the scene with a large detachment of police. He quickly deployed his men behind the Sixth Massachusetts Regiment—that is, between them and the bulk of their assailants. Kane personally drew a pistol and shouted "Keep back, men, or I shoot!" This finally drove back the mob, and the battered soldiers proceeded to Camden Street without further violence. By the time the troops left Baltimore at 1:00 P.M., four soldiers were dead and three dozen were wounded. As they left the city, one luckless Southern sympathizer named Robert W. Davis, evidently unaware of what had happened, raised a cheer for Jefferson Davis and the South. He was instantly shot dead from the window of the train by one of the infuriated Massachusetts men. Back in Baltimore at least twelve citizens were dead and a large, undetermined number were wounded. The frightened unarmed Pennsylvania militia never even left the President Street station, and those who had not already fled in panic were hastily sent back to Philadelphia by train.

The situation on the afternoon and evening of April 19 was explosive. No word had come from Washington on Brown and Hicks's entreaty that no more troops be sent through the city. The mayor called a mass meeting for Monument Square that evening and invited several leading citizens to speak. All the addresses were designed to quiet the crowd, but the excitement was clearly out of hand. The speeches met with loud cheers or groans and hisses, depending on how the audience interpreted the words. Brown's own speech was the firmest; he said that the authorities had matters under control, and that no more mob violence was either necessary or tolerable.

Hicks followed Brown to the rostrum and made a remarkable and uncharacteristic speech; the strain of the situation was clearly affecting him. He faced a hostile crowd there in the square. Very possibly his life was in danger.[127] More impassioned than usual, he stood next to the state flag and announced his position, that he ardently desired to see the Union preserved. At this, angry shouts came from much of the crowd. Shaken, the governor continued:

I coincide in the sentiment of your worthy mayor. After three conferences we have agreed, and I bow in submission to the people. I am a Marylander;

[127] See Radcliffe, *op. cit.*, pp. 54–55.

I love my State and I love the Union, but I will suffer my right arm to be torn from my body before I will raise it to strike a sister State.[128]

This declaration was so completely out of line with Hicks's steady Unionism both before and after the nineteenth that critics later charged him with hypocrisy and going back on his word. Hicks, however, obviously spoke in the passion of the moment and in a certain amount of fear. He was surrounded by his enemies, hemmed in by the demands of duty, expediency, and panic. Five days of feverish activity, trips to Washington, and hard decisions had nearly drained him. For a while it seemed as if he were cracking under the pressure. He did not go back to his hotel after the meeting, but at Brown's invitation went to the mayor's home; it might not have been safe for him to stay at the hotel.[129] When a group of city leaders arrived at Brown's for an emergency conference late that night, they had to meet in Hicks's bedroom because the governor was too stricken to stand.

The civic leaders who met at Brown's home were desperate to prevent more bloodshed, and they adopted a desperate expedient. It was agreed that the railroad bridges north and east of the city would be burned to prevent the arrival of any more troops by train. Hicks reluctantly approved the action, or at least he could not summon the strength to resist the unanimous determination of the others.[130] The destruction of key bridges on all major approaches to Baltimore was completed by midafternoon on the twentieth. Maryland Home Guard troops and Baltimore police did the job. Some private demolition teams were at work, too.

The next two days were all confusion in Baltimore. "Anxiety, alarm, and rage have taken possession of the town," wrote Kennedy.[131] "A time like that predicted in Scripture seemed to have come when he who had no sword would sell his garment to buy one," said the normally prosaic Brown. He added that Saturday, April 20, "was a fearful day in Baltimore. Women, children, and men, too, were wild with excitement."[132] In a special Saturday morning session the city

[128] Brown, *op. cit.,* p. 56. There is a small disagreement on Hicks's exact words. Instead of referring to "sister states," the *Baltimore American,* April 21, 1861, quoted Hicks as using the word "brother." Radcliffe, however, whose research seems quite thorough, agrees with Brown's version. Such a reference to "sister states" would be in tune with the rhetoric which was current in Maryland that winter.

[129] Brown, *op. cit.,* p. 58.

[130] Some controversy exists over the exact nature of Hicks's approval of the bridge-burning plan. See *ibid.*; and Radcliffe, *op. cit.,* pp. 56–57.

[131] John P. Kennedy, Journal, April 20, 1861, Kennedy Papers.

[132] Brown, *op. cit.,* pp. 60, 75.

council agreed to borrow half a million dollars for "city defense." The money was pledged by local bankers within a few hours. Fifteen thousand men were temporarily deputized into the city police force, and three-fourths of them were supplied with arms. The idea was to keep the peace, though many had volunteered with expectations of leading the fight against any additional federal troops. Colonel John J. Robinson, in command of the federal garrison at Fort McHenry, firmly believed he was going to be attacked on the twentieth. Henry Winter Davis told his friend DuPont that "on Sunday 21st Baltimore was veritably *crazy*."[133]

Armed men—some organized militia from the Maryland counties and some freebooters—began to arrive in the city that weekend.[134] They kept coming all during the next week and were a dangerous addition to the city's volatile atmosphere. At least one of the militia companies, a Frederick unit under Captain Bradley T. Johnson, had been invited to come. On the night of April 19 Marshall Kane sent a frenzied telegram to Johnson which said: "Streets red with Maryland blood; send expresses over the mountains of Maryland and Virginia for the riflemen to come without delay. Fresh hordes will be down on us tomorrow. We will fight them and whip them, or die."[135] When the board of police commissioners discovered Kane's indiscretion, they seriously considered discharging him. His act could easily have brought retribution from Washington, many felt.[136] As it turned out, Kane stayed on the job for the time being, only to be arrested later by the federal government.

The ensuing negotiations between Maryland authorities and the federal government were very confused.[137] Brown and Hicks had difficulty communicating with each other, and their efforts were consequently uncoordinated. Emmissaries and telegrams shuttled back and forth between Annapolis, Baltimore, and Washington. Senator Anthony Kennedy and Congressman J. Morrison Harris acted solely on their own initiative, independently of Brown and Hicks, which confused the situation even more. Basically, Marylanders all insisted that no more troops should or could be sent across the state. The Lincoln administration in turn insisted that for the defense of the

[133] Davis to Samuel F. DuPont, April 29, 1861, DuPont Papers; italics in the original.

[134] Units came from Baltimore, Anne Arundel, Howard, Talbot, Cecil, Carroll, Prince George's, and Frederick counties.

[135] Brown, *op. cit.*, p. 70. Johnson was later a Confederate general.

[136] *Ibid.*

[137] The details of trips to Washington, dozens of telegrams, missed appointments, conferences, and so on are not worth going into here. See Brown, *op. cit.*; and Radcliffe, *op. cit.*

capital such troop crossings were absolutely essential. A compromise was reached. The Lincoln government pledged that no more troops would be sent through Baltimore. Instead, the units would embark on steamers at the north end of the Bay in safely Unionist Perryville, then go by water to Annapolis. From Annapolis it was a short trip to Washington on the Annapolis and Elk Ridge Railroad. In return the Baltimore authorities would try to prevent their citizens from leaving the city to harass the troops. In addition, a group of Pennsylvania militiamen who had come as far as Cockeysville, north of Baltimore, were prudently held up and then rerouted.

Without question the decision to send troops through Annapolis prevented Maryland from seceding. Another clash in Baltimore would have propelled Maryland out of the Union. For a time after the April 19 riot, "Union sentiment temporarily disappeared," in the opinion of Mayor Brown.[138] Union men were afraid to avow themselves. Even the Minute Men, a Unionist club, hauled down its Stars and Stripes and replaced it with the Maryland flag. Henry Winter Davis, who always belittled his opponents, admitted that he was "very much astonished at the fury of the passions" which had given "for the moment the mastery" of Maryland to the forces of "weakness and wickedness."[139]

Thanks to the caution of the Lincoln administration, that mastery was short-lived. The excitement cooled and Unionism reasserted itself. By April 26 John P. Kennedy reported that the city was considerably calmer.[140] By April 28 "the tide had turned," the Fort McHenry commander remembered; "Union men avowed themselves and the stars and stripes were again unfurled and order was restored."[141] By the twenty-ninth Henry Winter Davis had shifted from extreme despair to cautious optimism, Unionists now being "masters of the state" once more.[142] Some Marylanders felt a purging effect. Davis reasoned that "the outbreak of the nineteenth has opened the eyes of our people as nothing else could; it has greatly strengthened us [Unionists] and I feel now more confidence than ever in the resolute loyalty of Maryland under all circumstances."[143] One Marylander significantly noted that the riot had pointed up Maryland's vulnerability to attack. The South had been clamoring for Maryland's help for months, he said, but had stood by helplessly at that point when Maryland seemed ready to act; the South could not, did not, rise to

138 Brown, *op. cit.*, p. 64.
139 Davis to Samuel F. DuPont, April 29, 1861, DuPont Papers.
140 John P. Kennedy, Journal, April 26, 1861, Kennedy Papers.
141 Beall, *op. cit.*, p. 51.
142 Davis to Samuel F. DuPont, April 19 and 29, 1861, DuPont Papers.
143 Davis to DuPont, May 5, 1861, *ibid.*

the crisis.[144] By May the *Frederick Examiner* was calculating that "secession is a sick man in Maryland."[145]

The bloodletting of April 19 has often been misunderstood. Unionism was dominant in Maryland except during that one brief, inflammatory encounter. When Maryland secessionists were unable to use the Baltimore riot to move Maryland out of the Union, the game was up; they would not get a second chance. Furthermore, the riot itself was not entirely attributable to offended Southern sympathies.

Baltimore's heritage of riots and roughhousing had more than a little to do with April 19. Those who had given the city an unenviable reputation as "mob town"—the unemployed, the street gangs, the fire-house clubs, the riff-raff and drunks, and on-leave sailors—were still numerous in Baltimore. Jobless men were even more plentiful than ever that winter because of the business recession. Though many respectable citizens took part and many honest motives stirred the crowd, the naturally unruly types who had come to infest the city magnified the disorder. Mayor Brown, for example, found it necessary to close all the bars in Baltimore on Monday, April 22; surely this indicated that not all the trouble was grounded in outraged principles. Unemployed men used the disorder as an opportunity to "confiscate" goods and supplies. The toughs found the situation a convenient excuse to obtain arms and ammunition. The business community was seriously alarmed about looting, and possibly feared a renewal of the fighting for this reason more than for any other.[146] What began as pro-Southern indignation grew and sustained itself on other discontents. As time passed, some Marylanders lost pride in the defiant patriotism of the riots and found them instead a source of embarrassment. "The affair of the nineteenth was deplorable," wrote one chagrined Baltimorean. "It put us completely in the wrong before posterity, to say nothing of the pecuniary damage."[147] "An armed mob" did the damage, the *Cecil Whig* complained.[148] To Henry Winter Davis "a mob guarded by police and secessionists" was to blame.[149] "Would to God," lamented the *Frederick Examiner,* "it had never happened."[150]

144 "O.P.O." to the *Cecil Whig,* June 8, 1861. The Confederate government did think of aiding Baltimore. On April 22 Jefferson Davis telegraphed Governor John Letcher of Virginia: "Sustain Baltimore if practicable. We will reinforce you." Dunbar Rowland, ed., *Jefferson Davis, Constitutionalist: His Papers, Letters, and Speeches,* 10 vols. (Jackson: Mississippi Department of Archives and History, 1923), 5:65.

145 May 1, 1861.

146 Catton, *op. cit.,* pp. 94–95.

147 Anonymous letter to Thomas H. Hicks, May 4, 1861, Hicks Papers.

148 April 27, 1861.

149 Davis to Samuel F. DuPont, April 29, 1861, DuPont Papers.

150 April 24, 1861.

IV

The complicated and confusing events after the April outburst reveal Maryland's halting progress toward acceptance of its position within the Union and the demands that this position would make. This progress could be seen on several fronts at once—in the popular mind, in the governor's increasingly warm relations with the Lincoln government, in the unexpectedly inactive course of the General Assembly, and in the success of federal military operations in the state.

For confirmed Unionists, expressions of their belief became easier after the first of May 1861 as secession became an ever remoter possibility. Unionists were also emboldened by the obviously solicitous surveillance of the federal government and the presence of federal troops. Unionism reappeared first in Western Maryland, where a special election to fill a vacancy in the Washington County Assembly delegation was won handily by unconditional Unionist Lewis P. Fiery, a former American turned Republican. Unionists also carried the municipal elections in Cumberland.[151] A Union convention met on May 2; though this meeting did little, it helped to coalesce Union sentiment and make it public.[152] Mass meetings throughout the state petitioned the General Assembly to avoid treasonable obstruction of the federal government. On May 7 Mayor Brown disbanded the special defense force of fifteen thousand in Baltimore and told the city council that in his opinion the people of Maryland had decided to submit to the Washington government.[153] The city council accordingly asked the legislature to repair the railroad bridges so hastily demolished three weeks earlier. In Baltimore and across the state U.S. flags were brought out of the closets where they had been temporarily hidden.

For most Marylanders, however, acquiescence in the duties of remaining in a Union at war was difficult. For these persons a middle ground was needed temporarily, and that middle ground was called "armed neutrality." Maryland had been traveling down the path of moderation, compromise, and halfway measures for a decade, and her citizens could not change overnight. Although the time for compromise was past and the crisis of allegiances was at hand, many Marylanders made one last attempt to evade the choice; in effect, they asked to remain in the Union, but to be excused from the fight against the Southern states. Under the concept of "armed neutrality" these Marylanders sought to retreat within their own borders, defend their own soil, and wash their hands of the rest of the conflict.

As a phrase, "armed neutrality" dated back in the Maryland press

151 Radcliffe, *op. cit.*, p. 94.
152 *Baltimore American*, May 3, 1861.
153 *Baltimore Sun*, May 7 and 8, 1861.

at least to November 1860, but the idea became both well defined and popular in the spring of 1861.[154] A major ingredient in it was that curious local attachment which is so hard for twentieth-century Americans to comprehend. The state flag for a time replaced the national banner on Maryland public buildings. Even more important to armed neutrality was the difficulty of choosing sides. "Neutrality is the only antidote of Revolution now," cried the *Frederick Examiner;* "it is our only safety." Any other course would be "Ruin, ruin, ruin."[155] The *Baltimore American* was another leading advocate of armed neutrality. When breaking the news of the firing at Fort Sumter, the paper urged Maryland to "stand aloof."[156] A correspondent to the *American* urged on April 19:

> Say to the Southern Confederacy; you must not pass over our soil to invade the federal capital. Say to the [United States] government; we are loyal citizens. The public property shall be safe and protected in our borders. We will keep our troops to guard our State. We ask of you a truce until Congress meets. . . . Hold, and we will act as *mediators.*[157]

Both the governor and the legislature also offered at various times to serve as mediators in the conflict, either alone or in concert with other border states. Armed neutrality was the essence of the proposals Hicks took to Washington—that is, that Maryland troops be left in Maryland. Throughout the spring Hicks had spoken of a concert of neutral border states as the proper antidote to the crisis.[158] He later told the special session of the General Assembly, "I honestly and most earnestly entertain the conviction that the only safety of Maryland lies in preserving a neutral position between our brethren of the North and of the South."[159]

Armed neutrality, of course, was impossible politically, geographically, and militarily. But it was a useful fiction because it postponed a choice, a conscious recognition of taking sides, until the federal government was able to consolidate its position in the state. The president and his administration were wise in not insisting at the outset that Maryland firmly and unequivocally declare that it would participate fully in the war to restore the Union. Armed neutrality,

154 *Frederick Herald,* November 27, 1860. Neither the idea nor the term "armed neutrality" was unique to Maryland. Kentuckians, for example, tried the same approach.

155 April 30, 1861.

156 April 13, 1861.

157 *Ibid.*; italics in the original.

158 *Cecil Whig,* January 19, 1861; and *Baltimore Sun,* January 21, 1861.

159 Maryland General Assembly, *House and Senate Documents,* 1861, document "A."

as genuinely and as earnestly as it was advanced by so many persons, simply served to buy time for Unionism.

One of the first public figures to abandon armed neutrality was Governor Hicks. In his correspondence with the Lincoln administration in late April and into May he said he saw a change in public sentiment in Maryland toward the Union, and his own tone became quite cooperative.[160] On April 29 he issued a proclamation warning Marylanders against enlisting in the numerous military companies springing up around the state, because these groups "[are] subversive of good order, and in the present excited condition of the public mind, are well calculated to imperil the public peace."[161] The governor also tried unsuccessfully to invalidate the commissions of some state militia officers he suspected of being Southern sympathizers.[162] On May 4 he moved to enroll the troops Lincoln had asked for in his April 15 proclamation. On May 30 he instructed Colonel E. R. Petherbridge of the state militia to collect from the local militia units all arms and accoutrements belonging to the state; this was obviously a move to disarm potentially disloyal military groups.[163] He also called upon Marylanders to deliver up all state-owned arms to Petherbridge.[164] Furthermore, Hicks stocked the collected arms at Fort McHenry and the state armory at Frederick, but not at the other state arsenal in Easton, on the pro-Southern Eastern Shore.[165]

While Marylanders tried to straighten out personal loyalties and Hicks became increasingly friendly with the Lincoln administration, the General Assembly was meeting in special session at Frederick. Hicks had been forced to convene the legislature in the wake of the April 19 bloodshed. If he had not done so, extralegal steps would have been taken to convene either the legislature or a state convention, and Hicks had to avoid that. Coleman Yellott, state senator from Baltimore County, had drafted a letter to the other members of the General Assembly asking them to meet for consultation in Baltimore.[166] The *Sun* concluded that, if Hicks did not yield on calling a special session, "a spontaneous demonstration of the people" would initiate "revolutionary proceedings."[167] That same afternoon Hicks resignedly summoned a special session to meet on April 26 in Annapolis:

160 This correspondence is in the Letterbook of the Executive, Hall of Records, Annapolis, Md.
161 *Baltimore Sun,* May 2, 1861.
162 Radcliffe, *op. cit.,* p. 89; and *Baltimore Sun,* May 8, 1861.
163 Thomas Hicks to Colonel E. R. Petherbridge, May 30, 1861, Hicks Papers.
164 Moore, *op. cit.,* 1: 347–48.
165 Radcliffe, *op. cit.,* p. 98.
166 *Ibid.,* p. 52.
167 April 22, 1861.

he later protested that he did so because he had no choice.[168] A special election in Baltimore on April 24 filled the ten delegates seats vacated by the House in 1860 because of fraud. Given the excited condition of the city, only a "Southern rights" ticket was in the field: turnout was slight.[169] Also on the twenty-fourth Hicks moved the session to Frederick to avoid any possibility of a clash between the legislature and the Washington-bound federal forces. Not incidentally, Frederick was also more safely Unionist than Annapolis.

Unionists feared the worst when the General Assembly met on April 26 in the German Reform church in Frederick, but as it turned out the legislature behaved moderately. The day after they convened the Senate unanimously passed an "Address to the People of Maryland" in which they denied that they had the right to consider an ordinance of secession.[170] The House concurred by a vote of 53 to 12.[171] No further statement issued from the legislators for two more weeks, as the Committee on Federal Relations struggled with the task of drafting resolutions that were acceptable to the diverse shades of opinion present at the session. In the meantime the Assembly sent a three-man delegation to Washington to protest the military occupation of parts of the state.[172] Finally, on May 9 the Committee on Federal Relations produced its resolutions. These resolutions declared that Maryland would have no part of a war against the South but would remain neutral, that the military occupation of the state was "a flagrant violation of the Constitution," and that the Confederate States should be recognized. But the resolutions also said "that . . . it is not expedient to call a sovereign convention of the state . . . or to take any measures for the immediate reorganization and arming of the militia."[173] The House adopted these resolutions by a vote of 43 to 12.[174] Indignant rhetoric aside, these resolutions, coupled with those of April 27, clearly meant that Maryland was not going to secede; the legislature first denied that it had the power to consider secession, and then refused to call a convention which would have had the power.

The legislature was reduced to impotence by the unexpectedly sharp divisions of opinion within its own body and by its lack of

[168] Maryland, General Assembly, *House and Senate Documents,* 1861–1862, document "A."

[169] Only 9,244 votes were cast, as contrasted with over 30,000 at the last presidential election.

[170] Maryland, Senate, *Journal,* 1861, p. 8.

[171] Maryland, House of Delegates, *Journal,* 1861, p. 22.

[172] The delegation consisted of Otho Scott, Robert McLane, and William J. Ross.

[173] Maryland, General Assembly, *House and Senate Documents,* 1861, document "F."

[174] Maryland, House of Delegates, *Journal,* 1861, p. 106.

effective influence on the course of events. The first special session adjourned on May 14, and by the time it reconvened on June 4 the federal authorities and Governor Hicks were so firmly in control of the state that the legislators could do nothing.

The initiative had passed to the federal government in the last week of April, and the Lincoln administration acted with careful firmness. Upon the decision to go to Washington via Annapolis, General Benjamin F. Butler seized the town and the Baltimore, Annapolis, and Elk Ridge Railroad terminal.[175] Annapolis was no less hostile than Baltimore to the sight of federal troops, but it was a great deal more manageable in size. By May 5 Butler had the entire railroad under control, including the tracks. On the fifth the general occupied the Baltimore and Ohio Relay House seven miles from Baltimore, where the Baltimore, Annapolis, and Elk Ridge tracks join the B. & O. line to Washington. The next step was to occupy Baltimore itself, and Butler used the cover of a violent thunderstorm to enter the city on May 13.[176] He immediately fortified the commanding heights on Federal Hill. So calm and resigned had Baltimore already become that no resistance whatsoever was offered. The elaborate preparations and plans for defending the city at a cost of $500,000 were nowhere in evidence. Baltimore acquiesced quietly, and Maryland was definitely secure for the Union.

The General Assembly was the only group which did not resignedly accept the situation. The subsequent course of the legislature in the summer and fall of 1861 was painfully tragic. The governor and the federal authorities were so completely in control that the legislators could only work themselves into an impotent fury, which made them seem more and more treasonable. Furthermore, with the writ of habeas corpus suspended in Maryland by order of the military authorities, the individual members placed themselves in danger of arbitrary arrest.[177] The first legislator was arrested by the federal

[175] See Benjamin F. Butler, *Private and Official Correspondence of General Benjamin F. Butler*, 5 vols. (Norwood, Mass.: Plimpton Press, 1917); and by the same author, *Butler's Book* (Boston: A. M. Thayer & Co., 1892).

[176] See *ibid.*; and Radcliffe, *op. cit.*, pp. 90–93.

[177] For a full discussion of the suspension of the writ of habeas corpus in Maryland, see James G. Randall, *Constitutional Problems under Lincoln* (New York: D. Appleton & Co., 1926). That the right to a writ of habeas corpus could be suspended in case of civil war was clear, but who should do the suspending? The prohibition against suspension appears in Article I, section 9, of the Constitution, which deals with the powers of Congress. But with Congress not in session in the spring of 1861, Lincoln assumed many extraordinary powers, including that of suspending the writ. Furthermore, he delegated this authority to military commanders in the field, to use at their discretion, thereby confusing the issue even further.

authorities after the temporary adjournment in May 1861. He was Ross Winans, "southern rights" delegate from Baltimore, an iron manufacturer who had supplied the Baltimore Home Guard with guns and pikes. He was formally charged with treason, but was released later that year. In September the military authorities seized the remainder of the Baltimore delegation, along with three other legislators and Congressman-elect Henry May of Baltimore. Mayor Brown also was apprehended, a fate he certainly did not deserve. These unfortunate men were incarcerated at various federal forts for lengths of time ranging from a few months to over two years, all without formal charges being brought against them.

These arrests, which caused so much bitterness both at the time and subsequently, were unnecessary.[178] The U.S. government met resentment but no serious resistance in Maryland after the end of April. By May pro-Southern Marylanders had quit trying to take their state out of the Union and were concentrating instead on fleeing South as individuals. The four regiments asked for by Lincoln were recruited by early June, without qualification as to their place of service.[179] In a special election held on June 13, pro-Union candidates carried sixteen of Maryland's twenty-one counties.[180] Although this election was affected by federal intimidation, the point is that federal control was firm.

Unionism, it would seem, was always uppermost in Maryland. Barring the April 19 riot, the record of Maryland shows more fear of the consequences of war than it shows any entrenched treason. The entire "armed neutrality" notion was the product not of disloyalty but of dismay. By 1861 Maryland had evolved into a pattern of life so different from that of the Southern states that secession was never more than a distant possibility.[181]

By summer, 1861, a new phase in Maryland's life and politics was beginning.[182] The war blotted out the old issues and came to dominate

178 General L. C. Baker, undercover agent for the Lincoln administration, claimed that the Maryland legislature was infested with traitors and that secession ordinances would be passed in September 1861. L. C. Baker, *History of the United States Secret Service* (Philadelphia: By the author, 1867), pp. 85–86. This makes no sense at all, but apparently some believed it.

179 Radcliffe, *op. cit.*, pp. 95–96.

180 The five recalcitrant counties were Talbot, Worcester, St. Mary's, Charles, and Calvert.

181 Earlier works by Seabrook, Beall, Freasure, and Catton, cited above, agree that Unionsm was stronger than secession sentiment.

182 A first-rate analysis of Maryland politics during and after the war is Jean H. Baker, *The Politics of Continuity: Maryland Politics from 1858 to 1870* (Baltimore: The Johns Hopkins University Press, 1973).

every aspect of life. The weak party structure of the 1860 election collapsed completely by the spring of 1861. The resulting political vacuum was filled by a "Union" party of Republicans, Constitutional Unionists, war Democrats, and loyalists of all types. The confused decade of the 1850s had finally ended in blood and a resolution of sorts. The crisis of allegiance was over—Maryland was Unionist in sentiment, it is clear, though its choice was made manifest by its acquiscence to federal force rather than entirely by its own actions. Marylanders moved into a new era of war and readjustment.

CONCLUSION

Looking back from 1861 at what he had endured, the average Marylander would have been surprised and undoubtedly dismayed. A great deal had happened; a great many hopes had been dashed and fears fulfilled. This average Marylander would not have had it come out as it did. His search for a comfortable allegiance had been futile.

Marylanders as a group could be counted as sectional conservatives in the 1850s. This sentiment was as logical as it was obvious. Lacking a clear sectional identity, Maryland lacked a sectional allegience, and avoiding conflict was a primary concern for its citizens. Marylanders consequently accepted a role in national politics which was comparable to their role in the national economy—as brokers, middlemen, traders between the sections. Marylanders generally supported the Compromise of 1850 and conservative parties and candidates who stressed the artificiality of the sectional crisis—notably, the American party and Millard Fillmore and the Constitutional Union party and John Bell.

Maryland's conservatism was touched by a certain impotent desperation. At times it seemed that Marylanders were seeking to solve all problems by sheer incantation of their belief in the soundness of the Union. Henry Winter Davis's recipe for settling the slavery issue—"be silent on it"—conveyed impatience and exasperation with the debate, but it also pointedly failed to offer any usable suggestions toward solution of the crisis. Maryland's only positive contributions to quieting the North-South struggle were limited. Senator James A. Pearce led the Senate Whigs away from Henry Clay's Omnibus Bill in 1850 and helped save the Compromise. Maryland's congressional delegation generally supported the Kansas-Nebraska Act in the vain hope that it would restore unity. In December 1860 Congressman Davis was crucial to the operations of the Committee of Thirty-Three. Short of that, Marylanders had nothing to offer toward national peace except rhetoric and a record of voting for conservatives.

The failure of conservatism in the 1850s was a national phenomenon, and Maryland's experience may help to explain it. For one thing, conservatives lacked any program beyond the Compromise and the too-late Crittenden Compromise of 1860-1861. Whether or not sectional differences were soluble, Unionists had surprisingly few solutions to offer. Conservatives did not anticipate crises, but tended to ignore them until they were overwhelming. Second, conservative Unionist candidates at the national level—notably Fillmore and Bell—were singularly colorless and uninspiring figures. And in Maryland's case the cause of Unionism was tragically bound up with nativism.

The conjunction of nativism and Unionism was not an illogical one. Nativism grew on the fears of certain Americans—whether rational fears or not—that their nation was drifting into a loss of character and purpose. Immigrants and Catholics were tangible symbols of all that seemed alien and un-American; they could be blamed for urban crime, social unrest, divisiveness, and corruption in politics. To combat this presumed threat the nativists exalted a mythic past and urged Americans to gather beneath the Star Spangled Banner once more. Having invoked the national spirit in the face of an "alien" threat, nativists moved easily to evoke the same spirit against domestic disruption. The same superpatriotism which served as a shield against foreigners was ready for use against disunionists. Nativists and Unionists shared a similar alarm and a similar solution.

When nativism paled as an issue, the Know-Nothings switched emphasis to a Unionism without missing a political beat. In doing so they earned a great deal of scorn from historians for being hypocritical and untrue to their principles.[1] This change was startling to some Marylanders, especially diehard nativists like the Reverend Andrew Cross; but, considered dispassionately, the switch was both rational and understandable. All parties adapt themselves to changing needs and conditions. The move from violent xenophobia to conservative Unionism was in the best interests of Maryland and the nation. Although the sudden abandonment of xenophobia was ironic and possibly embarrassing to the Know-Nothing leadership, it seems unjust that the American party should be condemned both for advocating nativism and for dropping it, or for not continuing to perform as a club instead of as a political party.

In the end, however, the alliance with nativism proved damaging for Unionism. During the period of Know-Nothing hegemony many

[1] See Laurence Frederick Schmeckebier, *History of the Know Nothing Party in Maryland* (Baltimore: N. Murray, 1899); and Mary St. Patrick McConville, *Political Nativism in the State of Maryland* (Washington, D.C.: The Catholic University of America, 1928).

worthy politicians who might have contributed to the quality of Maryland's conservative statesmanship either dropped out of politics or were pulled into the Southern rights orbit of the Democratic party. For instance, some former Whigs, like John P. Kennedy, went into semi-retirement, and others, like Senator James A. Pearce, became Democrats. Other causes besides nativism contributed to the political disaffection of some conservatives—factors like the increasing rowdiness of party politics—but the connection with nativism definitely tended to give Unionism a bad name. This guilt by association was especially damaging late in the decade and climaxed when Constitutional Unionist John Bell was denied Maryland's electoral votes, principally because the association of his conservative party with defunct nativism cost him thousands of votes in Baltimore. The transfer of Maryland's eight electoral votes from Breckinridge to Bell would not have affected the outcome of the presidential election, but it would have better represented the frustrated Unionism that was clearly a majority sentiment among Marylanders. At the very least, if Marylanders had been on record as Bell supporters, the Lincoln administration might not have reacted so suspiciously toward Maryland in general, and Baltimore in particular, especially since a tenuous bond of sympathy existed between some Bell supporters and the Republicans.

The interaction of local and national issues in the 1860 election emphasized the complexity of the issues Marylanders had confronted in the 1850s. At other times during the decade similar overlap occurred. In the period 1850–1852, for example, the combination of national and state issues hastened the end of the party which claimed the allegiance of at least half of all voting Marylanders. Just when the national Whig party was seriously divided over sectional issues the Maryland Whigs found themselves additionally embarrassed by the question of constitutional reform. In consequence the reorganization of Maryland's politics around the Know-Nothing party was speeded up. This reorganization was also more thorough; if the American party had encountered a strong Whig organization—and the Whig party was once powerful in Maryland—the nativists would have had to accommodate themselves to the moderating influence of Whiggery in order to succeed. This, in turn, would have made the American party more into what historians have often erroneously (in Maryland's case) assumed it to be, Whiggery redivivus. Had this moderation of nativism occurred, then the debilitating stigma of rampant nativism might have been avoided and conservatism in Maryland would have had a sounder base and a more influential voice.

Maryland party realignments in the 1850s offer another insight into the complexity of the decade. The Whigs collapsed because of national party divisions, local party weakness, the disappearance of old issues, and the inability of some of their leaders to adapt to the changes in political style. The vacuum created by their passing was filled by the Know-Nothings, but behind that simple substitution lay countless individual shifts in party identification. By the time these shifts were completed—by 1856 or 1857—the old Whig stronghold in Southern Maryland had gone Democratic while Baltimore had gone from Democratic to Know-Nothing. In the spaces between the shifting party organizations, furthermore, independent candidates operated with better than usual success, especially from 1851 through 1854. Also, one of the most striking features of Maryland politics in the 1850s, the influential reform movement in Baltimore, grew from independent action and only after rising to power made an alliance with the regular party system. Not since the 1820s, and not again until the Progressive era, would political independents have so much scope.

These dislocations show that the economic and social issues which had defined the party balance before 1850 had changed. Issues like banks, tariffs, and internal-improvement spending no longer formed the basis for political identification, nor did considerations of social class carry as much weight as formerly. Instead, Marylanders were, for a time, politically identified in federal elections by whether they valued the Union or Southern rights first. On the state level the Union issue was muted and the question of corruption in the Know-Nothing stewardship became paramount, as the Democratic campaign of 1859 and the reform issue indicated. These two levels of issues, state and national, became entangled in the presidential election of 1860 to the advantage of Breckinridge.

Baltimore remains the fascinating enigma of Maryland life—feared, admired, and, above all, powerful. Only a great deal of laborious study will ever unlock the secret of the city's turbulent street gangs and their relationship to politics. The social structure of Baltimore is shrouded in shifting ward boundaries, inadequate statistics, and the mass anonymity that was one of the city's terrors to contemporary Marylanders. The metropolis grew and changed so quickly that generalizations drawn about 1850 need to be rejustified for 1860. The safest conclusion is that the city usually controlled the results of Maryland's elections, and that no assumptions about what Marylanders did is entirely safe until city and counties have been checked separately.

Above all, examination of a single state in the decade before the Civil War should reawaken a sense of the complexity of the historical situation. Facile assumptions about what the "South" or "North" did, and why, seldom stand unchallenged before the details of more localized history. The conclusions drawn from a close examination of people's lives are not those to be drawn from perusing senatorial rhetoric. Such important outbursts as the Know-Nothing crusade are too often lost in the traditional overview of the decade, an overview which has been conditioned to serve as prelude to a war which no one at the time really knew was coming. The 1850s contained more than the roots of the war, as important as those were. Choosing between North and South was not the only test of allegiances that Marylanders, like other Americans, had to make. The sectional choice was confused by the others, by choices between tradition and change, city and country, openness and suspicion, localism and nationalism. Even when the firing on Fort Sumter reduced and narrowed the options, the matter of allegiances was not simple.

BIBLIOGRAPHICAL ESSAY

Maryland source materials may have discouraged potential researchers. Jean H. Baker, for example, notes that Walter Lord contemplated a book on Maryland's Know-Nothings but abandoned the project because of the lack of information. The paucity of secondary studies on the state reflects—and possibly has grown from—the scarcity of primary sources.

Below is a selective listing of the materials that were most useful in the preparation of this book, arranged by type of source and subject. For the sake of brevity, the *Maryland Historical Magazine* (published by the Maryland Historical Society) is cited as *MHM*.

Bibliographies

In addition to the standard reference works in American History, see *The Manuscript Collections of the Maryland Historical Society*, compiled by Avril J. M. Pedley (Baltimore: Maryland Historical Society, 1968). Also handy is Eleanor Phillips Passano, *An Index to the Source Records of Maryland* (Baltimore: Privately printed, 1946).

Manuscript Collections

Two outstanding personal collections were valuable in my research on Maryland in the 1850s—the John Pendleton Kennedy Papers (Peabody Institute Library, Baltimore) and the Samuel F. DuPont Papers (Eleutherian Mills Historical Library, Greenville, Del.); the DuPont Papers contain voluminous correspondence from Henry Winter Davis. Many other useful collections are housed in the Maryland Historical Society, Baltimore, including the papers of James A. Pearce, Brantz Mayer, Reverdy Johnson, S. Teackle Wallis, Thomas H. Hicks, Benjamin C. Howard, and Robert W. Garrett. The Society also has a collection of political broadsides and election tickets. At the Library of Congress, Washington, D.C., the papers of Montgomery Blair, John W. Garrett, Justin S. Morrill, Reverdy Johnson, and Abraham Lincoln were useful.

Official Documents

For the workings of the Maryland delegation in Washington, see the *Congressional Globe.* Also, both the House and Senate of the Maryland General Assembly published a sketchy *Journal* of their proceedings for every session, as well as a volume of *Documents* relevant to that session. The Executive Letterbook is housed at the Hall of Records, Annapolis. For studying the constitutional convention of 1851, see *Proceedings of the Maryland State Convention to Frame a New Constitution* (Annapolis: Riley & Davis, 1850); note that the publication date on this volume should read 1851.

Newspapers

The great Baltimore dailies are the best single source for Maryland history in this period—the *Sun* and *American* most notably. The *Sun* was extensively used in this study because it was the largest circulating and most influential newspaper in the state, and remained as neutral in its politics as any paper in this period was likely to be. Other significant Baltimore papers include the *Patriot* (Whig) and the *Clipper* (Know-Nothing). All other papers used were weeklies—the *Baltimore County Advocate* (Towson, Md.), the *Planters' Advocate* (Upper Marlboro, Md.), the *Upper Marboro Gazette,* the *Worcester County Shield* (Snow Hill, Md.), the *Port Tobacco Times,* the *Frederick Herald* and *Frederick Examiner,* the *Republican Citizen* (Frederick, Md.), the *Herald of Freedom and Torch Light* (Hagerstown, Md.), which was also known at various times as the *Herald* or the *Herald and Torch,* and the *Cambridge Democrat.* Broken but reasonably complete files of these papers for the 1850s can be found at the Maryland Historical Society or the Enoch Pratt Free Library, Baltimore. Widely scattered numbers of other local weeklies also are available.

Statistical Sources

The most complete sources of demographic statistics are, of course the U.S., Bureau of the Census, *Seventh Census of the United States* (Washington, D.C.: GPO, 1850), and *Eighth Census of the United States* (Washington, D.C.: GPO, 1860). Joseph C. G. Kennedy, *Historical Account of Maryland* (Washington: Gideon & Co., 1852), was written by a census official and drew on census materials. Richard Swainson Fisher, *Gazetteer of the State of Maryland* (Baltimore: J. S. Waters, 1852), also used census data. Election statistics come from the newspapers most easily, and may be checked with the manuscript election returns in the Hall of Records, Annapolis. For a quick review of Maryland's behavior in presidential elections, county by county, see W. Dean Burnham, *Presidential Ballots, 1836–1892* (Baltimore: The Johns Hopkins Press, 1955).

Descriptions

A large body of descriptive materials, mostly travelers' acounts and reminiscences, was valuable in providing an accurate mental picture of Maryland in the mid-nineteenth century. A comprehensive bibliography of travelers' descriptions is Bernard C. Steiner, *Descriptions of Maryland,* The Johns Hopkins University Studies in Historical and Political Science, ser. 22 (Baltimore: The Johns Hopkins Press, 1904). Among the more useful reminiscences are John C. French, "Poe's Literary Baltimore," *MHM,* 32 (1937): 101–12; John H. B. Latrobe, "Reminiscences of Baltimore in 1824," *MHM,* 2 (1906); 113–24; "A Maryland Tour in 1844: Diary of Isaac Van Bibber,"*MHM,* 39 (1944): 237–68; and Henry Stockbridge, "Baltimore in 1846," *MHM,* 6 (1911): 20–34. M. Ray Della, Jr.'s "An Analysis of Baltimore's Population in 1850," *MHM,* 68 (1973): 20–35, is valuable for its statistical thoroughness.

Local Histories

The state of Maryland has just commissioned a scholarly state history, but until it appears the only available state and local histories are the old ones, which reflect the interests, style, and scholarship of the nineteenth century. The best of the state histories are J. Thomas Scharf, *History of Maryland* (Baltimore: J. B. Piet, 1879); and Matthew Page Andrews, *History of Maryland, Province and State,* an old study which was recently re-released (Hatboro, Pa.: Tradition Press, 1965). Many Maryland counties have been described in local histories. The better local histories include J. Thomas Scharf, *History of Baltimore City and County* (Philadelphia: L. H. Everts, 1881); and, by the same author, *History of Western Maryland* (Philadelphia: L. H. Everts, 1882). See also Thomas J. C. Williams, *History of Frederick County, Maryland* (Frederick: L. R. Titsworth & Co., 1910); his *History of Washington County, Maryland* (Chambersburg, Pa.: J. M. Runk and L. R. Titsworth, 1906); and Will H. Lowdermilk, *History of Cumberland* (Washington, D.C.: J. Anglim, 1878).

Biographies

Biographies of leading Maryland figures in the 1850s are scarce, and many of those that do exist are badly outdated. For capsule biographies there are the cumulative directories of prominent men. In addition to the biographical sections of local and state histories, see *The Biographical Cyclopedia of Representative Men of Maryland and the District of Columbia* (Baltimore: National Biographical Publishing Co., 1879); Heinrich E. Buchholz, *Governors of Maryland* (Baltimore: Williams & Wilkins, 1908); and Wilbur F. Coyle, *The Mayors of Baltimore*, reprinted in book form from the *Baltimore Municipal Journal* in 1919. Various city directories for Baltimore are useful as a source of occupational information about otherwise obscure individuals.

The more notable studies of individual Marylanders include: Philip Bohner, *John Pendleton Kennedy, Gentleman from Baltimore* (Baltimore: The Johns Hopkins Press, 1961); Carl Brent Swisher, *Roger B. Taney* (New York: Macmillan, 1936); and Samuel Tyler, *Memoir of Roger Brooke Taney* (Baltimore: John Murphy Co., 1872). The Tyler study contains some autobiographical material. Autobiographical material also forms the early chapters of Bernard C. Steiner, *Life of Henry Winter Davis* (Baltimore: John Murphy Co., 1916). A good biography of Davis is badly needed, and hopefully one of the several studies in progress will fill that need; a full-length treatment by Gerald S. Henig is due to appear in late 1973. In the meantime Davis's own *Speeches and Addresses* (New York: Harper & Brothers, 1867) is a help. A Marylander who rose to be postmaster general of the United States under Grant received a cursory study in Elizabeth M. Grimes, "John Angel James Creswell, Postmaster-General" (Master's thesis, Columbia University, 1939). See also Bernard C. Steiner, "Brantz Mayer," *MHM*, 5 (1910): 1–18; and, by the same author, "James Alfred Pearce," *MHM*, 16 (1921): 319; 17 (1922): 33, 177, 269, 348; 19 (1923): 13, 162.

Political Studies

In addition to the general political studies in which Maryland receives notice, some works dealing specifically with politics in the state are invaluable. Among the most worthwhile are Mark H. Haller, "The Rise of the Jackson Party in Maryland, 1820–1829," *Journal of Southern History*, 28 (1962): 309–26; Richard P. McCormick, *The Second American Party System* (Chapel Hill: The University of North Carolina Press, 1966), esp. pp. 154–73; and W. Wayne Smith, "Jacksonian Democracy on the Chesapeake," *MHM*, 62 (1967): 381–93. Older works which also help are Bernard C. Steiner, *Citizenship and Suffrage in Maryland* (Baltimore: Cushing & Co., 1895), and, also by Steiner, "The Electoral College for the Senate of Maryland and the Nineteen Van Buren Electors," *American Historical Society Annual Report, 1895,* pp. 129–71. For another perspective on the 1836 crisis treated in the Steiner article, see A. Clark Hagensick, "Revolution or Reform in 1836: Maryland's Preface to Dorr's Rebellion," *MHM,* 57 (1962): 346-66. See also James Warner Harry, *The Maryland Constitution of 1851,* The Johns Hopkins Studies in Historical and Political Science, ser. 20 (Baltimore: The Johns Hopkins Press, 1902); Charles James Rohr, *The Governor of Maryland: A Constitutional Study,* The Johns Hopkins University Studies in Historical and Political Science, ser. 40 (Baltimore: The Johns Hopkins Press, 1932); and Elihu S. Riley, *A History of the General Assembly of Maryland, 1635–1904* (Baltimore: n.p., 1905). New and useful are three articles from *MHM,* 67 (1972): Eugene H. Roseboom, "Baltimore as a National Nominating Convention City" (pp. 215–24); Betty Dix Greenman, "The Democratic Convention of 1860" (pp. 225–53); and Donald Walter Curl, "The Baltimore Convention of the Constitutional Union Party" (pp. 254–77). A summary of state politics from 1851 to 1856, Douglas Bowers, "Ideology and Political Parties in Maryland, 1851–1856," *MHM,* 64 (1969): 19–217, is compact and essentially agrees with the conclusions in this volume.

The Know-Nothings

General studies of the Know-Nothings help to put the Maryland movement in perspective; so do studies of nativism in other states. The basic studies of nativism in America during the last century are Ray Allen Billington, *The Protestant Crusade, 1800–1860* (Chicago: Quadrangle Books, 1964); and John Higham, *Strangers in the Land* (New Brunswick: Rutgers University Press, 1955). W. Darrell Overdyke has written *The Know-Nothing Party in the South* (Baton Rouge: Louisiana State University Press, 1950). A highly dramatized account of the Know-Nothings can be found in Carlton Beals, *Brass Knuckle Crusade* (New York: Hastings House, 1960).

Works which examine the Know-Nothings in other states include Warren F. Hewitt, "The Know-Nothing Party in Pennsylvania," *Pennsylvania History,* 2 (1935): 69–85; Carl F. Brand, "History of the Know-Nothing Party in Indiana," *Indiana Magazine of History,* 18 (1922): 47–81, 177–207, 266–80; Louis D. Scisco, *Political Nativism in New York State,* Columbia University Studies in History, Economics, and Public Law, no. 13 (New York: Columbia University, 1901). For further reference consult the excellent bibliography in Billington's *Protestant Crusade.*

Several works focus directly on the Know-Nothings in Maryland. The best general account, although outdated both in style and methodology, in Laurence Frederick Schmeckebier, *History of the Know Nothing Party in Maryland* (Baltimore: N. Murray, 1899). This work is often cited as part of The Johns Hopkins University Studies in Historical and Political Science, ser. 17 (Baltimore: The Johns Hopkins Press, 1899). It appeared in both forms, as Murray was the printing agent for The Hopkins Press and simply issued the study in separate book form. Biased but useful for supplementing Schmeckebier is Sister Mary St. Patrick McConville, *Political Nativism in the State of Maryland* (Washington, D.C.: The Catholic University of America, 1928). See also Benjamin Tuska, *Know Nothingism in Baltimore, 1854–1860* (New York: Broadway, 1925). Extremely well conceived is Jean H. Baker, "Dark Lantern Crusade: An Analysis of the Know-Nothing Party in Maryland," (Master's thesis, The Johns Hopkins University, 1965). Mrs. Baker's bibliography also is excellent. No study of Maryland nativism is complete without this work.

The voluminous nativist literature in Maryland is well represented by Anna Ella Carroll, *The Great American Battle* (New York: Miller, Orton, Mulligan, 1856); and Friedrich Anspach, *Sons of the Sires* (Philadelphia: Lippincott, Grambo & Co., 1855).

Aside from the works of Higham and Billington cited above, the best place to begin an examination of the immigrants and Catholics who were the objects of nativist distaste is in Dieter Cunz, *The Maryland Germans* (Princeton: Princeton University Press, 1948), a very competent study of the major foreign element in Maryland, and in Robert Joseph Murphy, "The Catholic Church in the United States during the Civil War Period, 1852–1866," *Records of the American Catholic Historical Society of Philadelphia,* 39 (1928): 272–344. The *Records* have several usable minor articles on nineteenth-century American Catholics and their difficulties with nativist opposition.

Economic Studies

Transportation was the major factor in the economic development of Maryland. To study this subject see, for a start, Edward Hungerford, *The Story of the Baltimore and Ohio Railroad* (New York: G. P. Putnam's Sons, 1928); Walter S. Sanderlin, *The Great National Project: A History of the Chesapeake and Ohio Canal,* (The Johns Hopkins University Studies in Historical and Political Science, ser. 64, no. 1 (Baltimore: The Johns Hopkins Press, 1946); and *idem,* "The Maryland Canal Project," *MHM,* 41 (1946): 51–65. For a look at the trade patterns developed by this transportation system, consult Laura

Bornholdt, *Baltimore and Early Pan-Americanism,* Smith College Studies in History, no. 34 (Northampton, Mass.: Smith College, 1949); and William B. Catton's well-done "The Baltimore Business Community and the Secession Crisis, 1860–1861," (Master's thesis, University of Maryland, 1952), which is concerned with more than trade patterns but which analyses them very well nonetheless.

No examination of Maryland's economic situation before the Civil War is complete without Avery Craven, *Soil Exhaustion as a Factor in the Agricultural History of Virginia and Maryland, 1606–1860,* University of Illinois Studies in the Social Sciences, no. 13 (Urbana: University of Illinois, 1926).

Labor's role can be pieced together from several articles. Very useful is Richard B. Morris, "Labor Controls in Maryland in the Nineteenth Century," *Journal of Southern History,* 14 (August 1948): 385–400. A good study of one large laboring group can be found in Katherine A. Harvey, *The Best-Dressed Miners: Life and Labor in the Maryland Coal Region* (Ithaca: Cornell University Press, 1969). See also M. Ray Della, Jr., "The Problems of Negro Labor in the 1850's" *MHM,* 66 (1971): 14–32; and, in another look at labor and the race question, Clement Eaton, "Slave Hiring in the Upper South," *Mississippi Valley Historical Review,* 46 (1960): 663–78.

Maryland Negroes

This study is essentially centered on white Marylanders as the primary decisionmakers in the 1850s; Maryland's black population figures primarily as an influence on the mind of the whites. A good study of Maryland's blacks is needed, but for the present we will have to work with two standard old volumes: Jeffrey R. Brackett, *The Negro in Maryland,* The Johns Hopkins University Studies in Historical and Political Science, extra vol. 5 (Baltimore: The Johns Hopkins University, 1889); and James M. Wright, *The Free Negro in Maryland 1639–1860,* Columbia University Series in History, Economics, and Public Law, vol. 97, no. 3 (New York: Columbia University Press, 1921). See also Stanton Tiernan, "Baltimore's Old Slave Markets," *Baltimore Sun,* September 13, 1936; Elwood L. Bridner, Jr., "The Fugitive Slaves of Maryland," *MHM,* 66 (1971): 33–49; and the studies by Della and Eaton cited above in the section on economic history.

Maryland and the Election of 1860

Only a few secondary works are of much help on Maryland in the election of 1860. See Ollinger Crenshaw, *The Slave States in the*

Election of 1860 (Baltimore: The Johns Hopkins Press, 1945); and Reinhard C. Luthin, *The First Lincoln Campaign* (Cambridge, Mass.: Harvard University Press, 1944). One good reference is Willard King, *Lincoln's Manager, David Davis* (Cambridge, Mass.: Harvard University Press, 1960); David Davis was a cousin of Henry Winter Davis. Brand new and very competent is Jean H. Baker, *The Politics of Continuity: Maryland Politics from 1858 to 1870* (Baltimore: The Johns Hopkins University Press, 1973).

The Coming of the Civil War in Maryland

A wide variety of sources are necessary for a proper understanding of the secession winter and the crisis of decision in Maryland. A good start, beyond the legislative debates, the Executive Letterbook, newspapers, and relevant manuscript collections, is George L. P. Radcliffe's *Governor Thomas H. Hicks of Maryland and the Civil War*, The Johns Hopkins University Studies in Historical and Political Science, ser. 19 (Baltimore: The Johns Hopkins Press, 1901). Next best is Carl M. Freasure, "Union Sentiment in Maryland, 1856–1860," *MHM*, 24 (1929): 210–24. See also George Beall, "The Persuasion of Maryland to Join the Federal Union," typescript, Maryland Historical Society, Baltimore. Invaluable is William B. Catton's work on Baltimore businessmen in the secession crisis, cited above among the works on economics. For the efforts of Maryland's secessionists, see William C. Wright, *The Secession Movement in the Middle Atlantic States* (Rutherford, N.J.: Fairleigh Dickinson University Press, 1973).

For the efforts of Marylanders in Washington the leading works focus on Henry Winter Davis and include Henry Adams, "The Great Secession Winter of 1860–61," in *The Great Secession Winter of 1860–61, and Other Essays*, ed. George Hochfield (New York: Sagamore Press, 1958); and David M. Potter, *Lincoln and His Party in the Secession Crisis* (New Haven and London: Yale University Press, 1942). See also Gerald Henig, "Henry Winter Davis and the Speakership Contest of 1859–1860," *MHM*, 68 (1973): 1–19. Marylanders also participated actively in the "peace conference" held in Washington in February, which was reported in Crafts J. Wright, *Official Journal of the Conference Convention Held at Washington City, February 1861* (Washington: M'Gill & Witherow, 1861); and in Lucius E. Chittenden, *Debates and Proceedings of the Conference Convention, 1861* (New York: D. Appleton & Co., 1864).

For the dramatic events of the spring of 1861, see George William Brown, *Baltimore and the Nineteenth of April, 1861* (Baltimore: N. Murray, 1887); Norma Cuthbert, *Lincoln and the Baltimore Plot,*

1861 (San Marino: Huntington Library, 1949); Frank Moore, ed. *The Rebellion Record,* 9 vols. (New York: G. P. Putnam's Sons, 1861–68); and the works by the most prominent military figure operating in the state that spring, Benjamin F. Butler, *Private and Official Correspondence of General Benjamin F. Butler,* 5 vols. (Norwood, Mass.: Plimpton Press, 1917), and *Butler's Book* (Boston: A. M. Thayer & Co., 1892).

An adequate picture of the events of the spring of 1861 cannot be obtained, however, without recourse to primary materials—newspapers, the letterbook and correspondence of Governor Hicks, legislative journals and documents, and the correspondence of leading figures like John Pendleton Kennedy and Henry Winter Davis.

INDEX

Library of Congress Cataloging in Publication Data

Evitts, William J 1942-

A matter of allegiances; Maryland from 1850 to 1861.

(The Johns Hopkins University studies in historical and political science, 92d ser., 1)

Bibliography: p.

1. Elections—Maryland—History. 2. Maryland—Politics and government—1775-1865. 3. Maryland—Economic conditions. 4. Maryland—Social conditions. I. Title. II. Series: Johns Hopkins University. Studies in historical and political science, 92d ser., ser., 1.
JK3893 1850.E84 320.9′752′03 73-19336
ISBN 0-8018-1520-7